Data Warehouse Management Handbook

Richard J. Kachur

PRENTICE HALL

Library of Congress Cataloging-in-Publication Data

Kachur, Richard.
    Data warehouse management handbook / Richard Kachur.
      p. cm.
    ISBN 0-13-083346-0 (cloth)
    1. Data warehousing—Handbooks, manuals, etc. I. Title.
QA76.9.D37 K33 2000.
658.4'038'0285574   99-052679
                                       CIP

Acquisitions Editor: *Susan McDermott*
Production Editor: *Eve Mossman*
Formatting/Interior Design: *Robyn Beckerman*

© *2000 by Prentice Hall*

Printed in the United States of America

10 9 8 7 6 5 4 3 2 1

ISBN 0-13-083346-0

9 780130 833464   90000

PRENTICE HALL PRESS
Paramus, NJ 07652

On the World Wide Web at http://www.phdirect.com

To my life partner and best friend, my wife Shirley
who supported me through this process

To my daughter Kyla who left Daddy alone to write

and to my dog Kye

Author Biography

Richard J. Kachur is an independent consultant dedicated to the discipline of knowledge management and data warehousing. He acted as a practice leader in data warehousing for two large consulting organizations before establishing his own firm.

Mr. Kachur also provides data warehousing services as an associate and lecturer to the Data Warehousing Institute, an international body of data warehousing professionals dedicated to this technology discipline. In addition, he currently writes for "Data Management (DM) Review" a magazine dedicated to Data Warehousing and Database Management. He currently provides a DW column through DM Direct.

Mr. Kachur's diverse background in information technology includes international data warehousing experience in the public and private sectors. He has advised on systems methodology consulting, project management, information systems planning, data administration, business process reengineering, enterprise data modeling, data warehousing, repository administration, and case technology management across North America and Europe.

Richard Kachur can be reached at horse.musket@attcanada.net

Contents

Section One

The Data Warehouse Value Proposition   1

Overview—3

Section Two

Infrastructure Development   81
Overview—83

Section Three

Design, Implementation, and Assessment:
The Data Warehouse Development Spiral 193

Overview—195

Section Four
_____

Data Warehouse Support and Maintenance   277

Overview—279

Foreword

DATA WAREHOUSE MATURITY
BY W. H. INMON

In the 1970s and early 1980s era of information processing, a database was thought to be a single source of data for all processing. Coming from the magnetic tape application oriented background of the 1960s, it is easy to see how this now arcane theory of database grew popular. Thus it was pure heresy in the mid 1980s when data warehouses started to spring from the earth that the notion of two types of database began to gain acceptance. The database theoreticians were sorely offended by this encroachment into what they perceived to be their private intellectual territory.

By 1990, data warehousing had taken hold, and today data warehousing has turned into conventional wisdom. The early theoreticians do not even bother to protest any longer. With the advent of data warehousing came many other things, some positive, some not so positive.

- The growth of the volumes of data placed a challenge on organizations as never before. For example, the word "terabyte" was not widely used prior to data warehouses. Today the word is commonplace.

- The different style of Data Warehouse processing was something the technicians of the corporation had never before seen. The lessons learned in OLTP had scant relevance to data warehousing and DSS processing.

- The world of data warehousing opened up information processing to a community of users who had heretofore never been able to effectively access corporate data. Marketing, sales, finance, and others came to love their data warehouses.

- Integration—with all of the complications and work that is required—faced the organization with no compromise. Looking the old legacy applications in the eye and once and for all confronting them was an unpopular, but very important stance required by building the successful warehouse.

- Tools for end user access and analysis appeared that add an elegance and grace never before seen. The OLAP, multidimensional, and end user reporting tools were a light year's leap into the future. It is doubtful that these advances would have been made without data warehousing.

- Vendors of traditional technologies tried to convince corporations that they had been doing data warehousing all along (after having strongly supported the single database concept).

- New issues arose as to corporate budgeting and alignment in support of the warehouse, and so forth.

It is true that data warehousing turned the world of information processing upside down. Things will really never be the same.

As data warehousing matures, it is inevitable that the corporation will start to address the issue of managing and coping with the data warehouse. An entirely new and different set of skills is required for the day to day management of the Data Warehouse environment.

Richard Kachur's book represents an important step in the maturity of the industry. Once the bloom of having a data warehouse is off the rose and the corporation settles down to the reality building, maintaining, and using a data warehouse, then the wisdom contained in these pages becomes invaluable.

What This Book Will Do for You

BACKGROUND

The business community is in the midst of a technology boom. The trend toward data warehousing to satisfy this growing demand for information has resulted in rapid technology growth in hardware and software sales, and services.

A large part of this technology trend relates to the use of the Internet to retrieve information contained in data warehouses. This technology shift is, in part, the result of movement away from purely data processing systems to knowledge enabled systems. These knowledge systems provide businesses with leverage so that their internal best practices obtain a competitive advantage in the marketplace. Significant users of this technology include retail giants such as Wal Mart, credit card companies such as American Express and VISA, and major banks and transportation institutions, which include Bank of America and United Airlines.[1]

Planning the design and construction of these huge, and often complex information repositories has led to a new discipline called data warehousing. Its role remains crucial in understanding, planning, scoping, and

---

[1] *Information Week*, February 24, 1997, John Foley and Lisa Nadile. The data warehousing boom shows no signs of a slowdown. The market is expected to grow 50% this year, to $5.7 billion, according to the Meta Group, a research firm in Stamford, Conn. Corporate users are leveraging data warehousing in creative ways. Credit card giant Visa International is launching several initiatives to help its member banks be more profitable. "There's almost nothing in the company that won't be touched by where we're going with data warehouses," says Deborah McWhinney, executive VP with Visa in San Francisco.

Visa is using data warehouses on several fronts, including target marketing, fraud and risk analysis, and financial reporting. It's also developing predictive modeling software to identify card holders who present a high risk for bankruptcy. The projects are part of Visa's Information Initiative, a strategy for applying IT to meet several business objectives. Says McWhinney, "Information is becoming a much bigger piece of what we offer our members."

delivering knowledge capital back to the enterprise in a timely and cost effective fashion.

The Data Warehouse Management Handbook addresses this critical need for practical, best practice material on how to plan, analyze, design, and implement data warehouses. This "hands on" guide provides best practice processes, methods, and deliverables, all taken from a vendor independent perspective.

This book is written for data warehouse practitioners, as well as for beginners, who require information on the data warehousing process. *The Data Warehouse Management Handbook* takes you step by step through this process, from inception to implementation. *The Data Warehouse Management Handbook* is a practical source book meant for you, the data warehouse project manager or technician whose company is currently utilizing or considering the application of this technology within its information systems environment. It will assist you in developing and delivering this business intelligence technology. The text addresses the concerns and challenges of data warehousing by clearly describing the overall functions and interactions of each architectural component. The companion CD ROM disk contains a selection of materials to aid the data warehouse practitioner in managing the data warehouse life cycle from planning to maintenance.

This extensive library of best practice materials will assist data warehouse project managers such as yourself in understanding the process of data warehousing and how to present and incorporate this technology into your company's business operations. It shows how to describe the process, define a business case, develop an architectural framework, strategize policy that will generate high return on investment, and present a rapid design and implementation process that will quickly enable this environment.

DELIVERY APPROACH

The Data Warehouse Management Handbook's primary purpose remains as a practical "hands on" source book that guides you through the daily process of building and maintaining a data warehousing environment. It is meant to sit at the elbow of every data warehousing professional.

The topics discussed include budgeting, Data Warehouse and data mart design, decision support technology, key performance measure identification, subject area data modeling and database design, metadata management, data quality management, data staging, business and IS user training, vendor selection, and system maintenance.

The Data Warehouse Management Handbook is organized into five sections.

- Section One introduces the key concepts behind data warehousing.
- Section Two addresses the development of the data warehouse.
- Section Three discusses the data warehouse design and implementation process.
- Section Four addresses maintenance and support considerations.
- Section Five completes the text with a collection of reference information as well as an enclosed CD ROM disk. The CD contains the required deliverable templates, spreadsheet forms, and sample presentations, which can be immediately employed to "quick start" one's own data warehouse development process.

DISCLAIMER OF LIABILITY

Contact Information:

E-mail: horse.musket@attcanada.net

Section One

---◆---

The Data Warehouse Value Proposition

OVERVIEW

In Section One we discuss a variety of topics related to understanding the features and benefits of this technology and how to justify the business investment.

We start with a definition of key concepts before moving on to describe a functional description of its components. Key concepts include data warehousing functional characteristics and implementation approaches and what options exist with this technology.

Key issues related to data quality management and metadata management are addressed as necessary grounding information. Until recently, little attention was paid to these two critical areas, which are among the most difficult to manage, but are essential for success.

Finally, we look into the most critical area of all—how to educate ourselves and our business users to the value of this investment and how to present it to our project champions and sponsors. In addition, we need to know how to implement a benefits measurement framework. In too many cases, benefits definition and measurement are the weakest area, making cost justification a shaky prospect. We look at the various types of benefits that are accrued and examine the various types of financial measures in use today: return on investment (ROI), net present value (NPV), internal rate of return (IRR) and cost displacement.

Section One stands alone and can be used independently or in conjunction with the other sections of this book. This section references a number of knowledge objects on the companion CD. Please consult Chapter 20, which describes the features and functions of these knowledge objects as managed by the Data Warehouse Assistant. The Data Warehouse Assistant contains a description of all the electronic material provided for your use and modification as you develop the necessary level of data warehousing awareness within your organization.[1]

---

[1] This is a single user license to use and make use of the author's supplied CD material. The vendor material is provided for review only, with all rights for this material remaining with the vendor.

◆

CHAPTER ONE

What Is a Data Warehouse?

DATA WAREHOUSE BASICS

The term *data warehouse* is probably one of the most maligned phrases in our industry today. To some, a data warehouse is an integrated collection of all transaction data that exist within a company, to be used to consolidate and analyze daily business transactions. To others, a data warehouse is an integrated store of subject matter data meant to address the anomalies and inconsistencies that exist across information systems. Still others view a data warehouse as a historical record of what occurred in the business and where this record is combined with external data to make sense of business climate at a specific point in time.

There is no right answer to this question. What is needed is a frame of reference that fits one's culture and implementation approach, allowing us to choose a definition that can be clearly and concisely articulated to the business community. The following chapters expand on this theme and suggest a process whereby this understanding can be defined and implemented in a coherent, managed, and timely manner.

Following this theme, we define a data warehouse as a repository of subject matter data, collected from internal as well as external data sources. This integrated repository of information is used to assist our business community in either retaining or obtaining a competitive edge in the marketplace by analyzing what has occurred within the business across time.

Data warehouses today are utilized to promote operational efficiency or to validate what has taken place. Very few, if any, warehouses exist today to extend our knowledge for competitive advantage.

With this understanding we initiate our process by first defining a set of rules or definitions which is based on our data warehousing perspective (operational efficiency, or business validation). First, we must define what we mean by a data warehouse as a repository of information based on these perspectives versus a data warehousing architecture that contains the necessary data loading and data access components.

- A data warehouse is an integrated set of subject matter data integrated within a database(s) repository.
- A data warehouse architecture is a set of business and technical topologies that, together, allow a data warehouse database(s) to operate in a cost efficient and timely manner.

Next, we must clarify the role our data warehousing environment or architecture will play in the business. Remember, a data warehouse can be couched in a number of different roles, so it is important to understand the functional role it should take. Again, there is no right or wrong answer here, only the best process or approach that is advantageous for our business.

Our data warehouse can operate as:

1. As an operational based repository containing short term data, which have been collected and integrated to support the day to day operations of our business.

2. To serve as a tactical view of our business that focuses on a key business activity with high value returns (e.g., customer relationship management). In such cases, a more local or data mart based view is selected, with a focus on high payback areas of our business such as marketing and product development and/or service delivery. Service delivery focused efforts concentrate on pushing out customer knowledge to the various types of customer integration points to improve sales and reduce customer churn.

3. As an enterprise intelligence engine, where the objective of our data warehousing effort implies a more strategic, cross line of business view. This

process implies a corporate approach where a cross line of business repository of knowledge is built up over time, to support the process of business intelligence.

In all three cases, we develop our data warehousing architecture based on a foundation of three key processes.

1. Data staging, or retrieving information from the best possible sources of data (internal or external), for repair, verification, consolidation, and loading into our warehouse.
2. Data management, or storage and formatting of this data, for easy and timely access by a variety of knowledge workers utilizing a wide range of tools.
3. Data access, or retrieval processing, where an integrated set of tools is used to interrogate the data collected and create new information for business analysis.

We develop and maintain this suite of data sets and tools within a distinct and separate environment from our house holding, or operational transaction processing systems environment (OLTP). We do this for three main reasons.

1. To improve performance, since data warehouses can result in creating an unpredictable and heavy demand for computing resources.
2. To isolate data, thereby freeing the warehouse from the limitations imposed by the business cycle (collect, verify, process, store, audit, and archive) as inherent within operational databases.
3. To insulate data, thereby ensuring as data is collected and managed across time that the context of this information is not lost. The greatest benefit of a data warehouse is the time variant nature of its design, where business rules in place when the data was first created are kept in the warehouse, providing useful background information into the meaning of the data. Transaction processing systems and ERP solutions cannot provide this contextual data. In these cases such solutions provide information based on current state business rules only as their information store is the operational (current state) database environment which is not time variant.

Figure 1–1
Sample Data Warehouse Architecture Footprint

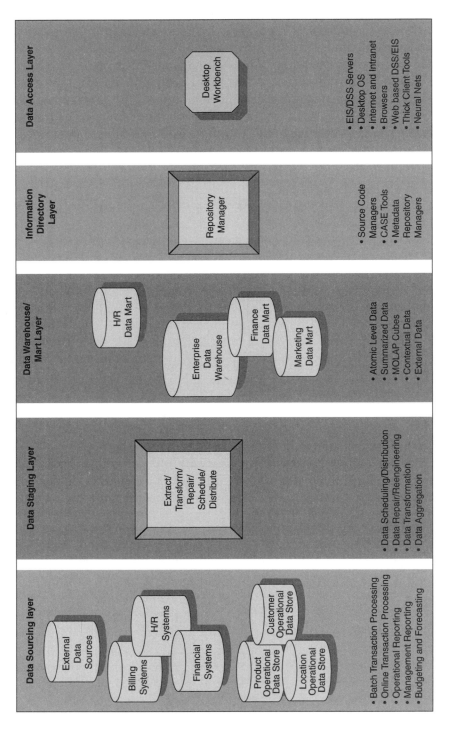

WHERE DOES DECISION SUPPORT FIT IN?

Much like the term data warehouse, decision support is another term that can mean just about anything. Again, it is important to understand the purpose for which we are collecting the data.

In a data warehousing context, decision support can imply the deployment of one of four options.

- Option One: Providing the ability to access operational data for management reporting.
- Option Two: Allowing knowledge workers to investigate sales/production performance results across time.
- Option Three: Determining patterns, issues, or trends emerging within our business or competitive community of which we may not be aware, thereby allowing us to be more proactive in our response.
- Option Four: Developing new business potential by creating a base of knowledge that will help us reinvent our business, allowing us to differentiate ourselves in the marketplace and establish new market share.

Any or all of these directions for decision support may be right for our business. If we select

- Option One: This approach results in our need to build operational data stores accessed by report writing tools.
- Option Two: Necessitates building either data marts or data warehouses to hold more time variant (longer term) data. This information is organized around a set of key business processes and accessed by a set of tools that allow us to view the data in different forms, from various aspects utilizing relational based online analytical processing (ROLAP) tools.
- Option Three: Requires more sophisticated predictive modeling and data mining, or MOLAP tools, for multidimensional analysis of patterns, trends, and emerging management issues.
- Option Four: Requires the deployment of business rule engines and advance technologies, such as neural nets, to investigate and chart the future directions for our business.

THE POLITICS OF DATA

If we wish to develop a useful and credible repository of data, we must ensure it is accurate and timely. The context of the data must be understood as well, especially when assessing past business results across multiple fiscal years. For example, what business rules were in use when this data was collected? We must also ask ourselves, what where the environmental, social, political, or economic events driving business demand at that time?

Traditionally, information systems organizations focused on supporting individual business areas such as marketing, accounting, or payroll. Each business area developed duplicate repositories containing common information about customers and products. Over time, these sources of information about assets, products, services, customers, and locations became out of sync, causing additional engineering of data collection procedures in an attempt to reconcile the data.

In the early 1980s, data management, facilitated by a data administration group, became popular as a vehicle to address the problem of data consistency. However, data administration enjoyed little success due to the political climate in most businesses. Early data warehousing efforts also failed, largely due to a lack of will on the part of the business to spend time, people, and money to correct, integrate, and repair their data assets. This situation still persists today and will not change for most businesses until competitive pressure such as the deregulation in the telecommunications industry, or environmental concerns (such as those raised over world CO_2 output), force businesses to change. Private sector businesses have the most to gain from improved data quality management, yet this sector suffer substantially in their level of data quality management.

To be successful in data warehousing from a data quality perspective, we must understand the level of data management maturity (discussed in Chapter Six) which exists within our business and to gauge what will be a practical starting point for our data warehousing effort.

Understanding the political climate, in terms of the "art of the possible" will help us set the stage for success. Chapter Four on data quality management describes how we gauge our level of business process maturity and determine what is possible, from a data management perspective, in our initial and successive data warehousing implementations.

Inconsistent and inaccurate data can lead to disastrous business decisions. Therefore, it is important that we verify the level of accuracy and consistency existing within our current source systems before we develop the data staging and data management layers of the data warehouse architecture. Maintaining credibility in our warehouse remains an essential key for ongoing success.

Data warehousing efforts often falter due to

- The magnitude of the business problem is not fully understood.
- Sponsorship does not exist or is incorrectly positioned.
- Little or no project infrastructure exists.
- Change management has been ignored or understated.
- Long term strategy or direction has not been established.
- A program management process is lacking.

Let us look into each one of these problem areas in more detail.

THE MAGNITUDE OF THE BUSINESS PROBLEM IS NOT FULLY UNDERSTOOD

Data warehousing initiatives start with requirement definition. However, this process is often short circuited as information management departments plunge into this technology. Without fully understanding the nature or importance of the business problem, it becomes a difficult task selecting and implementing a technology solution. A number of factors come into play that will ultimately affect what is delivered to the client.

1. What is the critical need of our client?
   - To improve operational efficiency?
   - To obtain a competitive position in the marketplace?
   - To invent a new market?
2. How will this technology improve business practices?
3. Will data warehousing costs justify the return on investment?
4. What will the impact of this technology be on the end users in terms of changing their job descriptions and rewards?

What can happen

In a telecommunications company, the data warehouse architecture was skewed toward delivering only one aspect of the business—current promotions and campaign management. Since only a limited aspect of the business was covered, the client is now faced with a credibility problem with its data warehousing program. Why? The client's significant investment in this technology failed to yield any tangible benefits.

To obviate this problem, ensure that a complete and accurate assessment of the business opportunity is undertaken in terms of publishing, distributing and understanding the impact of change on the business. A statement of requirements must contain recommendations for moving forward in a cost effective and efficient manner.

SPONSORSHIP DOES NOT EXIST OR IS INCORRECTLY POSITIONED

Visible, credible sponsorship is key to the success of any data warehouse project. Often, though, these initiatives address project sponsorship as a by product or afterthought. Buy in at the executive level is critical for success, especially when the data warehouse involves user groups across lines of business.

What can happen

A health care provider selected an IT approach, where the information services department took it upon themselves to sponsor the data warehouse program. With no executive end user buy in resource commitments slipped pushing the project dangerously over budget.

To ensure success, secure a viable and active project sponsor to establish a clear direction and business purpose for the data warehouse. Produce this agreement in the form of a project approach document or project charter, which describes what is expected from each party (business and information technology). The project approach document establishes the contract between IT and the business by explaining the approach, scope, costs, and time frame of the proposed investment.

LITTLE OR NO INFRASTRUCTURE EXISTS

Infrastructure is critical to the overall success of the data warehouse. Often, though, data warehousing initiatives fail to address the need for establishing a dedicated core team that can then direct and determine the eventual size and structure of the data warehouse organization, along with each department's roles and responsibilities.

What can happen

An insurance/finance company initiated a number of data warehousing projects that overlapped across business lines. With no core team, or program group in place, the cost of each data warehouse, in terms of duplicate data and technology, soared. Now the organization is challenged to return to basics and reestablish its system of record for each subject area while also trying to come to terms with the escalating costs of inconsistent and conflicting technology.

A dedicated data warehouse organization can also help kick start subsequent data warehousing projects. This team can oversee the long term direction of the data warehouse program as well as provide continued support for the first project. This core group contains experienced data warehouse project management personnel who have experience in or have been trained to understand data warehousing as a point of departure or change for not only the business but IT as well. Data warehousing implies a knowledge base rather than a transaction based perspective. Its critical success factors and key components imply a radical shift for most IT organizations. As a consequence of this process, a number of critical touch points exist for the data warehouse infrastructure.

- Data administration
- Database administration
- Methodology and CASE tools
- Network and communication
- Data stewardship and IT governance
- Information systems planning

CHANGE MANAGEMENT HAS BEEN IGNORED OR UNDERSTATED

Data warehousing affects the assessment and planning for future business activities as well as its day to day operations. It is important to understand the impact of the technology on customer touch points and how it is being applied in the business if people management problems are to be avoided.

What can happen

An insurance company did not pay heed to the challenges of change management, implementing a "closed loop" data warehousing process. The new system was to feed decision support information and suggestions to customer service representatives on how to improve customer needs. However, the customer service representatives' performance measurement program remained as it was, with individuals assessed on the number of calls completed in a day and not on how they addressed each call. The end result—a considerable investment in this technology had a minimal impact on the business. The overall data warehousing initiative was placed in jeopardy when the customer service representatives made little or no use of the enhanced system.

To ensure the infrastructure and end user issues are addressed as part of the overall delivery of the data warehouse, a change management assessment must be undertaken. This change readiness assessment, completed in conjunction with an overall assessment of the IT organization's, produces support and deliverables throughout the business. The results of this assessment form part of the business case or value proposition.

LONG TERM STRATEGY OR DIRECTION HAS NOT BEEN ESTABLISHED

Data warehousing is an architecture as much as it is a process. Therefore, emphasis must be placed on understanding the functions of this architecture, whether it is operational data store based and/or following a data warehouse approach. Without an architecture in place, the IT organization will implement a patchwork, inconsistent solution. Such an approach stresses the ability of the operations groups to provide and maintain the necessary level of support. The architecture also provides the IT organization with means to gauge the viability of vendor solutions. Establishing a framework and educating vendors to this framework leaves the business in charge rather than the organization falling victim to what the vendor(s) perceives as the appropriate course of action.

What can happen

An insurance provider had its business and IT departments separately consult and contract for services with a number of vendors, each of whom had his or her own architecture process, resulting in overspending on technology acquisition and causing maintenance costs to escalate.

Establishing a direction for the data warehouse is critical for long term success, due to its inherent complexity and far reaching implications to the business. We should develop the data warehouse architecture framework as part of data warehouse program plan, with a description for each architecture layer. These layers consist of

- Processor/server
- Network and communications architecture
- Source systems and operational data store
- Data staging
- Data warehouse subject area and line of business data mart
- Decision support/desktop and data mining application systems

A PROGRAM MANAGEMENT PROCESS IS LACKING

A program management function delivered as a program management office (PMO) is another key ingredient to success. For large scale data warehousing projects, a program office provides cross project direction, method and technology development guidelines, architecture planning, and project management support. However, program management is often overlooked in the push to rapidly deliver a data warehouse to the business. As is the case with the architecture, deploy the PMO in increments in size and scale that suits the development of the warehouse. Without a PMO, project issues such as interproject environment start up and support, interdependencies on other data warehousing, or operational systems initiatives are left to individual project teams to manage.

What can happen

A telecommunications company failed to establish a PMO when an uncoordinated program planning initiative resulted in varying and inconsistent project planning, staffing, and scoping processes. Addressing these issues consumed valuable time and delayed the staffing and start up of the data warehouse by three months.

Establish a PMO as part of the initial start up and planning process. Key functions to consider include

- Architecture planning and administration
- Development environment planning
- Business case and project charter development
- Change management
- Issue management
- Status reporting
- Program and project roles and responsibilities planning and deployment
- Training and education planning for IT and the business
- Methodology and CASE tool support
- Repository/metadata management
- Vendor management
- Marketing and communication management

WHAT KINDS OF BENEFITS CAN BE ACHIEVED?

Return on investment is only an aspect of the potential benefits that can be obtained from data warehousing. Successful data warehousing initiatives have yielded hundredfold return on investment returns in as little as six months to one year. The real benefits, however, lie with the impact such knowledge capital has on the business. Not only can a data warehouse promote operational efficiency, but it also leads to significant organizational change, where the business literally reinvents itself to become much more competitive and profitable. This is the real attraction in deploying this business intelligence driven technology.

Successfully marketing data warehousing to the business requires that the benefits be stated in tangible and intangible terms, where the data collected and new best practices lead to the knowledge management organization. In the knowledge management organization, business goes beyond data collection and moves into the realm of business enablement via the sharing of best practices (knowledge) throughout the enterprise. Achieving this goal requires a set of entrenched and supported data management practices that encourage sharing of expertise and information in a constructive and healthful manner. The traditional approach is to household knowledge and data along departmental boundaries where incentives are measured and rewarded on individual rather than on community success. This is another feature of successful data warehousing efforts where the compensation and incentive programs fall in line with the core competencies and direction of the business enabled by data warehousing.

◆

CHAPTER TWO

Components of a Data Warehouse Architecture

WHY AN ARCHITECTURE?

In managing the implementation of a data warehouse, numerous business and information system components must be considered, ranging from organizational support issues to database technology and network capacity. These components exist across a set of functional layers, which make up the data warehouse. These layers, with their shared components, form an integrated working system or architecture. Building and changing this architecture is accomplished in stages in support of the changing needs of the business.

Much like any other evolving architecture, these components consist of

- Hardware and software products
- Network and communications
- Retrieval, repair, and consolidation of data
- Storage, replication, and backup of data
- Access and formatting data
- Process management
- Information directory management

With these components in mind, it becomes difficult to select an "off the shelf" solution. This suite of products, or services, must address all the aforementioned items and, together, support the evolving information systems framework. Therefore, to develop the solution set that is right for our

19

company's needs, we must first understand the parameters of our own environment and prepare a shopping list, or blueprint, against which these various options can be measured. In addition, terminology utilized by the industry can also lead to confusion when selecting the right combination of products and services once our architecture is defined. As a necessary first step, then, we need to develop a conceptual architecture, or framework, that describes the roles of each component within our architecture. Once our functional definition (or blueprint) has been prepared, the staging, data management, data access, process management, and information directory layers which make up this architecture can be planned. Based on the scope, type, and size of our warehousing/data mart project, development and implementation timeframes are then determined for the seven components that exist these five layers of our architecture.

COMPONENTS OF THE DATA WAREHOUSE ARCHITECTURE

The data warehouse architecture consists of five major layers or properties.

1. Data staging
2. Data management
3. Data access
4. Infrastructure
5. Information directory

THE DATA STAGING LAYER

The data staging layer manages all data extraction, transformation, aggregation, cleansing, and distribution from business and external system data assets to the data management layer.

The data staging layer requires management of the following five components:

1. Hardware and software products
2. Network and communications

Figure 2-1
The Data Warehouse Architecture

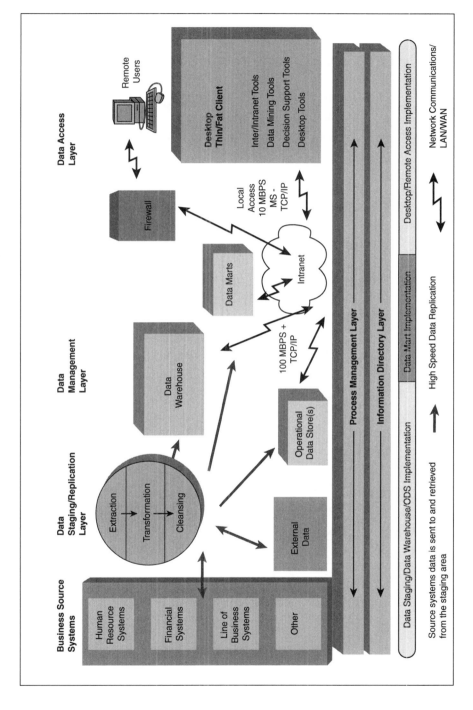

Figure 2–2
The Data Staging Layer

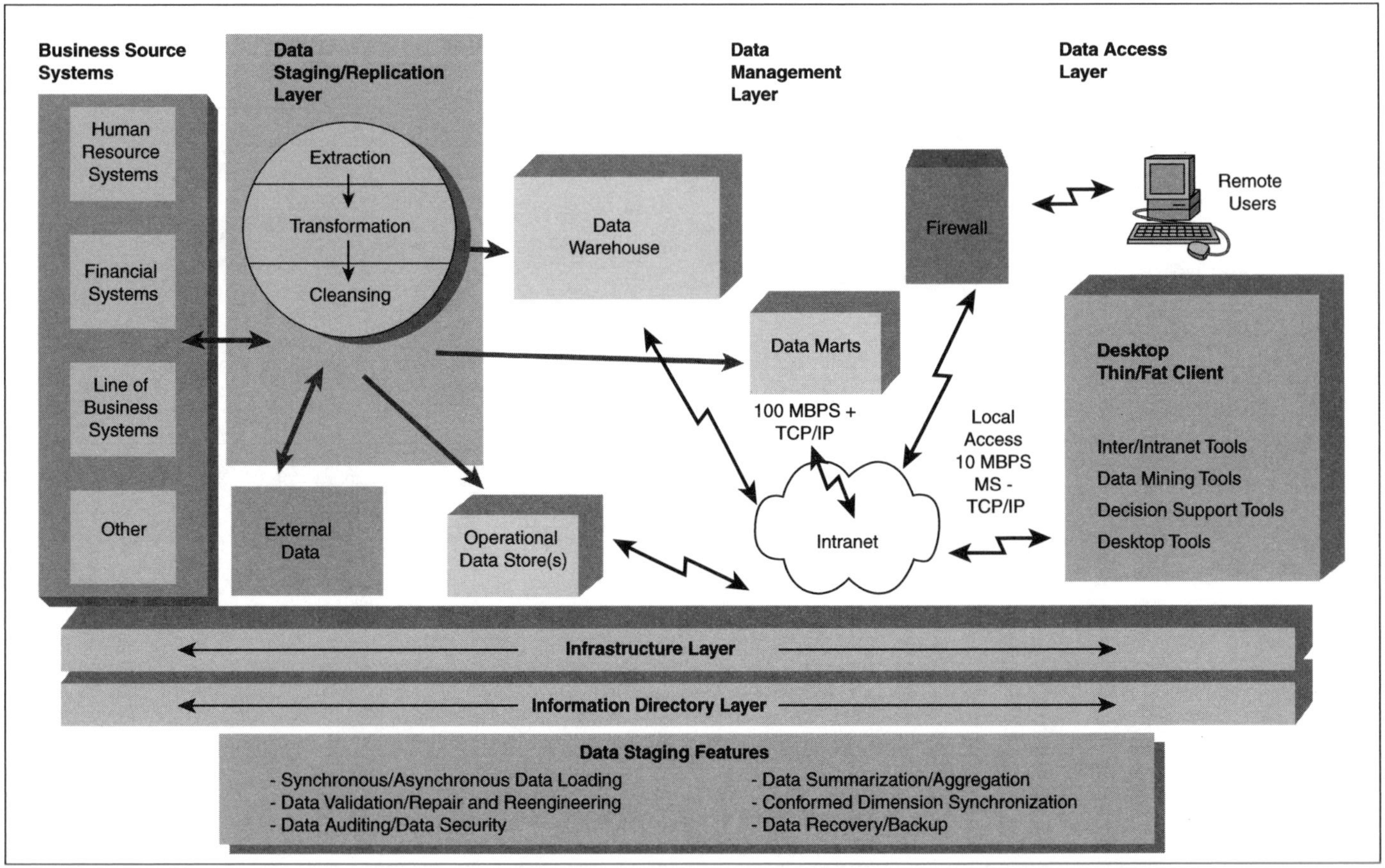

3. Retrieval, distribution, repair, and consolidation

4. Process management

5. Information directory management

THE DATA MANAGEMENT LAYER

The data management layer manages all storage, backup, and recovery of all data moved to the data warehousing environment. The data management layer manages the data warehouse, operational data store, and data mart databases.

The data management layer requires management of the following five components:

1. Hardware and software products

2. Network and communications

3. Storage and backup

4. Process management

5. Information directory management

THE DATA ACCESS LAYER

The data access layer collects, consolidates, and formats data collected from the data management layer. The data access layer is the business user's window into the total data inventory as maintained by the data management layer. In conjunction with the data management and information directory layer, this environment also manages data security.

The data access layer requires management of the following five components:

1. Hardware and software products

2. Network and communications

3. Access and formatting

4. Process management

5. Information directory management

Figure 2–3
The Data Management Layer

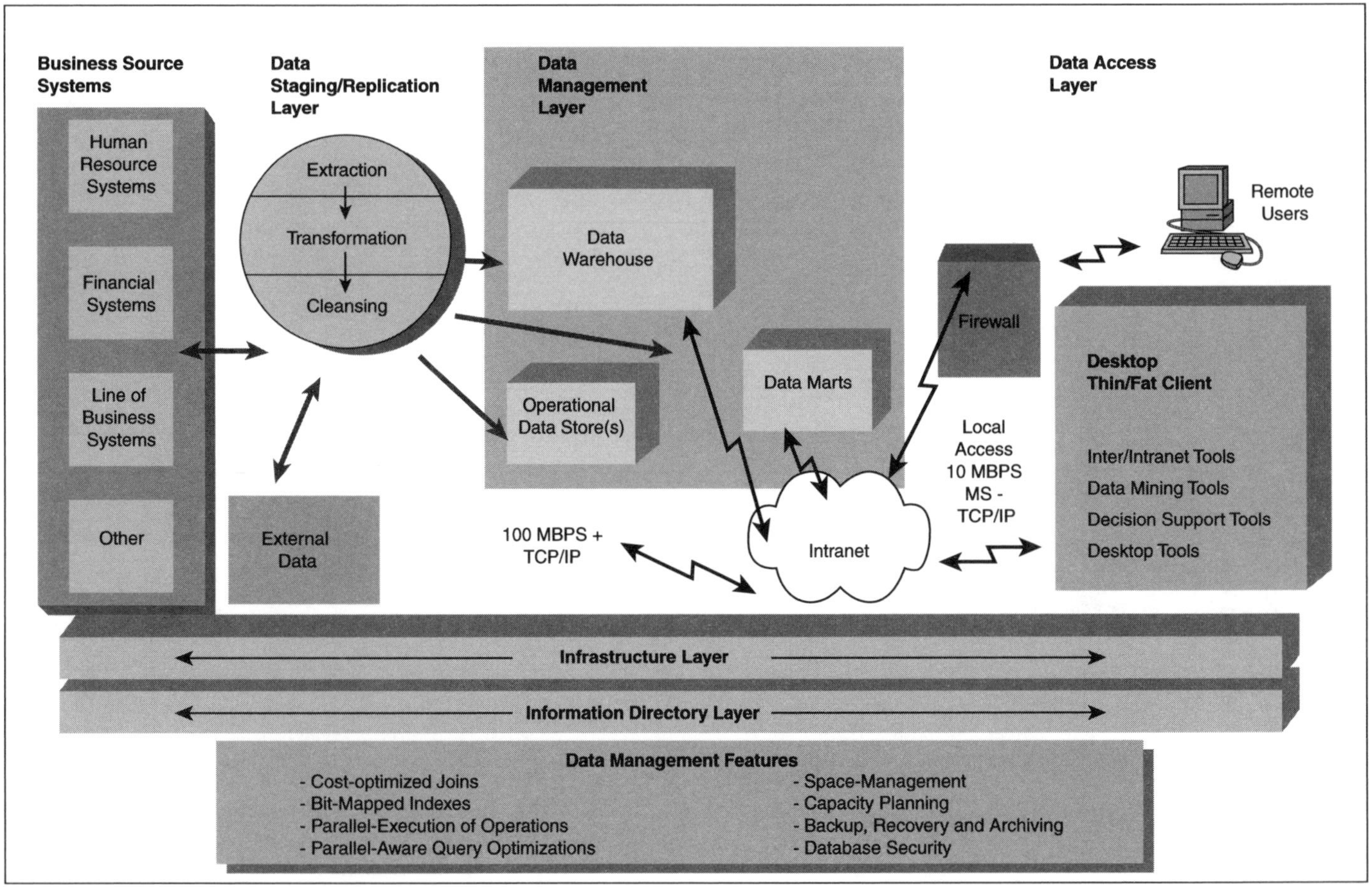

Figure 2–4
The Data Access Layer

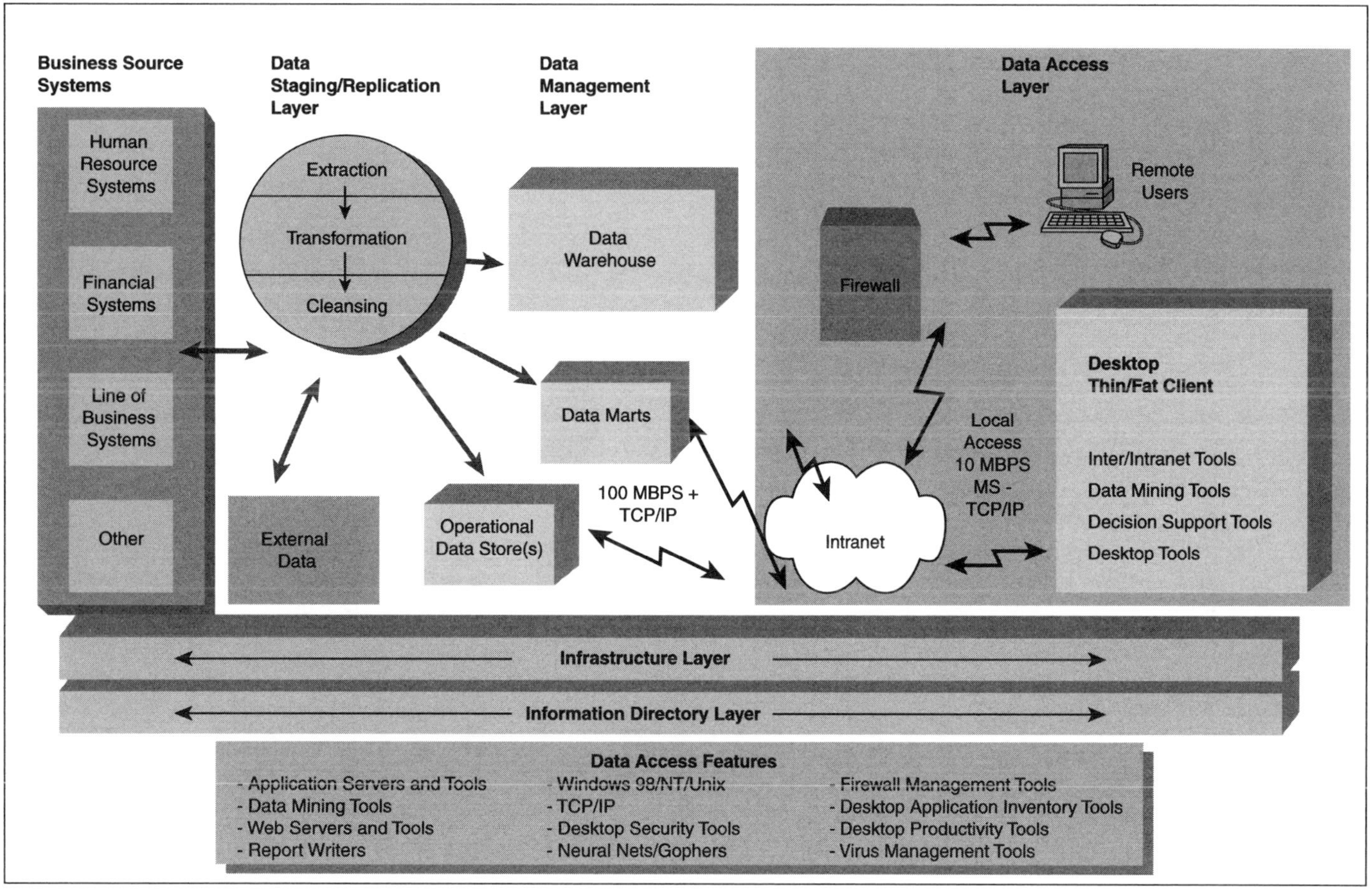

Business Source Systems
- Human Resource Systems
- Financial Systems
- Line of Business Systems
- Other

Data Staging/Replication Layer
- Extraction
- Transformation
- Cleansing
- External Data

Data Management Layer
- Data Warehouse
- Data Marts
- Operational Data Store(s)

100 MBPS + TCP/IP

Data Access Layer
- Remote Users
- Firewall
- Intranet

Local Access 10 MBPS MS-TCP/IP

Desktop Thin/Fat Client
- Inter/Intranet Tools
- Data Mining Tools
- Decision Support Tools
- Desktop Tools

Infrastructure Layer

Information Directory Layer

Data Access Features
- Application Servers and Tools
- Data Mining Tools
- Web Servers and Tools
- Report Writers
- Windows 98/NT/Unix
- TCP/IP
- Desktop Security Tools
- Neural Nets/Gophers
- Firewall Management Tools
- Desktop Application Inventory Tools
- Desktop Productivity Tools
- Virus Management Tools

INFRASTRUCTURE LAYER

Probably one of the most important, yet often forgotten layers of the data warehouse architecture is the infrastructure layer. This layer manages the methodology and tools required to build and maintain the data warehouse architecture. It includes all project management procedures and defines the required end user processes used to access and maintain the data in the data warehouse. The infrastructure layer also manages all required hardware and software selection, certification, and product maintenance and support. This infrastructure layer directs the development and deployment of all necessary support group procedures and required data warehouse organizational infrastructure in terms of skills, roles, and responsibilities. This layer further addresses organizational development issues, in terms of organizational change management for business users and IT support personnel. Training programs are also managed at this layer of the architecture.

The infrastructure layer requires management of the following three components:

1. Hardware and software products
2. Process management
3. Information directory management

INFORMATION DIRECTORY LAYER

The information directory layer manages the three schema metadata directory/repository and all required links to the other layers of the architecture. All metadata for the data warehousing environment is managed here. This layer also addresses all data administration and data stewardship issues that arise out of the collection, definition, and use of metadata.

The information directory layer requires management of the following three components:

1. Hardware and software products
2. Process management
3. Information directory management

Figure 2-5
The Infrastructure Layer

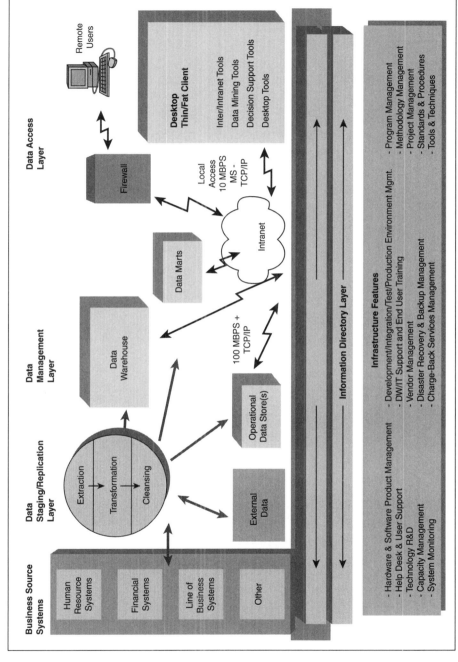

Figure 2-6
The Information Directory Layer

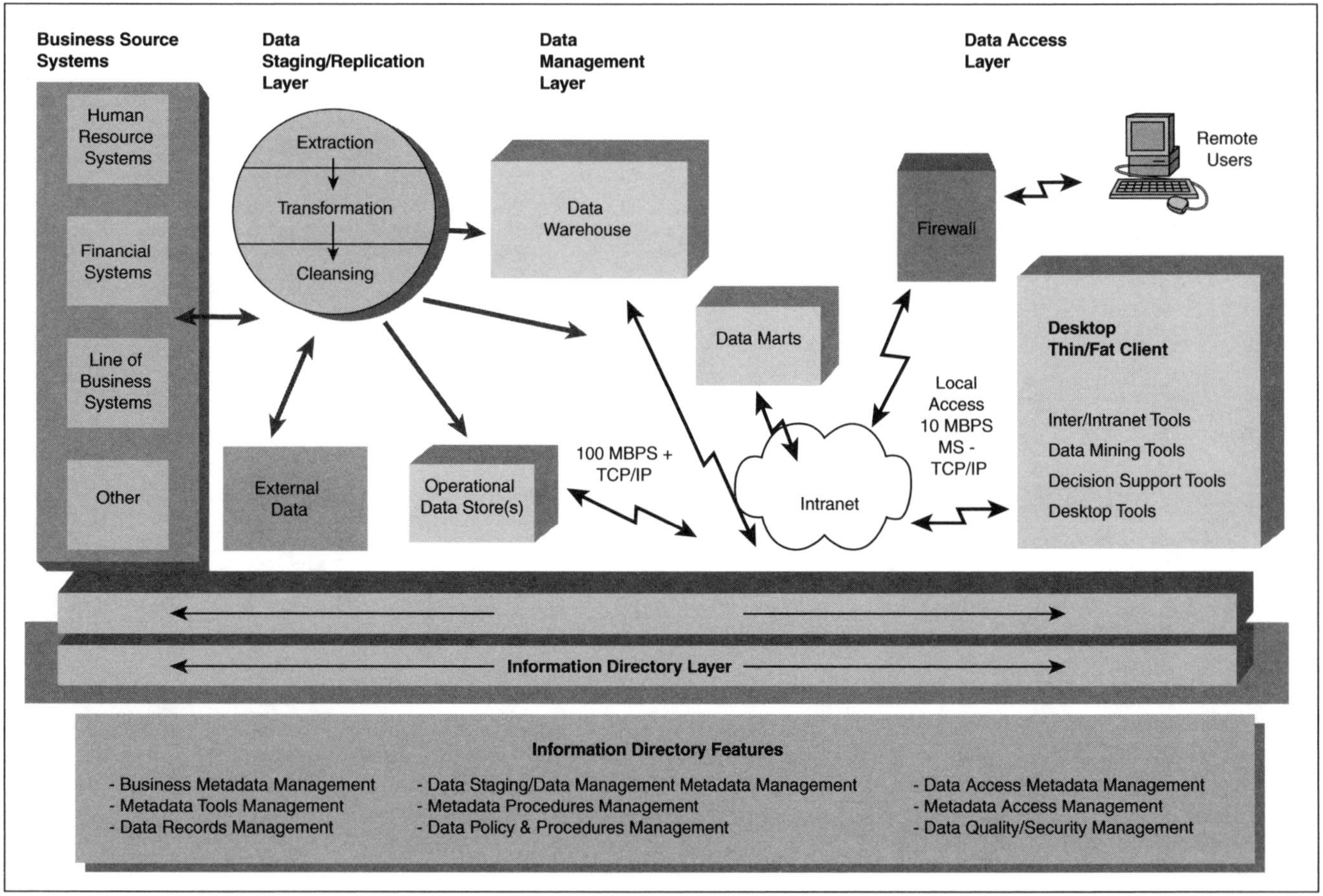

Each layer of the data warehouse architecture requires management of several components that support the five layers of the architecture (data staging, data management, data access, infrastructure, and information directory as described above). Each component contains a number of different features as itemized here.

1. Hardware and software products and services
   a. Requirements preparation and selection of product version or service (in the form of a request for information (RFI), request for quotation (RFQ), request for proposal or service (RFP)
   b. Product certification (testing)
   c. Product release staging to the production environment
   d. Product version/release maintenance
   e. Product training and use
   f. Consultant selection and review
   g. Vendor management
      i. *Vendor financial analysis*
      ii. *Vendor reference verification*
      iii. *Industry and market surveys and evaluations (i.e. Gartner, Seybold, MetaGroup)*

2. Network and communications management
   a. Logical network address flexibility (protocol compatibility)
   b. Physical network capacity management (bandwidth)
   c. Inter/Intranet requirements

3. Retrieval, distribution, repair, and consolidation
   a. Identification and management for system of record locations
   b. Data extraction from business source and external systems
   c. Data verification and repair
   d. Data aggregation
   e. Data replication and distribution

4. Storage and backup
   a. Logical and physical database design

    b. Database security

    c. Database tuning

    d. Database journaling

    e. Database backup and recovery

    f. Database archiving

    g. Database disaster recovery

5. Access and formatting

    a. End user interface standardization

        i. Browsers

        ii. E mail

        iii. Interactive media (video conferencing)

        iv. Desktop (e.g., Microsoft Office, Lotus Works)

        v. System of record selection, consolidation, translation, and formatting from database sources

    b. End user tool suite selection

        i. Decision support/executive information systems management tools

        ii. Multidimensional analysis/data mining tools

        iii. Predictive modeling tools

6. Process management

    a. Methodology and supporting tools selection and implementation

    b. Development/test/production environments design and implementation

    c. Project office management

        i. Cross project controls and communication

        ii. Cross data warehouse/data mart projects with other business systems

        iii. Project planning and budgeting guidelines

        iv. Project administration and reporting guidelines

            (1) Change management

            (2) Issue management

            (3) Knowledge management (skills transfers)

    d. Project communications (awareness presentations, distributing project updates)

7. Information directory management

    a. Repository planning and analysis (three schema modeling)

    b. Repository product(s) selection and customization

    c. CASE tool/business intelligence/data staging/database management metadata integration process design and implementation

    d. Roles and responsibilities for data warehousing

    e. Data security procedures

       i. Data sensitivity guidelines

      ii. Data access authorization guidelines

     iii. User profile maintenance guidelines

    f. Data stewardship procedures

       i. Stewardship process setup and management guidelines

      ii. Roles and responsibilities

     iii. Data certification procedures

    g. Data analysis processes

       i. Data administration procedures

      ii. Data modeling guidelines

     iii. Data definition guidelines

     iv. Data format guidelines

        (1) Electronic

        (2) Paper

        (3) Video

        (4) Microfiche

    h. Data quality procedures

       i. Data content guidelines

      ii. Data context guidelines

     iii. Data currency guidelines

DEVELOPING A DATA WAREHOUSE ARCHITECTURE

Developing a data warehouse architecture requires planning for the immediate, or short term needs (one to two years), as well as satisfying long term direction for knowledge management services. With this approach we are able to leverage our initial technology investment and not have to replace it when a subsequent data warehouse iteration is developed.

The key to selecting and implementing an architecture for data warehousing requires following one of two approaches:

1. Implementing the architecture by layer(s)
2. Implementing the architecture by segment(s)

IMPLEMENTING THE ARCHITECTURE IN LAYERS

Implementing the architecture in layers requires the deployment of a scalable infrastructure. This provides services across the retrieval, storage, and access layers enabling long term growth. To provide scalable growth, most organizations now opt for a three tier architecture approach where the storage and application software and the hardware components are managed by separate servers. These hardware and operating system combinations consist of mainframe, minis, and NT or Unix based servers.

In building the architecture in layers we consider five components.

1. Hardware and operating system software that have the capacity to scale up from symmetrical multiprocessing (SMP)[1] and clusters to massively parallel processing (MPP)[2] to nonuniform memory access (NUMA)[3] when required.

---

[1] A typical SMP architecture allows for the sharing of up to 16 processors through a common system bus, which accesses global system memory and an I/O controller.

[2] MPP architectures manages disk and memory access multiple nodes: Each node is a mini SMP system with its own dedicated memory, processors, disk, and operating system. These types of architectures can support up to 64 modes.

[3] NUMA takes advantage of the benefits of the SMP and MPP architectures. MPP system building blocks are very similar to MPP nodes except that memory is shared across all blocks. This architecture provides a single system image for memory and disk access. NUMA is seen to be the architecture of the future.

2. Database software that manages data into the terabyte range and scale up from clusters and SMP to massively parallel processing machines managing very large databases (VLDB)s. An initial database layer contains a data staging component to collect and prepare the data for loading into the warehouse and a data warehouse/data mart to house the data (often on the same server). With successive iterations, or based on capacity management thresholds for both storage and access, these two architecture components eventually migrate to separate servers.

3. Access software for decision support analysis that can operate in a thin client mode or can start as a fat client on a local server and desktop environment and scale up to three tier running on dedicated application servers.

4. Retrieval data access software scales from using ODBC to TCP/IP protocols accessing internal and external data sources. This middleware draws knowledge objects from internal systems directly or through dedicated data lines, connected to off site services or facilities. The architecture alternatives vary based on criticality and currency of the data. Access to real time data is the most complex of all, where up to the minute results are required for business analysis. Often real time data access requires routines to be either written in house or by services provided by real time data management vendors.

5. Metadata management software that addresses source code and data definition management requirements that scales up to the needs of an object oriented environment with data types expanding to include image, voice, and video.

Data staging services encompass software and procedures developed to manage the data extraction, cleansing, and aggregation of business and external data. Advanced data staging services also include an adjunct service called data reengineering where legacy data is repaired in the operational systems databases before it is migrated to the data staging environment.

Process and information directory services are initially provided by the data warehousing staff. Over time, these services are split into operational support (for ongoing care and maintenance of the data warehouse) and help desk support (who provide integrated call center assistance). The data warehousing staff initially provides these services as it assists them in understanding the nature of the environment they have built before passing it onto others for management.

IMPLEMENTING THE ARCHITECTURE IN SEGMENTS

Implementing the architecture in segments involves an evolutionary approach where the target is the total data warehouse environment. The data warehouse environment is implemented either from the access layer in or from the data management layer out.

DATA WAREHOUSE ARCHITECTURES DEVELOPED FROM THE ACCESS LAYER IN

The access layer in approach requires careful planning of each line of business data mart (DM) or operational data store (ODS). Each data mart, or operational data store, must retrieve data from an integrated data staging area. By staging data centrally, one of the biggest problems with marts and operational data stores is avoided unsynchronized data.

DATA WAREHOUSE ARCHITECTURES DEVELOPED FROM THE DATA MANAGEMENT LAYER OUT

Building the data warehouse from the data management area out involves developing and deploying operational data stores. The operational data store(s) (ODS) acts as an initial staging area for integrated subject matter data. Developing the data management layer in this way is most often chosen by firms entering into data warehousing since it provides initial exposure to components of this technology without assuming either the financial or end user risk of data credibility in a fully defined enterprise level service.

The method we choose will largely depend on the information management maturity level[4] within the business.

---

[4] The maturity model consists of five layers—Initial, Repeatable, Defined, Managed, and Optimized. Businesses are usually assessed at being at one of these five layers and progress over time up the scale. Data warehouses are most successful at the Managed or Optimized level where the true business benefits can be measured and achieved.

Figure 2-7
The Information Systems Maturity Model

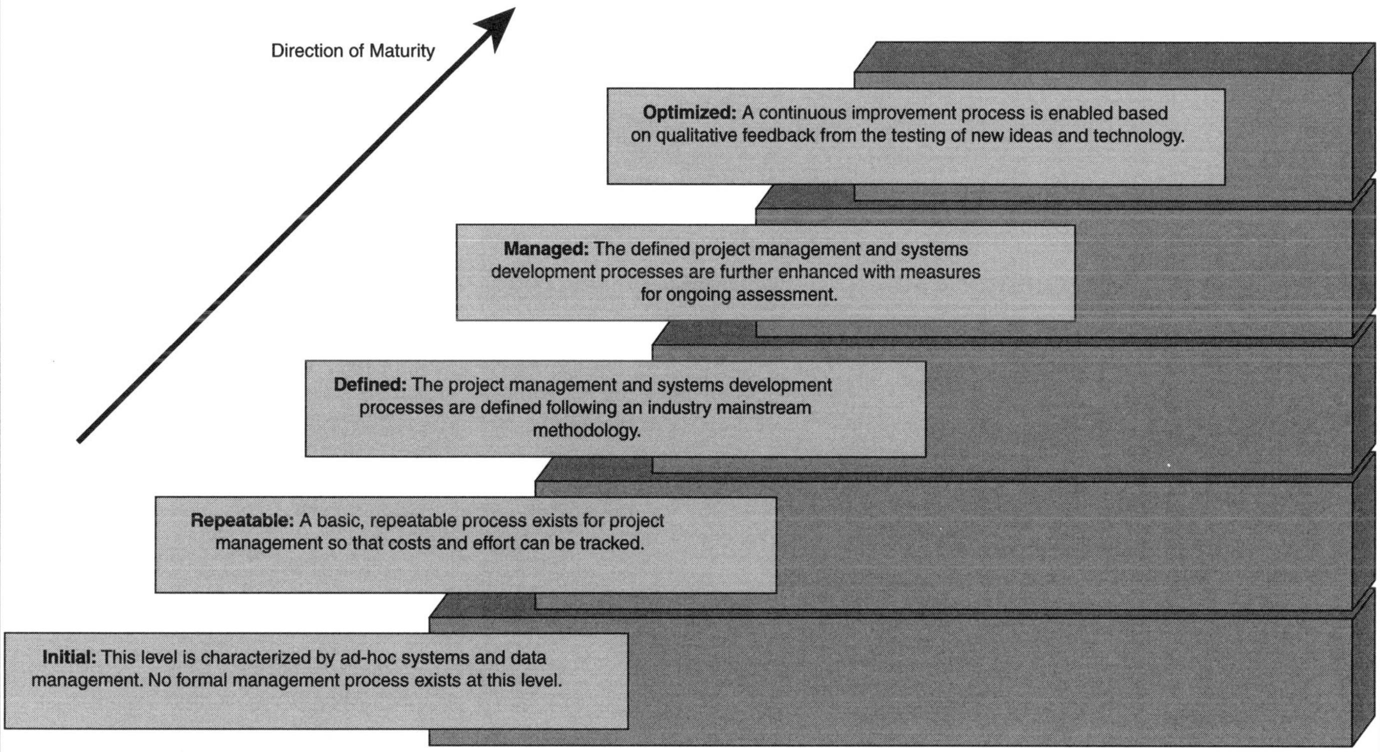

Direction of Maturity

Optimized: A continuous improvement process is enabled based on qualitative feedback from the testing of new ideas and technology.

Managed: The defined project management and systems development processes are further enhanced with measures for ongoing assessment.

Defined: The project management and systems development processes are defined following an industry mainstream methodology.

Repeatable: A basic, repeatable process exists for project management so that costs and effort can be tracked.

Initial: This level is characterized by ad-hoc systems and data management. No formal management process exists at this level.

Source: Carnegie Mellon University

The most common order of development for the data warehouse involves

1. Building a set of operational data stores, which are fed from a common data staging area. These operational data stores are accessed by report writing software and decision support software. Limited drill down and analysis is available with the suite of decision support tools utilized at this time (due to the short term nature and volatility of the data stored in the ODS environment).

2. This architecture is extended to include online analytical processing (OLAP) multidimensional data servers for data mining applications, usually for customer relationship management purposes. At this time, or later in the process, the enterprise data warehouse is developed with its updates also coming from the data staging area.[5] At the same time, access to the operational data store environment changes to one of near term detailed management status reporting. The decision support software is repointed to access the data warehouse for historical cross lines of business data as well as the ODS environment for near term current detail data. Often this stage is expanded to include what is called "closed loop" data warehousing where customer knowledge is collected and presented back to the various customer touch points for use by the customers or by customer service representatives.

3. The final stage establishes a data warehouse monitoring and data archiving process where stale data that has not been accessed for a period of years (to be specified by the organization) is purged from the warehouse and placed in archive. Data warehouse monitoring is required for ongoing capacity management and planning of the data warehouse database growth.

Throughout this process, the information directory layer is enhanced. The first implementation usually deals with internal schema and external schema metadata management.[6] With successive iterations, the data warehouse metadata management expands to embrace the conceptual layer to provide better business understanding of metadata to the broader base of end users.

---

[5] This concept of data staging is referred to as the "hub and spoke," where the hub of the wheel is the data staging environment, with all internal and external data (the spokes) feeding information into a set of tables for data correction, cleansing, and aggregation. A set of load tables is then prepared to feed a data mart, data warehouse, or operational data store with its required data updates.

[6] For an explanation of the various layers of metadata, please consult Chapter 3.

CHAPTER THREE

Understanding Metadata Management

WHAT IS METADATA?

The textbook definition of metadata is "data about data." Metadata acts as a describer of persons, places, things, and business events. We use metadata on a daily basis to make sense of our world.

In information technology systems, metadata is often confused with actual data. Real world examples of metadata include

- What a library card catalog is used for
- The description requirements for products and services offered by a company in their marketing materials and employee handbooks
- The explanation behind a product change, in terms of who made it and when it should take effect
- The purpose and role of legislation in running government
- Why intersections are marked for street crossing

Metadata exist everywhere in the business world as well; therefore, it must be managed as part of any data warehousing project. Data warehousing utilizes metadata to describe the information it collects from transaction processing systems. Metadata also explain the business context behind the data to the users of the data warehouse.

WHAT ARE THE VARIOUS KINDS
OF METADATA?

In data warehousing, metadata is referred to as "technical" (technology system influenced) or "business" focused.

TECHNICAL METADATA

Technical metadata cover the data movement, translation, aggregation, and presentation of data. Technical metadata support the technology implementation of the warehouse. Some traditional examples include

- Database system catalogs where electronic file and record layouts are stored
- Data dictionaries
- Database designs (schemas)
- Automated source code management systems

BUSINESS METADATA

Business metadata focus on what the information means to the business. Business metadata define information about the business and what this data means. This is largely an artificial division as most products blur the line between the two categories.

Complexities around metadata are further aggravated by how the various ERP and third party vendors have developed their metadata management repositories, confusing actual data with metadata. For example, a number of vendors treat a translation algorithm as metadata. An algorithm is, in fact, data, not metadata. The metadata for the algorithm include purpose and intended use in the business. The programming code, or formula, that describes how the algorithm actually works is the data (or information).

The confusion between business and technical metadata and the overlaps between them are addressed by describing what it is about metadata that we want to manage. In data warehousing, we are concerned with what the data mean in our warehouse, where it came from, and how it should be presented or translated. Following a three schema* architecture approach to metadata management, we seek to manage

1. Internal metadata: information about the physical location, type, and movement/translation history
    - For internal schema metadata managers, we look to data extraction/translation and movement tools. The internal schema describes.
        - Changes to the data's structure and size
        - Translation, repair, and aggregation history
        - Naming conventions in use at the time
        - Data metrics such as how many rows and how fast the data is growing

2. External metadata: information about how metadata is represented or displayed to end users
    - When referring to external schema metadata we are looking at the metadata managed by the various front end decision support and executive information system tools. The external schema describe
        - How the data is being accessed and changed for presentation purposes
        - Their ownership history

3. Conceptual metadata: information about the business meaning and context of the data
    - The difficult part is the conceptual schema metadata layer. Here we look to traditional repositories, source system catalog managers, office automation/Internet software, and other available sources where business information and ownership/stewardship regarding the data is managed and presented to the business users. It is the conceptual layer that ties it all together and gives meaning to information about what the data mean in the warehouse. Contextual and content related information is managed by the conceptual schema. Contextual information assists the end user in understand-

*A three schema approach describes information technology as being conceptual (business driven), internal (database defined) or external (user access driven).

ing the nature and timing of the data in terms of its history and intended use. The conceptual schema describes contextual information about

- Organizational descriptions and their changes across time
- Product and or service descriptions and their changes
- Pricing policies and procedures currently enforced
- Market segmentation and product/service distribution descriptions
- External contextual data such as economic, geographic, meteorologic, competitive, technological, consumer, or political events.

With a three schema perspective, it becomes easier to break down the problem of metadata management and look to tools and processes to manage each aspect. The more mundane, but essential who, what, when, where, and how, in terms of how the data is extracted, repaired, summarized, aggregated, and staged into the data warehouse or data mart, is shared across the internal and external metadata schemas.

THE METADATA AUDIENCE

Regardless whether we follow a business/technical view of metadata or a three schema view, the traditional audience of metadata management remains the IS practitioner and not the end user. Few, if any metadata tools today are engineered with the business end user in mind. The history of data processing, due to time and product pressures, reduced metadata management to a "nice to have" or "we'll get to it later" status. The challenge of implementing a metadata management process, therefore, is not a technology issue, but rather one of breaking with past habits and perspectives. If the business does not view information about its knowledge assets as a necessary commodity worth managing, then our efforts to enable a metadata management process will not meet with complete success. The end user, or the group that can contribute the most to capturing and enabling the use of metadata, is often left out or not consulted. Therefore, to extend the metadata audience, we must consider not only the technology factors in play but the human ones as well. We must also consider expediency and cost as it relate to metadata management. Like any other asset worth managing, metadata require intensive capital and resource investments. Metadata can quickly become a management nightmare if not approached in an organized and informed manner.

METADATA MANAGEMENT METRICS

Metadata management can become a daunting process. If, on average, a business manages 10,000 data fields in the various records and repositories, the metadata catalog, as a rule of thumb, must track for *each data field* a minimum of

- 8+ internal schema fields (source, target, size, structure, algorithm, frequency of update, growth, version definitions)
- 4+ external schema fields (user, security level, location, local view structure)
- 8+ conceptual schema fields (name, description, synonym, homonym, definition/change date, effective date/until date, comments, business rule)

In other words, $(20 \times 10,000$ fields) equates to 200,000 metadata definitions!

These numbers are staggering and pose a real challenge for effective metadata management. It becomes an essential first step to target those parts of the metadata architecture that provide the highest return to the business at the lowest cost. In terms of timeframe and cost, the internal schema data remain the least costly to collect and automate since it can be extracted from database catalogs. The conceptual schema metadata remain the most time consuming and difficult to manage since we must gain consensus across the entire business for the properties of each corporate metadata definition. Data administrators have been wrestling with and failing the conceptual metadata challenge for more than two decades, due to the poor level of data management that exists within most organizations. Our challenge in tackling the metadata management problem is to first understand our organization's strengths and weaknesses in establishing and maintaining sound data management practices before deciding on an implementation approach.

DEPLOYING METADATA MANAGEMENT

In deploying metadata management, look at it as an ongoing process, much like any other facet in our data warehousing environment.

To succeed in metadata management we must strive to

1. Understand where our organization fits in the information management maturity cycle by conducting a review of[1]
   a. Data dictionaries/CASE tools
   b. Business systems documentation
   c. Data management/data architecture/models

2. Educate our business and technology users to the importance of metadata management.

3. Plan the scope of implementation to enhance the delivery of the first or subsequent iterations of our data warehouse architecture by
   a. Obtaining a data warehouse program sponsor/steward for metadata
   b. Creating a project/program charter for metadata (separate from the data warehouse/data mart approach documents)[2]

Once we understand where we are able to achieve success by assisting data warehousing projects in managing the metadata, then an enabling process in terms of procedures and tools can be considered.

In evaluating a metadata management process we must then establish

1. A set of business/technical roles and responsibilities[3]

2. A process to be followed, or interfaced with, on each data warehousing project and a suite of tools, whether standalone or integrated directly within the data warehouse architecture, to manage the metadata

---

[1] Consult the Data Warehouse Assistant on the CD ROM disk for a metadata evaluation checklist form. The capability maturity model charts the progress of IS from initial to repeatable, defined, managed, and optimized levels of performance.

[2] Consult the Data Warehouse Assistant on the CD ROM disk for a sample metadata management charter.

[3] Please consult Chapter 7 for a detailed description of the roles and responsibilities of the metadata administrators and assistants.

METADATA MANAGEMENT PROCESS

The following activities should be considered when developing a data warehouse project plan. These activities need to be integrated within each data warehouse or data mart development life cycle.[4]

1. Planning Phase

   - How metadata is to be collected and maintained during project planning and end user analysis (internal and external data, structured and unstructured data)

2. Design Phase

   - How metadata is to be collected and integrated across various data warehouse management and end user decision support and data mining tools

3. Implementation Phase

   - How metadata is to be provided to end users and IS support personnel who maintain the data warehouse and tailor the metadata view provided by the semantic layer of the various decision support and executive information system tools

Embedded within each data warehouse/data mart project lie the information directory functions of planning, developing, and deploying a metadata management process that every data warehouse/data mart project can then utilize. A project approach document for metadata management defines metadata management as a separate infrastructure building process.

A metadata approach document or charter will contain:

1. Purpose and objective of metadata management

2. Scope of initial implementation

3. Risks and issues associated with the approach

4. Project dependencies (data warehouse/data mart supported initiatives)

5. Technology selection/change process

---

[4] Consult the Data Warehouse Assistant on the CD ROM disk for sample data warehouse life cycle plans.

6. Infrastructure (staffing) and skills requirements
7. Project work plan and costs
8. Benefits to the business (tangible and intangible)

The activities required to complete the technology selection, implementation, and supporting procedures are itemized here. These activities are completed as part of a metadata management approach workplan[5]

Metadata Repository Definition and Support Task List

1.1. Develop a project approach
    1.1.1. Initiate repository project and establish budget
    1.1.2. Refine repository approach document
    1.1.3. Review and approve program approach and program plan
    1.1.4. Initiate repository project
1.2. Confirm the project approach
    1.2.1. Confirm three schema architecture approach
    1.2.2. Package three schema approach for review and approval
1.3. Conduct a metadata services analysis and design
    1.3.1. Develop metadata management metamodel requirements
    1.3.2. Prepare for review and approval
1.4. Develop a metadata management construction approach
    1.4.1. Prepare repository requirements in support of data warehouse projects
    1.4.2. Prepare vendor findings for review and approval
    1.4.3. Develop repository management procedures
    1.4.4. Prepare metadata management services for review and approval
1.5. Construct a metadata management service
    1.5.1. System test repository management procedures
    1.5.2. Prepare developed services for review and approval

---

[5] Please consult the Data Warehouse Assistant for a sample project approach document, project plan, and deliverable descriptions.

1.6. Implement a metadata management service

1.6.1. Conduct production procedure training

1.6.2. Establish the production metadata management environment

1.6.3. Conduct production installation

1.6.4. Hand over production access and end user support processes

1.7. Provide ongoing support and maintenance

1.7.1. Implement repository process monitoring and control

1.7.2. Conduct repository review and assessment

Common roles found in metadata management include

Figure 3–1
Metadata Management Roles Descriptions

Role	Description
Metadata Project Manager	• Manages the project • Maintains project approach document and project plan • Facilitates all milestone and status meeting reviews • Tracks all issues • Tracks all change requests • Responsible for the overall quality of the deliverable
Metadata Project Champion	• Controls business aspects of the project • Participates in developing the project approach • Directs the formal review process • Resolves issues and change requests • Provides human resources • Approves all work products
Technical Architects and Support Technician(s)	• Acts as a specialist in data warehousing technologies for process, technology and, organizational change • Provides technology leadership in process innovation/ reengineering current procedures.

Repository Administrator(s)	• Establishes repository management strategies
	• Leads the documentation of repository requirements
	• Validates the future direction for repository services
Metadata Trainer(s)	• Develops and conducts business and technology user training
	• Develops the training plan

Typical deliverables over and above the metadata management service include

Figure 3–2
Metadata Management Deliverable Descriptions

This table contains a description for the various types of metadata management (MD) project deliverables.

Major Deliverables	Description
Project Approach	Outlines the current scope, objectives, deliverables, facilities and resources for the Metadata Management Project
Work Plan	Describes the tasks, timing, and resources required to complete the release of metadata management services
Metadata Briefing Material	Metadata management project status and briefing materials
Metadata Team Training Material	End user and support group training material produced during the Metadata Management Project
Status, Issue and Change Management Reports	Any status or issue/change management reports related to the Metadata Management Project
Metadata Repository Requirements Definition	Requirements definition document describing three schema metadata, and metadata procedure requirements
Repository Test Scripts and Expected Results	Test procedures and expected outcome documentation to match against actual test runs of metadata loading/ synchronization

Major Deliverables	Description
Support & Maintenance User Documentation	Software and support procedure maintenance guides for ongoing repository management by the metadata administrators and technical support specialists
Business User Training Material	Training material solution sets for access to business and technical metadata
Repository Product Selection Criteria and Process	Repository evaluation criteria developed from requirements and the metadata model and the evaluation process
Repository Product Selection Results	Results collected during the metadata software evaluation process
Repository Procedures	Repository procedures used to manage the automated and manual processes of metadata process management
Repository Code/Software	Repository programs and or software used to manage metadata in electronic form

METADATA MANAGEMENT REPOSITORY(S)

The metadata repository(s) acts as an integrator of metadata collected across all three schemas (conceptual, internal, and external). As part of the technology selection process for metadata management, a physical (single tool) or virtual (multiple tool) repository is assessed for its ability to satisfy the following external, internal, and conceptual criteria. The process of collecting and stating these requirements is addressed by utilizing a meta model. This model states the metadata objects (entities) and business rules (associations) required for maintenance across the repository architecture. Once stated, the repository meta model (or data model of metadata requirements) is translated into our tool requirement checklist.[6]

---

[6] For documentation on metadata requirements, consult the Data Warehouse Assistant on the CD ROM disk and open the documents titled, "Metadata Repository Standards" and "Conceptual Schema Metadata."

Tool evaluation criteria to consider in selecting a metadata repository tool include

Figure 3–3
Metadata Repository Selection Worksheet

For	[Project Name]
Date Completed	[Date Completed]
Product Name:	[Product Description, Release Date, and Version]

Features: *SCORE*	**Undesired Level** *0 or 1*	**Minimal Level** *0 or 1*	**Preferred Level** *0 or 1*
Architecture			
Architecture	One Tier 0	Two Tier 0	Three Tier 0
Server Environment	MVS/VMS 0	NT 0	UNIX 0
Client	DOS 0	Windows/Window for Workgroups 0	Windows/NT or Unix 0
Configuration Management	Server based only 0	Fat client based only 0	Configurable across servers with thin clients 0
Meta Model Management			
Meta Model Documentation	Not Provided 0	Paper Doc/Online 0	Online/Multimedia/ Web enabled 0
Case Tool/DSS tool Integration	No metadata sharing 0	Limited/static metadata sharing 0	Full meta model sharing 0
Integration	Static/standalone 0	Load & update 0	Dynamic/integrated 0

Features: *SCORE*	Undesired Level *0 or 1*	Minimal Level *0 or 1*	Preferred Level *0 or 1*
Entity Control			
Customization Level	Proprietary 0	Limited object enhancements 0	Fully customizable 0
Check in Check Out	Not available 0	Exclusive check in/out 0	Shared and exclusive check in/out 0
Version Control	None 0	Model Level 0	Object Level 0
State Control of Objects	None 0	Manually across project life cycle 0	Automatically across project life cycle 0
Database Management			
Database Engine Support	Proprietary 0	Flat/file non relational 0	Relational 0
Database Integrity	Limited 0	Proprietary integrity 0	Open RDBMS integrity 0
API Integrity	No standard API 0	CODASYL compliant API 0	Object oriented compatible API 0
End User Access/ Security Control			
End User Access	Separate Tool 0	Report writer 0	Web compliant browser 0
Access/Security	Not available 0	Proprietary 0	Customizable 0
Ease of Use	Text doc 0	Online doc 0	Online doc & help 0

Features: *SCORE*	Undesired Level *0 or 1*	Minimal Level *0 or 1*	Preferred Level *0 or 1*
Vendor Management			
Stability in Market (Length of time in business)	Less than 1 year 0	Less than 3 years 0	3 or more years 0
Reference Sites	Not available 0	Available but not in same industry 0	Available in same industry 0
30 Day Trial and Evaluation Copies are available	Not available 0	Available for a 30 day fee 0	Available with no evaluation fee 0
Total Score	0	0	0
Product Score Across Columns	0		

METADATA REPOSITORY TOOLS

The following describe a sample of metadata management products, covering various aspects of the internal, external, and conceptual schema metadata management.

Table Legend: X = Supports, P = Partially supports

Vendor	Internal	External	Conceptual
Carelton Passport	X	X	P
ETI Extract	X	X	P
IBM DataGuide	X	X	
Meta Agent	X	X	
Informatica Power Mart	X	X	P

Vendor	Internal	External	Conceptual
MicroStrategy DSS Architect	P	X	
Oracle Designer/2000	X	X	P
Platinum Repository with DataShopper	X	X	P
Prism Directory and Warehouse Managers	X	X	P
SAS	X	X	P
PineCone Metadata Manager	X	X	P

CHAPTER FOUR

Data Quality Management

MAINTAINING CREDIBILITY THROUGH DATA QUALITY MANAGEMENT

A number of perspectives come to mind when trying to understand the data quality management process. Is data quality important only to the data warehouse or should house holding systems be improved as well? The traditional, or reactive approach, verifies corporate, or common data, only after it is collected from the data entry systems before being fed back to these systems in a modified form. The proactive approach requires changes, sometimes extensive, to the data entry systems themselves to solve the problem of data consistency and accuracy at the source. Others see this process as establishing technical rigor over how information is collected, verified, and transported only to the data warehousing environment. These perspectives, when taken together, cover a wide range of business and technology issues requiring extensive and dedicated efforts to ensure success.

To understand our perspective on data quality we must define what it is we hope to accomplish. A crucial first step is to lay out a set of ground rules in establishing our framework to deliver value (in this case timely, accurate, and consistent data) to our family of business users.

To ensure data warehousing success, our focus on data quality centers on the collection and processing of data to serve the needs of our data warehouse end users and not every knowledge worker in the business.

Data warehousing is not responsible for the total quality management effort of an organization, nor should it assume this task. Not all of our house holding systems, or subject areas, will populate our environment, so it is important to maintain this perspective as we define our approach to data quality management. Therefore, for our purpose in developing and maintaining a data warehousing environment, data quality management must focus on implementing a process by which credible, accurate, and timely information is extracted from a *preferred subset* of internal and external sources. It is these few critical systems that must become the focal point of our efforts.

THE HIGH COST OF LOW QUALITY DATA

A data warehouse is all about credibility, in terms of the information collected and its relevance in the business community for actionable decision making. Poor data quality in internal source systems such as inaccurate, conflicting, or missing information leads to erroneous and costly business assumptions. Lack of timely information also results in slow reaction to changes in the business climate, contributing to lost opportunities and reduced sales. In dealing with this problem data warehousing projects invest 70 to 80 percent of their total project time and resources. Without this effort, doubt over the validity and accuracy of the data stored in the warehouse often causes projects to fail. Credibility is essential. Not only must the data be quality assured before it enters the warehouse, but it also must be audited to prove the correct sources were selected when doubt creeps into the minds of our business users. In concert with any data warehousing initiative, a data quality management process is essential for the success of the data warehousing initiative.

In developing a data quality management process for data warehousing we must

1. Understand the content and location of our data sources and be able to adapt to change our best sources for data by proactively identifying new sources

2. Involve the business users in defining standards and guidelines for the definition and use of the data

3. Influence the ongoing data rehabilitation efforts of the business by influencing the development, or restaging, of house holding systems

4. Develop and maintain an integrated process in support of the data staging, data management, and information directory layers of the architecture

HOW DO WE START?

We initiate our data quality management process by proactively supporting a data warehousing project. Involvement in a project gives us an immediate perspective on how broad the data quality net can be cast and how effectively it can be implemented.

A project context provides four key inputs.

1. A list of subject areas for detailed inventorying and investigation

2. Prioritization of business processes or business areas to be supported

3. The means to test drive a suite of data quality technology and procedures

4. A starting point for setting up a data quality program, chaired by a standing committee, where data is regularly reviewed and certified on an ongoing cross project basis

In undertaking an inventory of the current source systems[1] we are concerned with targeting our assessment against a list of internal and external source systems from which we expect to obtain the necessary data. At this stage we define, through metadata investigation and data sampling, a list of valid conceptual (or business) data to map against the internal (or data storage view) and the external (application system views) of our data sources.[2]

---

[1] Consult the Data Warehouse Assistant on the CD ROM disk for knowledge objects containing the "Source System Survey Form," "Source Systems Assessment" spreadsheet and "Source Systems Assessment Report."

[2] Consult the Data Warehouse Assistant on the CD ROM disk and open the "Data Quality Map" spreadsheet to view how this information is collected.

CONCEPTUAL SCHEMA METADATA MAPPING

As part of the ongoing data quality management process, we establish what features (or properties) are important for us to measure and monitor. At the attribute, or business level, we are concerned with

- A definition and all homonyms and synonyms this field is known under from a business perspective.
- Property description in terms of the size, form, and number of occurrences this field contains (e.g., a last name attribute field would contain the surname of a person to a certain limit or size. Nor would this last name field ever be reused or used for some other purpose, such as to record a group or business or association name).
- Business rule information dictating how the data is created, maintained, accessed, and its lifetime value (how long it can be retrieved or calculated in its current form before a context change is required). Data has a life span, after which it ages where the value of the information can no longer be compared to current standards or environment (e.g., currency comparisons and value, average or mean temperatures, product descriptions).
- Administration information such as who created this data, who the subject area champion is, and the timeframe when this field went into use (managed by repository version control features).

This information is captured in the form of a metadata data model that is input to the overall metadata management process. This information defines the requirement model for data quality management and, to a large extent, metadata management. In establishing our requirements (metadata standards) for data quality for attribute or entity definitions we ensure six properties are addressed.

1. Singularity of definition for each attribute and entity
2. Completeness of description from a three schema perspective
3. Timeliness of the information
4. Level of required data quality
5. Life cycle value of when the data will mature and when it can be aged

6. Certification in terms of level of approval/use within the organization for this information

INTERNAL SCHEMA METADATA MAPPING

Once our business or conceptual schema properties are defined, we then map them to the physical files. This mapping is usually a one to many association, where one attribute or conceptual field will map to multiple data elements or columns. This mapping is augmented at the record, or table level, where database files, records, or tables are mapped to its owning conceptual schema entities. Definitions are collected from the available database catalog definitions to verify the information collected. Data reengineering tools are employed to verify the content of each field reviewed so that it can be checked against the internal and conceptual schema metadata definitions.

EXTERNAL SCHEMA METADATA MAPPING

With external schema mapping, we are concerned with how the data is presented to other application systems and business users (internal or external). As in the internal schema mapping, we map the form and content of each external schema field back to its owning conceptual schema definition.

BUSINESS USER OWNERSHIP

It is essential to establish some level of end user or business buy in to the management of the company's second most critical asset (data). The business community must assume ownership of the data quality process for data warehousing. Each subject area champion should feel comfortable defending the level of quality of his or her subject area's data as contained in the data warehouse. Again, within the world of data warehousing, we limit our view to the immediate priority of identifying and moving essential business data from internal and external systems into our data warehousing environment for business intelligence investigation. Our subject area champions in the business should be held accountable for data quality only to a similar extent.

We start our data quality management process at the inception of each data warehousing initiative. Once the scope and timeframe for the initial set of data warehousing delivery cycles are understood and agreed to by management, it is time to identify and contract line of business data champions. We contract these individuals within each line of business as this becomes part of their official duties and responsibilities upon which their individual performance and compensation package will be based. Without this employment commitment, the data stewardship process often falters and fails. Once these individuals are identified, they must be trained to their new duties and assigned responsibilities as part of the ongoing support program for data warehousing.

Four essential roles and responsibilities in establishing a data quality management process include

1. Data quality administrator
   a. The administrator is tasked with liaisons with the business and technology communities in terms of implementing the required recommendations. This role can form part of the responsibilities of a corporate data manager or data administrator.
   b. This person (or group) is responsible for maintaining the oversight committee meeting agenda, providing all required information for their review and approval.

2. Subject area champion
   a. Responsible for attending each oversight committee review meeting, recommending action on tabled agenda items and approving changes to existing corporate conceptual schema based metadata.
   b. Responsible for coordinating and completing periodic data quality review audits of his or her subject area and for being involved in any data quality management process from a rehabilitation or data warehousing implementation perspective.

3. Data oversight committee (encompass all the identified subject area champions and is administered by the data quality administrator)
   a. The data oversight committee is scheduled to meet on a regulated basis and is tasked with reviewing and approving cross line of business metadata or critical metadata identified by the data quality administrator.
   b. This committee certifies each common or corporate level metadata definition for implementation within the business and technology communities.

4. Data owner or knowledge worker
   a. Responsible for the day to day collection and management of current and new data on behalf of the organization.
   b. Is usually measured and rewarded along departmental or line of business boundaries only and does not usually maintain cross line of business responsibilities.
   c. These personnel must be educated and made aware of changes to any data collection or management activities that affect the business processes they perform and the information systems they access.

INFLUENCING DATA REHABILITATION

Data rehabilitation involves all procedures where existing source systems data files are repaired, reorganized, and restaged within the transaction processing, or house holding systems environment. This process also includes any changes to these source systems data collection processes in terms of how data is captured at the point of contact, processed, made available for review within the context of operational data management, and tagged for archiving after completing its span of business cycles.

Data rehabilitation, as it impacts data warehousing, encompasses

- The timing of when data will be repaired (or restaged) causing current data extraction and repair processes for the warehouse to change
- Identification of when new source systems will be made available (internal or external)
- Identification of alternative sources within the existing list of internal or external systems for more timely, accurate, or relevant data

IMPLEMENTING A DATA WAREHOUSING DATA QUALITY MANAGEMENT PROCESS

The data quality process follows a logical flow in support of the data warehousing project(s). From a project management standpoint a typical data quality management process includes the following project tasks.

1. Data quality core team staffing and environment definition, resulting in
   1.1. Core team roles and responsibilities definition and staffing
   1.2. Core team technology environment definition
   1.3. Core team education and training

2. Business intelligence systems business case verification and prioritization resulting in
   2.1. Subject area definition and business process dependency definition
   2.2. Subject area to information system database(s) mapping

3. Data quality standards and procedures definition (initial) resulting in
   3.1. Data quality mandate (program charter)
   3.2. Data quality procedures, milestones, and deliverables definitions[3]
   3.3. Data quality standards and enabling technology definitions

4. Business users education and awareness setting
   4.1. Initial data stewardship program definition
   4.2. Executive buy in and steering committee design
   4.3. Invited business core team member list confirmation
   4.4. Business core team training

5. Data quality procedures integration within the project life cycle
   5.1. Data warehouse data quality staffing and training
   5.2. Data warehouse development team procedure and technology implementation

6. Prioritized subject area data inventorying and assessment based on business case verification resulting in one or more of the following deliverables
   6.1. Data inventory/data sampling review
   6.2. Data rehabilitation strategy
   6.3. Data warehouse data staging approach
   6.4. Data warehouse data management approach
   6.5. Data warehouse user access approach

---

[3] Consult the Data Warehouse Assistant on the CD ROM disk for "Introduction to Data Quality Management."

7. Data quality standards and procedures changes (based on feedback achieved during the project(s))

7.1. Data quality process review and assessment

7.2. Data certification program action plan (or a list of updates to be added to an already in place program)

DATA QUALITY TOOLS

A growing list of tools are available in today's market that provide a considerable value added proposition, from a timing and cost perspective to the data quality management process. Tools in this arena deal with the investigation, repair, or reengineering of data within the existing source systems environment.

Data quality investigation tools include

- Group 1 Software, NADIS
- ISI, Innovative Edit
- Postal Soft, ACE

Data quality audit tools include

- QDB, Analyze
- SSA
- Unitech ACR Plus

Data quality reengineering tools include

- Apertus, Enterprise Integrator
- DB Star
- PT, InfoRefiner
- ISI, Innovative Batch Scrub
- Trillium
- Vality

◆

CHAPTER FIVE

Determining Business Value

HOW CAN WE MEASURE SUCCESS BY VALIDATING OUR INVESTMENT?

Probably one of the most difficult areas in data warehousing is the determination and measurement of business value. Traditionally, data processing systems were approved for capital investment based on operational efficiency. Even today, a number of data warehousing investments are approved following this approach. However, the true value obtained in data warehousing is the leveraging of the data and knowledge base that exist within each business to differentiate themselves and stand out in the marketplace. To be a leader in business innovation means leveraging all the assets of the corporation to maximum effect. With this goal in mind, some proponents of data warehousing have claimed hundredfold to thousands of percent improvement in their return on investment (ROI).[1] Proving this investment potential by establishing and implementing realistic measures is one of the primary challenges facing data warehouse managers.

---

[1] An IDC study reported average payback periods of three years for an investment cost of 2.3 million resulting in 401% ROI. One firm reported 1,600% ROI. Half of the firms surveyed reported ROI in excess of 160%, a quarter indicated returns of over 600%.

ESTABLISHING AN APPROACH

Establishing a strategy for business investment in this technology requires adopting one of two approaches. The first addresses an information technology direction while the second addresses core business values.

THE INFORMATION TECHNOLOGY APPROACH

Approaching data warehousing investment from this direction involves the traditional validation of business value based on primarily operational efficiency. This approach involves justifying ROI based on leveraging or extending the current information systems architecture within an organization. Such a strategy involves discussion around

- Client server implementation
- Package selection integration
- Business process improvement of house holding systems such as financial and human resources
- Strategic systems planning

CORE BUSINESS VALUES APPROACH

This approach is business driven and involves supporting the key processes of the organization. Unlike the traditional IT approach, providing technology in support of core business values identifies where the real ROI exists. For our business case, it is this approach that yields the largest returns on investment since deploying data warehousing technology as a business enabler results in

- Data cleansing of core subject areas such as product, customer, location, and vendor to improve accuracy of corporate data
- Leveraging improvements to supply chains
- Enabling and improving the customer relationship management process
- Kick starting marketing strategy and product and service improvements

- Assisting the business in reengineering itself by providing audit, or tracking, information at the various stages of business redevelopment

RISKS AND ISSUES FOR BUSINESS CASE DEVELOPMENT

Whether our approach involves an IT investment strategy or a business driven approach, we are faced with considerable challenges since IT traditionally has difficulty with establishing and measuring business benefits when they champion the data warehouse.

The major challenges facing the information technology organization include

- Little or limited core business knowledge
- Lack of understanding of the major pain areas of the business
- No training or experience in business benefits identification and measurement

Since the major value in data warehousing exists in identifying and measuring business improvement through the deployment of this technology, it is more practical to adopt a business first approach. We do this by

1. Engaging key business directors and managers in, not only sponsoring, but actually participating in the development of a business case for data warehousing

2. Engaging non IT personnel with experience in business case development.

3. Harvesting business input from a cross section of the core business community who will be directly or indirectly affected by the adoption of this technology and its business process and organizational change components

Our goal as a data warehouse manager is to

- Educate the business as to the benefits of data warehousing
- Assist in the selection of the right business areas and source systems to enable with this technology
- Measure and retain the benefits of this approach

THE BUSINESS CASE DEVELOPMENT PROCESS

The vehicle by which we educate management to the need for a data warehouse is by publishing a business case. The business case should be presented and confirmed by management prior to the start of our data warehousing project. A business case lends validity, understanding, and, most important, visible support for the data warehousing process. The business case development process covers the initial development of a business case, followed by actual deployment and measurement of expected benefits in the business environment. A number of different approaches exist; however, each follows these ten steps:

1. Establishing a business/IT core team

2. Educating the core team and defining the business case development and deployment process and expectations (outcomes)

3. Starting the process by identifying and prioritizing the pain areas of the business and key business representatives to participate in business benefits development.

   a. These individuals should be taken from a cross section of the targeted business area (i.e., marketing)

   b. Questions posed to this group should be validated by the core areas business management group to determine the appropriate priority areas for discussion

4. Conducting business opportunity and measurement sessions involves

   a. Setting objectives for each session

   b. Following the agenda and reaching conclusions at the end of each session

   c. Collecting and evaluating session responses as input to subsequent sessions

   d. Developing business benefit measures for publication in the business case

   e. Implementing a communication mechanism to keep attendees informed of project progress once these sessions are concluded

5. Establishing a measurement framework for each benefit

   a. This activity is completed during the joint sessions and validated with core business managers who are responsible for business performance. Measures need to be developed for both tangible and intangible benefits and must involve collecting both quantitative and qualitative returns

6. Developing a justification approach

   a. Return on Investment (ROI)

   b. Net Present Value (NPV)

   c. Internal Rate of Return (IRR)

   d. Cost Displacement

   A number of different approaches exist. Choose the one that is right for our organization since all possess certain limitations:

   i. *A return on investment (ROI) process does not recognize non-financial benefits. It encourages conservative investment strategies and does not offer a complete business picture*

   ii. *A net present value (NPV) approach provides improved financial measures, but still encourages low risk options. It does not address nonfinancial indicators, which can skew the overall evaluation process*

   iii. *Internal rate of return (IRR) approach is similar to the preceding and utilizes internal hurdle rates where small cash outflows could affect the expected outcomes*

   iv. *Cost displacement deals more with operational efficiency improvements and requires precision in determining the actual estimated cost reductions*

7. Publishing findings in the form of a business case

   a. Upon conclusion of the business benefits sessions, conclusions are published and distributed to the project champions and/or steering committee for review, amendment, and approval

8. Reviewing and revising our findings and obtaining approval to proceed with a prototype investment

   a. Iterating through prototype development and deploy in production

9. Deploying the measurement process and gathering benefit returns on an ongoing basis for up to one year after deployment of the prototype system

   a. Measuring investment against projected targets on a rolling six month basis

   b. Measuring results and proactively provide input to prototype refinement, adjust benefit measures, mechanisms

10. Adjusting measurement framework and providing input to the second iteration of technology deployment (subsequent prototype[s])

ESTABLISHING BENEFITS

Establishing benefits is difficult to accomplish when the core business value involves the ability to improve the decision making capability of an organization. However, improved decision making results in substantial cost savings to the majority of companies implementing data warehouses. Many of these cost savings result from the identification of patterns, trends, and mistakes from past actions and decisions. For example, an insurance carrier can more accurately predict the type and cause of insurance fraud by unscrupulous third party agents and their customers by collating claims information filed by classes of customers against targeted third party adjusters. This pattern would not have been recognized if customer data from multiple disparate systems were not merged and summarized in a data warehouse.

Some factors contributing to a company's inability to complete a business case involve:

- The inability to measure the dollar savings of improved decision making
- Doubt over the value added provided by the warehouse once made available to the business community.

As a starting point for benefits identification and measurement, the following set of tables provide examples across industry lines and business processes.

Business Activity	Benefit	Measure
Product and Service Marketing	Improved target marketing by 6% Increased new accounts by 20,000	Number of accounts increased by 20,000 by the end of the next fiscal year
Customer Service and Support	Reduced processing time by $650,000 a year Reduced paper costs by $250,000 a year	Reduced training costs, less processing errors, and improved customer satisfaction levels through customer surveys
Customer Productivity Analysis	Reduced query time from two hours to two minutes.	Provided current and comprehensive view of each customer
Product/Service Development	Reduced product or service development time from nine months to four weeks	Created eight to ten new products and marketing programs and provided management with a product development analysis system
Supply Chain Management	Decreased costs by $1 million annually	Reduced inventory costs and the need for volume discounts
Insurance Claims Processing	Reduced fraudulent claims by $3,500,000 and increased rates by $850,000	Reduced risk through the development and deployment of an exposure and loss model Measured premium increases, thereby reducing losses
Inventory Management	Reduced required shelf space by 6% per quarter	Reduced out of stock conditions, measured on a monthly basis
Manufacturing	Reduced costs by $1,200,000 a day through improved product distribution Reduced the number of required buyers by 50% by providing access to their own sales results	Improved ability to perform timely stock replenishment, gained better understanding of customer demographics, and improved pattern/trend analysis through ability to see daily sales by item

Business Activity	Benefit	Measure
Insurance	Improved product bundling	Bundled and measured three new product offerings in the first year
Customer Service	Improved customer retention and product sales by providing more information to customer contacts	Double the length of time taken by sales agents in sales and service calls over the first year
Manufacturing/Inventory	Reduced costs by $3,200,000 a year through product shrinkage and loss reduction	Improved ability to track all shipments from distribution centers to stores by providing a tracking and analysis system

RANKING PRIORITIES

Depending upon the scope of the business case, benefits investigation determines value drivers across one or more business areas. It is important to target business value drivers that reflect the core competencies of the business. These benefit priorities will vary by industry as illustrated here.

Insurance priorities include

- Fraud detection
- Premium growth
- Product bundling
- Customer cross and up selling of related products and services

Financial priorities include

- Credit card and portfolio fraud
- Account management and diversification
- Instrument management
- Real property analysis and acquisition
- Corporate customer segmentation analysis

Retail priorities include

- Customer relationship management
- Product and service development and deployment
- Product distribution
- Customer retention

BUSINESS MEASUREMENT

Once the business priorities are determined and the financial and business management measures have been developed, the required outcomes are refined in terms of deployed procedures and activities that monitor success on an ongoing basis. These implemented measures focus on

- Identifying productivity improvement areas that are important to the business
- Measuring financial benefits as only one part of the process (the others being establishing business competitive and organizational or structural efficiency improvements)
- Holding the business accountable for ongoing measurement collection and analysis for the data warehouse financial analysis will result in
  - Having the ability to measure the productivity level of business management
  - Promoting operational efficiency through reducing physical infrastructure and resource costs
  - Measuring business diversification resulting in increased shareholder value
  - Avoiding capital or discretionary costs due to required purchases or taxes

For a private sector enterprise, return on management equates to revenue less operating costs, shareholder equity, purchases, and acquisitions and taxation.

For a public sector enterprise, return on management equates to fees or licenses collected, less overhead staffing costs, and benefits and materials purchases.

CRITICAL SUCCESS FACTORS

In enabling the development, deployment, and measurement of business benefits, some critical success factors come into play.

- Defining the required roles, skills, and training requirements
- Focusing on business process, data access and usage, as well as empowerment of business users
- Determining infrastructure and distribution needs early on in the process
- Developing a road map for success
- Establishing and maintaining effective communication with management and business users
- Adopting an iterative process for prototyping, learning, reengineering, and refining warehouse benefits measurement process

PREPARING THE BUSINESS CASE

In completing the necessary information for the preparation and delivery of the business case, we look into competitive advantage assessment cost avoidance and options assessment as well as due diligence compliance such as risk mitigation assessment. These items are developed in terms of our overall recommendations and are stated as a set of objectives that follow an analysis method such as SWOT ([S]trength, [W]eaknesses, [O]pportunites and [T]hreats analysis).

We begin by establishing the criteria for success by defining key business measures and metrics coming out of our business case development sessions. If we adopt a SMART approach to the definition of our goals, we develop these objectives:

- (S)imple
- (M)easurable

- (A)chievable
- (R)elevant and
- (T)ime Constrained

Our objectives under a SMART approach address such items as

- Improving profit
- Increasing market share
- Enhancing internal productivity
- Managing the balance between profit or capital generation and costs

If we cannot identify SMART objectives we create a weak business case, reflecting only a pure technology approach. This type of process misses the mark in identifying and highlighting to management the real underlying business benefits.

ANTICIPATING THE POTENTIAL IMPACT ON OPERATIONAL CASH FLOW

As a next step we consider the anticipated impact on cash flow as part of our due diligence process. This activity focuses on the following.

PROFIT GENERATION AND ENHANCEMENT

This involves determining expected revenue as well as better assessing impacts on complementary or competing products and services.

COST DISPLACEMENT AND REDUCTION

Cost displacement and reduction are important for warehousing projects that focus on eliminating duplicate or redundant business processes and systems and/or on improving the level of data quality by eliminating redundant data collection mechanisms. This also includes the promotion of data stewardship whereby core business subject areas such as customers and products are cleansed. Some quantifiable measures include resources and infrastructure that are eliminated or redeployed.

COST AVOIDANCE

Cost avoidance measures focus on including any costs that can be reduced or eliminated by the investment. Often this involves financial forecasting. This measure is a key indicator for data warehousing projects promoting operational efficiency as their primary goal.

VALUE RESTRUCTURING

Value restructuring focuses on the elimination of low return activities with the resulting savings being fed into operational reduction. Business users are often enabled to spend more time doing higher value work as a consequence of the adoption of the improved operational or business intelligence processes.

MEASURING THE IMPACT ON LONG TERM BUSINESS GROWTH

Measuring impact on long term profitability involves the following:

OVERALL FIT

Overall fit involves assessing the degree to which the proposed investment supports established or emerging corporate goals, objectives, and critical success factors. At a minimum, it describes the association between the proposed investment and the goals and objectives.

COMPETITIVE ADVANTAGE

A number of factors impact the ability of the business to compete. Our business measures and metrics focus on business differentiation enabled through our proposed technology investment. Sources of competitive advantage are realized from

1. Changing business focus
   - Involves enabling best practices, in terms of new ways of working with business partners, making it more difficult for new competition to enter the market

2. Improving product or service offerings
   - Objectives enabled through business measures and metrics whereby significant performance improvements are realized in customer retention, service delivery, product and service cross and up sell, and product bundling

3. Providing new or enhanced products or services
   - Business objectives include extending or reinventing the business through a series of new product or service offerings

4. Impact on customer service
   - Customer service impacts identify risks or issues concerned with how the proposed investment affects the level of customer satisfaction. Oftentimes this measurement area is overlooked, resulting in falling market share.

DEFINING THE COST AND IMPACT OF THE PROPOSED INVESTMENT

We next determine the anticipated costs and its proposed impact on our investment recommendation. This usually involves the following.

DESCRIBING THE PROPOSED INVESTMENT

Here we identify the proposed investment in sufficient detail so that

- It is understood by business users and technology management
- Proposed benefits are clearly defined against the investment
- Due diligence is addressed by performing a preliminary financial analysis of the proposed investment

THE INVESTMENT ALTERNATIVES

It is important to describe alternatives to the proposed investment and to highlight any other possible quick wins that can be enabled or monitored by the deployment of data warehousing. The proposed alternatives provide enough details to illustrate why the proposed investment should be chosen.

As part of our analysis we include

- A description of our alternatives in comparison to what is being proposed;
- An assessment of whether or not another alternative can achieve some of the objectives of the proposed investment; and
- Documentation of these alternate approaches to the same project.

ADOPTING AN IMPLEMENTATION STRATEGY FOR DATA WAREHOUSING

We now address the proposed implementation method in terms of the key set of activities described earlier in this chapter.

In our business case for data warehousing we describe the

1. Business activities in terms of a project plan that outlines our work steps and key milestones
2. The timeframe and expected deliverables for the phases of the investment
3. The required supporting infrastructure from a people, process, and technology perspective through each phase of the proposed investments implementation including sales and promotion approach and strategy, training, data quality management needs, and supporting technology considerations.

EVALUATING THE POTENTIAL IMPACT OF DATA WAREHOUSING ON THE ORGANIZATION

We must consider the potential impact of our proposed investment solution on the existing organizational framework and business culture. Areas to change include

- Policies and procedures
- Remuneration and rewards
- Training and career development

ESTABLISHING RISK ANALYSIS

This activity involves articulating risks associated with carrying out the proposed investment include

1. Project and Organizational Risk

   For example:

   - Will the information technology organization be able to successfully execute the project?
   - Can the organization manage the business changes required to implement the investment?

2. Managing Uncertainty

   We define our level of comfort in terms of how well the benefits for the project will be understood by the business and communicated to the affected parties.

3. Technical Uncertainty

   This area involves gauging our ability to embrace the new technology and is usually completed by performing an information maturity assessment detailed in Chapter 6. We state our technical uncertainty in terms of the layers of the architecture and our ability to cope outlined in Chapter 6.

CONDUCTING FINANCIAL ANALYSIS

We use financial analysis as a tool for making decisions about the allocation of infrastructure and human resources. This analysis is geared toward determining the viability of the anticipated incremental cash flow of the project. Financial analysis is an iterative process. It provides one way to measure anticipated project outcomes.

Figure 5–1
Data Warehouse Financial Analysis

[Project Name]	Calculation	6 Months	YEAR 1	YEAR 2	YEAR 3	YEAR 4	YEAR 5
OPERATING CAPITAL INFLOW							
Additional Revenue	0.00	0.00	0.00	0.00	0.00	0.00	0.00
Increased Revenue from Existing Sources	0.00	0.00	0.00	0.00	0.00	0.00	0.00
Lost Revenue from Existing Sources	0.00	0.00	0.00	0.00	0.00	0.00	0.00
TOTAL OPERATING CAPITAL INFLOW	0.00	0.00	0.00	0.00	0.00	0.00	0.00
OPERATING CAPITAL OUTFLOW							
Deployment Operating Costs	0.00	0.00	0.00	0.00	0.00	0.00	0.00
Ongoing Operating Costs	0.00	0.00	0.00	0.00	0.00	0.00	0.00
Anticipated Cost Savings	0.00	0.00	0.00	0.00	0.00	0.00	0.00
TOTAL OPERATING CAPITAL OUTFLOW	0.00	0.00	0.00	0.00	0.00	0.00	0.00
NET OPERATING CAPITAL	0.00	0.00	0.00	0.00	0.00	0.00	0.00
CAPITAL							
otal Investment	0.00	0.00	0.00	0.00	0.00	0.00	0.00
Potential Salvage	0.00	0.00	0.00	0.00	0.00	0.00	0.00
Anticipated Capitalized Labour Costs	0.00	0.00	0.00	0.00	0.00	0.00	0.00
NET CAPITAL	0.00	0.00	0.00	0.00	0.00	0.00	0.00
TOTAL NET CAPITAL	0.00	0.00	0.00	0.00	0.00	0.00	0.00
NET PRESENT VALUE							
Discount Rate	1						
Discount Factor	1						
Present Value of Cash Flow	0						
Cumulative Present Value of Cash Flow	0						
erminal Value	0						
NET PRESENT VALUE	0						
Internal Rate of Return	0						
Discounted Payback Period	1						

After collecting this information it can be validated against our proposed list of prioritized objectives, which are enabled by a set of agreed to measures and metrics. All of this is then published for distribution, review, and approval in the form of a business case document.[1] The business case document presents the economic and business benefits (tangible and intangible) of the proposed investment for management review and approval.

With the publication and approval of our business case we are ready to proceed with establishing the necessary infrastructure discussed in Section Two.

---

[1] For a sample template that includes the topics discussed here, please consult the Data Warehouse Assistant on the CD ROM disk.

Section Two

✦

Infrastructure Development

OVERVIEW

In Section One we reviewed the features and benefits of data warehousing by educating ourselves and our users to its business and technology implications. In Section Two we prepare for the deployment, or enhancement, of our data warehousing environment. Establishing or extending this environment requires us to consider five foundation setting activities:

1. Assessing our current business and technology capabilities
2. Establishing or augmenting our organizational infrastructure
3. Selecting a project approach
4. Adopting a set of guidelines for success in terms of best practice methods and tools
5. Selecting a direction for deploying or enhancing our delivery architecture ("Think big but start small" approach).

These five critical activities are often overlooked or undervalued in the rush to embrace this technology. Without an architectural framework and a set of methods and tools backed by a program management process, our data warehousing effort will struggle to survive since

1. We do not have a clear understanding of our strengths and weaknesses within our IT organization and the business. We cannot answer a fundamental question—"Are we ready?"
2. We will not set in place the necessary core team to develop or enhance our capacity to deliver data warehousing technology to our users.
3. We will not have a clear idea what type of delivery (project) approach we should adopt. The end result is that we end up revisiting our project approach and project plan a number of times.
4. We will grope with technology tools in an effort to determine how best to tackle the business problem through a time consuming process of trial and error.
5. We will not establish a clear direction for the future as we deliver the data warehousing project, since our blueprint or architecture will be defined from a project standpoint and not from a program or long term perspective.

Section Two describes the foundation activities of the data warehousing process and our ability to deliver the necessary technology services on time and on budget.

As in Section One, this section stands alone and can be used independently or in conjunction with the other sections of this book. Section Two references a number of knowledge objects on the companion CD. Please consult Chapter 20, which describes the features and functions of these knowledge objects as managed by the data warehouse assistant. The data warehouse assistant contains a description of all the electronic material provided for your use and modification in your organization as you develop the necessary data warehousing program infrastructure.

CHAPTER SIX

Assessing Current Capabilities

ARE WE READY FOR DATA WAREHOUSING?

The ability to assess the business environment, culture, and climate are key areas to examine when considering the adoption, or enhancement, of decision support analysis processes. Environmental and cultural barriers can cause considerable delays or problems with the acceptance and deployment of this new wave of technology and business processes. To ensure success in our endeavor we should consider:

1. The maturity of our organization from an environmental and cultural perspective

2. How our organization manages itself in terms of business processes

3. What is on the horizon that may assist or inhibit our efforts

4. How we can move the organization (gently) toward becoming the business vendor in our industry

To complete these essential start up and monitoring activities we need to complete two key activities that allow us to develop a measurement baseline (for our people and the business processes they perform). This assessment provides us with a ruler to measure and monitor our data warehousing effort by taking an initial pulse of the organization, permitting us to chart our progress on an ongoing basis. These activities cover two important critical success factors of data warehousing.

- Organizational dynamics and measurement (measuring where people are and their ability, along with that of the organization, to adapt to change)
- Business process maturity analysis (where the business is on the competitive landscape and whether they are product or customer centric and whether or not their primary business concerns are tactical or inward focused, or strategic or outward directed)

ASSESSING ORGANIZATIONAL DYNAMICS AND MEASUREMENT

In assessing our business we look for a number of key organizational characteristics or features. These indicators provide a gauge of how effectively and rapidly our business users will be able to embrace the full benefits of this technology. Our organizational dynamics assessment indicates where we can achieve success from a people change management perspective. For example, if little knowledge sharing is recognized or promoted across the lines of business then our data quality management process may have to be limited to departmental based data clean up and verification, rather than to a subject area or corporate mandated consolidation.

In undertaking a rapid survey or organizational assessment in concert with or independent of the human resources department, a quick assessment of the target department or line of business should drive out the following characteristics:

- Attitude
- Communication
- Competence
- Empowerment
- Teamwork
- Training

This survey provides an insight to the ability our information technology and business partner project teams to embrace change and become more

knowledge aware. The survey can be completed in conjunction with the integrated end user organizational/business process assessment discussed here.
Initiating an organizational assessment involves three key areas.

1. Leadership philosophy
2. Collaboration and knowledge sharing
3. Communication

LEADERSHIP PHILOSOPHY

What is the leadership philosophy or approach for our organization? We must ask ourselves three key questions.

1. Is there an active mentoring, coaching, or facilitating process within our organization, that promotes
   - Freedom through control
   - Unity of purpose
   - Teamwork
   - Continuous improvement
   - Continued education and improvement
2. Are business users empowered by management to seek out new ways of completing or enhancing their business processes?
3. How does the business promote or enable its work force?
   - By employee empowerment, thereby, improving retention and the level of knowledge capital
   - By adopting an innovative work environment (time sharing, alternative work hours, home office).
   - Value added differentiation

If you answer no or does not exist to any or all of these questions, then the leadership process will surely mitigate against a supportive sponsorship enabled data warehousing approach that is the recommended vehicle for success.

COLLABORATION AND KNOWLEDGE SHARING

How does our organization operate when strategic or corporate projects are considered? Ask yourself these two questions:

1. Does the organization operate on a hierarchical or network based model. How flat is the organization from a management perspective? Is knowledge shared among teams and at all levels within the organization, or is it measured in terms of delivering value among teams?

2. How communicative are the various departments in sharing their knowledge and experience with others in different parts of the business? Is this joint knowledge sharing rewarded by informal recognition (lunches, outings, etc.) or formally, through employee reviews and awards?

A negative answer to these questions limits the overall impact and success of our data warehousing initiative. Ultimately this reduces our ability to deliver significant value and mitigates against any data warehouse delivery potential. These sorts of environments usually end up developing tactical reporting and analysis based legacy data marts, thereby creating problems for the future.

COMMUNICATION

Understanding how the organization communicates with itself and externally to the world at large speaks volumes to its ability to knowledge share. These three questions need to be addressed.

1. What internal or external communication mechanisms exist within our organization to publish and share knowledge across the business?

2. If communication mechanisms are available, how timely and current is the information (i.e., is this information produced on a monthly or weekly basis)?

3. In which direction does the information flow? Is the documentation produced policy and procedure based only from management, or does the information come from members of the various departments themselves, containing key insights, issues, or recommended corrections to business processes?

If the communication is minimal and infrequent and is published only by management, then our information management processes of our data warehousing effort will be adversely affected. This results in a minimal set of functionality being implemented, which makes it difficult to monitor and support, due to poor or unresponsive end users. These types of actions drive down the level of data quality and our ability to learn and react quickly to change in the business environment.

UNDERSTANDING BUSINESS PROCESS MATURITY

Business process maturity indicates how focused the organization is on the problems at hand (staying competitive and in business). Questions must be answered such as

1. Is the competition eroding our market share and if so, how?
2. How responsive are we to the changing needs of our customers?
3. What paradigm does our business follow? Is our business philosophy more product focused or more customer directed?
4. How can data warehousing become part of a continuous improvement process and not be looked at as a tactical reporting environment?
5. Where can information be collected to enable competitive advantage, resulting in our business becoming the business innovators within our industry?

To answer these questions we must first determine our level of process maturity by reviewing our current

1. Business value focus
2. Continuous improvement capability
3. Competitive advantage potential

BUSINESS VALUE FOCUS

Our customer focused assessment concentrates on how proactive and responsive the business is or wishes to become by utilizing these three criteria:

1. How are our customer service representatives measured? Are they rewarded based on the number of calls answered in an hour, or the amount of residual business they generated by cross or up selling?

2. What additional information from other lines of business on related products or services is available and how responsive are these business units in providing this information and keeping it up to date?

3. Does the customer truly come first and how does management illustrate this process?

Proactive response involves quickly directing critical customer care questions from the help desk to management when an important problem occurs. Does our organization exhibit any of these capabilities? If not, the value of customer care and the bringing of customer information together to provide the best service possible will not be realized or appreciated by our business. Nor will its economic bottom line considerations be easily rectified, such as poor customer service and increasing rates of customer churn, through dissatisfaction with products and services provided by our business.

ENABLING IMPROVEMENT

How does our business deploy continuous improvement capabilities? Ask yourself these four questions:

1. Is our past history based on purely operational efficiency and downsizing to stay economically viable? How quickly and efficiently are new products and services deployed to the market? How do we assess our capacity to improve our level of service while keeping costs down?

2. Are we proactive in understanding the changing nature of the market and our customers needs?

3. Do we employ proactive marketing programs, or simply react to advances being made by our competition? If so, how do we determine that a customer response was in reaction to a specific marketing program or campaign?

4. What has been the success rate in deploying new programs, products, or services; either to support the organization internally or to become more competitive in the marketplace?

If the answers we come up with here are not positive, then the time variant or historical aspect of our data warehousing efforts will not be viable or realistic for us to consider. This will result in a low value return on investment in a data warehousing solution rather than a tactical management reporting based approach. Lack of experience in a business process reengineering process and no human resource enabled change management process are clear indicators of a closed, regressive organization. In such cases our data warehousing efforts would be better directed at delivering current state management reporting data through operational data stores or localized data mart applications.

Competitive Advantage

Building on continuous improvement is the ability of the organization to be or become the business innovator in its field. Four issues need to be addressed in assessing competitive advantage.

1. What types of proactive and investigative business processes are in place in the planning and marketing areas of the organization?

2. How business aware is our organization to the market and the changing nature of our customers?

3. What matrix or cross line of business services or groups exist to exploit the knowledge capital within the organization to maximum effect?

4. What knowledge management processes (if any) exist within the organization? Does a rewards program exist?

Answers to these questions help determine where the business is headed and how competitive it shall remain.

WHAT LIES AHEAD

To complete our assessment and prepare ourselves for the impact of change on not only our business but also on our data warehousing environment, we need to be proactive in understanding

- What business changes are being considered in reaction to or as a result of changes in the marketplace. Is the business focused on long term cost reduction, increased productivity, and/or improved profitability through operational efficiency?

- The anticipated impact of data warehousing technology or business process improvement initiatives as we move toward becoming the business innovator in our field.

Some initial questions we can ask ourselves as technology enablers include

- Who are our customers?
- What do they need from us?
- What is our product or service to meet those needs?
- What are their measures and expectations of improved profitability?
- What is our process for meeting business needs?
- Does my product or service meet or exceed business needs and expectations?

The outcome of these questions provides us with an insight into how organizationally and process mature we are in our ability to enable the business through our technology products and services. What have we done to promote the process? Have we

1. Reviewed the customer relationship management technology in use or under consideration by our competitors?

2. Educated ourselves as to the business drivers and impacts of the market on our business and how technology has affected them?

3. Investigated the emerging potential of the Internet/intranet and multimedia to quickly provide knowledge to our business users?

4. Investigated the various types of external data sources and/or how they can be integrated within our proposed solution or how we could generate revenue through the definition or publication of our own service to customers and the world at large?

THE REVIEW PROCESS

In undertaking the business process maturity assessment, we adopt one of two strategies.

1. Extensive business review
2. Quick strike assessment

EXTENSIVE BUSINESS REVIEW

Extensive business review requires a two to three month engagement with a major consulting firm to provide the necessary expertise. This approach yields a wealth of information on the key people, process, and technology enablers and should be considered if the business is undergoing critical reengineering of its core functionality. However, the more effective and practical approach, due to the critical time constraints for data warehousing, is to adopt an incremental or focused approach.

QUICK STRIKE ASSESSMENT

The quick strike approach focuses on a surgical analysis in as little as three to four weeks and involves testing the business for key performance indicators. With this process we

1. Assign a critical core team of business and technology experts (no more than three core team members, comprised of a project leader/lead business analyst, organizational analyst, and technology analyst)
2. Collect available materials on the business, such as
   a. The current financial report
   b. IT business plans and software and hardware architecture definitions
   c. Reports, studies, or assessments conducted over the past business quarter
   d. Results of the organizational assessment discussed earlier in this chapter

  e. Industry surveys focusing on business performance improvement and technology advancement

  f. List of targeted managers, analysts, and knowledge workers, taken from a cross section of the business and supporting IT community

3. Conduct focused interview sessions over a two week period with one or two interviewees each focusing on the business survey questions following

4. Analyze and confirm results over a one week period to determine what type of going in position is most appropriate for the data warehousing project. The results of our assessment direct us toward considering

  a. A management reporting system running off an operational data store with minimal data quality management

  b. A data mart with line of business focused data quality management supporting limited product and service operational performance improvement or differentiation

  c. A subject area or strategic view with enterprise level data quality management focusing on product or service operational performance improvement or differentiation enabled by a data warehouse

Figure 6–1
Business Process Maturity Assessment

Taken By:[Your Name]

Taken On: [Survey Date]

Line of Business Name:[   ]

Interviewee Assessment

Name:[   ] Department:[   ] Local:

Assessment Category

Enter an "X" in the appropriate cells to complete the worksheet

Leadership Philosophy

What is the leadership approach for our organization?

1. Is there an active mentoring or coaching process within our organization which supports:

- Personal authority
- Unity of purpose
- Team metrics
- Continuous process improvement
- Education and awareness

2. Are business users empowered by management to enhance their business processes?

3. How does the business motivate its work force:

- By empowerment thereby improving retention and the level of knowledge capital
- By adopting an innovative environment through use of home or time sharing in the office
- Through value added activities

	Personality Assessment				Potential Supporter ?	
	Supportive	Not Involved	Opposes	Don't Know	Yes	No
	Yes	No				Total
		(2)	(1)	0		

Figure 6–2
Collaboration and Knowlegde Sharing

1. Is the organization hierarchical or network based. Is knowledge shared:							

Between departments and and at all levels within the organization

How is it measured in terms of delivering value between departments

2. How communicative are the various departments in sharing their knowledge and how is knowledge sharing recognised:

By informal events (lunches, outings, etc.)

Through reviews and awards

Connections and Communication

1. What mechanisms exist to publish and share knowledge across the business.

2. How timely and accurate are the current mechanisms.

3. How does the information flow (management down or worker up) and does it contain input from the knowledge workers

Business Value Focus

1. How are our Customer Service Representatives measured? Are they rewarded based on the number of calls answered in an hour, or the amount of residual business they generated by cross or up selling?

2. What additional information from other lines-of-business on related products or services is available and how responsive are these business units in providing this information and keeping it up-to-date?

3. Does the customer truely come first and how does management illustrate this process (do they walk the talk?)

Enabling Improvement

1. Is our past history based on purely operational efficiency or business validation. How are new products and services deployed to the market are we customer or product centric.

2. How do we understand the changing nature of the market, and our customers needs

3. Do we employ outbound marketing programs, or simply react (inbound) to customer queries. Do we lead or trail the competition in our industry.

4. What has been our success rate in deploying new products or services?

Figure 6–3
Competitive Advantage

1. What types of forward looking business processes are in place in our development of products and services			
2. How aware is our organization to the needs and make up of our customer base			
3. What matrix or cross-line-of business services or groups exist to exploit the knowledge capital within the organization to maximum effect			
4. What knowledge management processes (if any) exist within the organization and does a performance rewards program exist			
Survey Grand Total			

Survey Assessment Gauge

Enterprise Aware	Line of Business Capable	Operationally Focused
35 to 54	25 to 34	0 to 24

Note:

Each level should also support all the capabilities below it (I.e. an organization which is rated at "Line of Business Aware" should also be able to support "Operationally Focused Improvements).

Enterprise Aware

The organization should be able to adopt a corporate data warehouse approach and data quality management program, supporting services and product differentiation

Line of Business Aware

The organization should be able to adopt a focused improvement of a key product or service enabled by a data mart and limited data quality management

Operationally Focused

The organization should be able to adopt an operational reporting environment supported by an operational data store drawing data from a department.

♦

CHAPTER SEVEN

Establishing the Data Warehouse Organizational Infrastructure

The data warehousing process and, in some cases the data management function (of which it forms a critical part) can impose radical change on the I.S. organization. Conducting an organizational and business assessment (Chapter 6) assists us in measuring where we are and what is possible from the perspective of data management. We need to understand our going in position in terms of resource and budget commitments to this new or enhanced functionality and how it can be integrated within the rest of the I.S. organization. Our starting point and the nature of the work to be undertaken must also be understood before the process of laying out the required roles and responsibilities commences. This task is even more critical when considering the deployment of outside consultants. We must ensure that each internal or external (consultant) role has the necessary authority to carry out the assigned responsibilities and will be held accountable for all actions performed and deliverables produced.

Four necessary first steps include

1. Undertaking an I.S. survey to determine core cultural and people values and capabilities

2. Completing a current state assessment of the target business area (Chapter 4) to determine the level of end user knowledge management maturity

99

3. Educating ourselves to the type and nature of our intended development effort to answer the question of what type of data warehouse we should be building (Section One)

4. Establishing a going in position for the first/next increment of the data warehousing environment

GAUGING THE I.S. CULTURE

It is important to understand what has occurred and where we are from a data management perspective before attempting to implement or integrate this new core functionality in the organization. Two key questions to consider involve

1. Is there a data management group currently within I.S. and what has been its record of success?

2. What functions does it contain (some typical ones include data administration, data architecture and planning, database administration, data security, and records management)?

Rudimentary or primitive I.S. organizations that claim to possess a data management function address only the database management process, usually as an adjunct or part of their systems development organization.

When looking at our I.S. organization and current culture we need to consider how responsive we have been to the business in

- Establishing and communicating our I.S. vision/mission
- Successes in organizational redesign
- Our track record in resource planning (insource vs. outsource)
- Our ability to rapidly deploy quantitative, qualitative, and productivity enablers

We must consider how successful we have been in maintaining our level of core competencies and adding new ones in terms of

- Identifying new critical skills

- Obtaining training and acquiring new skills
- Establishing the required hardware, software, and network certification processes
- Staff acquisition and planning

To determine how we are going to attract and retain the right people we must first establish

- A recruiting program or process
- A career development opportunities
- An appraisal/performance evaluation process
- A rewards system
- A mechanism for culture change

It is also necessary to consider how we are going to develop our data warehouse strategic and tactical leaders in terms of

- Staff succession planning
- Career and supervisor mentoring
- Executive development managing

EVALUATING THE RESULTS OF THE CURRENT STATE ASSESSMENT

While we determine our response to the aforementioned I.S. organizational issues, we need to undertake a similar review of our business users (Chapter 6). Next, we must consider a context for implementation. What is it that our user community requires? Is it a management reporting environment or a data mart? We obtain key insight into the nature of our delivery environment by evaluating the results achieved from our business maturity assessment. From this assessment we determine what type of data warehousing environment the I.S. organization should implement. Based on our maturity assessment (Chapter 6), our business users will be at one of three levels of business maturity.

Figure 7-1

Data Management (Data Warehouse) Organizational Development Path

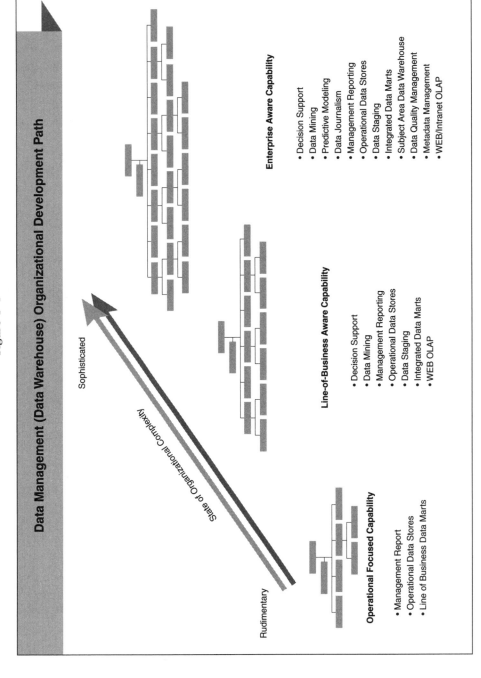

ENTERPRISE AWARE

The organization adopts a corporate data warehouse approach and data quality management program, supporting services, and product differentiation.

LINE OF BUSINESS AWARE

The organization deploys a focused improvement of a key product or service enabled by a data mart and limited data quality management.

OPERATIONALLY FOCUSED

The organization develops an operational reporting environment supported by an operational data store drawing data from a suite of line of business systems.

Organizations that are *Enterprise Aware* require the "full meal deal" of data management products and services illustrated on page 104.

Organizations that are *Line of Business Aware* favor the implementation of data marts with data being moved through either a data staging area and/or a centralized hub data warehouse to ensure that the subject area (dimensional) data being parceled out to the marts are synchronized.

Finally, organizations that are still operating at the operational or day by day stage of maturity require the least sophisticated data management organization of all as illustrated on page 106.

Figure 7-2
Enterprise Aware Data Management

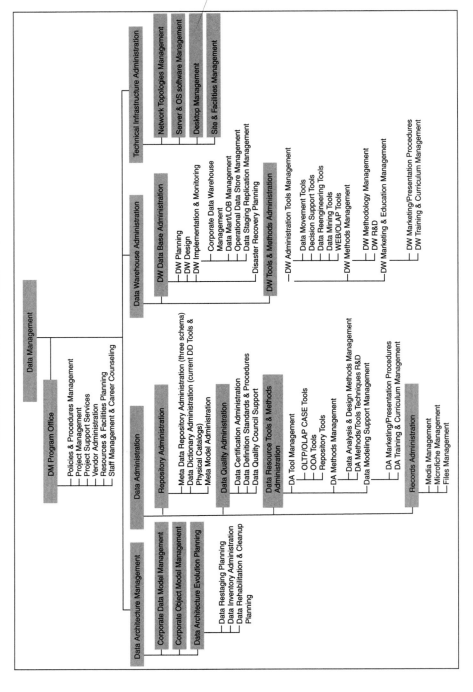

Figure 7-3
Line of Business Aware Data Management

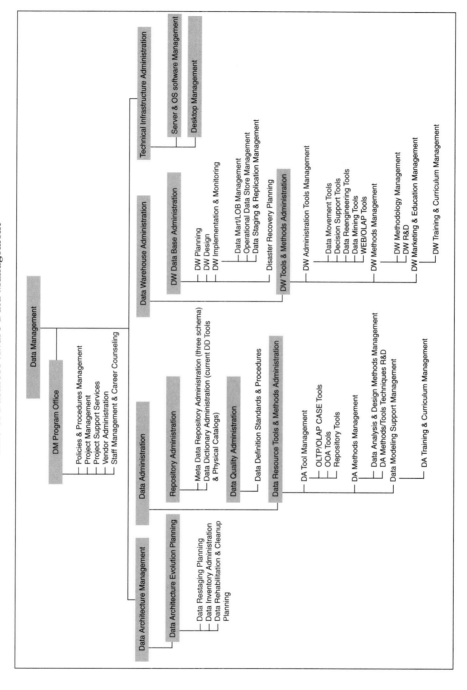

Figure 7–4
Operationally Focused Data Management

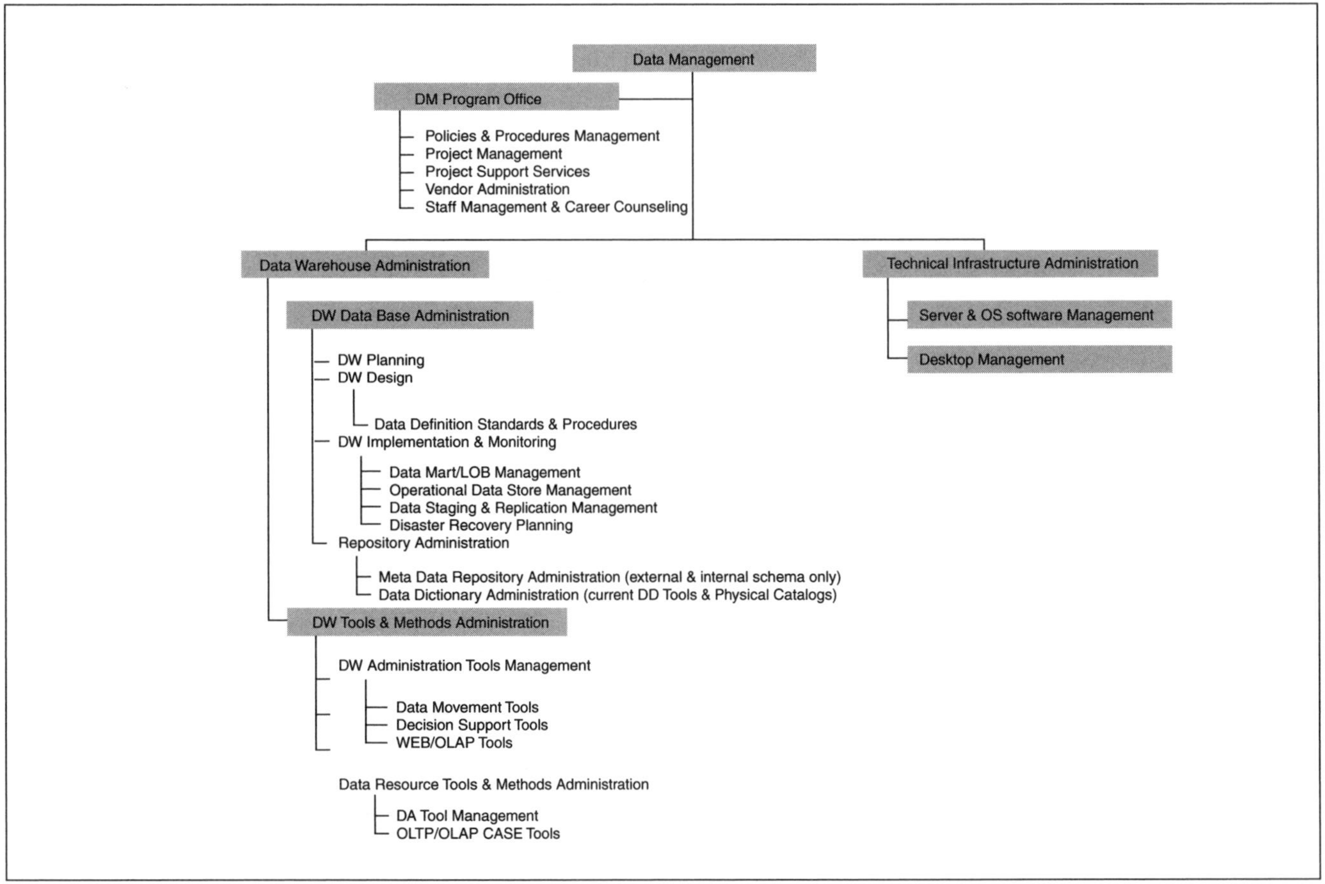

Data Management

DM Program Office
- Policies & Procedures Management
- Project Management
- Project Support Services
- Vendor Administration
- Staff Management & Career Counseling

Data Warehouse Administration

DW Data Base Administration
- DW Planning
- DW Design
- DW Implementation & Monitoring
  - Data Definition Standards & Procedures
- Repository Administration
  - Data Mart/LOB Management
  - Operational Data Store Management
  - Data Staging & Replication Management
  - Disaster Recovery Planning
  - Meta Data Repository Administration (external & internal schema only)
  - Data Dictionary Administration (current DD Tools & Physical Catalogs)

DW Tools & Methods Administration

DW Administration Tools Management
- Data Movement Tools
- Decision Support Tools
- WEB/OLAP Tools

Data Resource Tools & Methods Administration
- DA Tool Management
- OLTP/OLAP CASE Tools

Technical Infrastructure Administration
- Server & OS software Management
- Desktop Management

UNDERSTANDING THE NATURE OF OUR BUSINESS AND SETTING EXPECTATIONS

What is it that our user community is expecting us to deliver? Is it

- Improved management reporting
- Increased breadth of operational forecasting
- Reduced data collection costs and improved data consistency and accuracy
- Improved communication of best practices (knowledge) across the business
- Pushing information out to customer touch points and ultimately to customers and business partners
- Product and services campaign planning and management
- Business competitive assessment
- Business performance evaluation

Answers to these questions identify the business measurement requirements of our organization. By comparing these business measures against I.S.'s organizational capability and capacity for change, we determine the scope of our required organizational framework and its level of complexity.

CHOOSING THE RIGHT FUNCTIONAL CONTEXT FOR OUR DATA WAREHOUSE

Once we understand the level of business maturity and expectations, as well as our level of maturity and support within information services, we can map out our organizational structure. To deliver the various products and services required we establish the necessary program and project level functions.

ENTERPRISE AWARE DATA WAREHOUSING ORGANIZATIONAL REQUIREMENTS

For the Enterprise Aware Organization we coordinate cross line of business subject area implementations of data warehousing technology. These initiatives, due to their significant size and impact on the entire business, are usually implemented as a *program,* over multiple iterations or projects. At the enterprise level the staged delivery of a program management office addresses cross project management concerns such as

- Project planning and budgeting across project increments and multiple projects
- An integrated change management process
- The issue management and risk escalation process
- Program, project, and individual status reporting
- Roles and responsibilities of the various groups within the data management (data warehouse) organization
- Data management (data warehouse) training, mentoring, and education planning
- Data management (data warehouse) communication management

ENTERPRISE AWARE AND LINE OF BUSINESS AWARE DATA WAREHOUSE ORGANIZATIONAL REQUIREMENTS

The line of business aware organization focuses on vertical subject area requirements, where the dimensions of the organization are implemented in terms of how this line of business views its customers, services, and products. In such organizations, and in Enterprise Aware businesses, we need to consider how to adopt and deploy a data warehouse marketing process staffed with dotted line or direct reports business analysts. This internal marketing group

- Shops the knowledge collected and managed within the warehouse to other lines of business
- Provides internal education and awareness on this technology to other lines of business on an ongoing basis
- Identifies database marketing potential as a value add to the services delivered by the business, by reselling business knowledge to external vendors or business partners and, ultimately, to the customers themselves

Enterprise aware and to a more limited extent, line of business aware organizations must also consider how to adopt and deploy a data administration (data warehouse focused) function tasked with

- The development and management of the data warehouse data architecture and how they integrate within the overall data architecture of the business
- Metadata management
- Data warehouse data analysis processes, techniques, and technology (CASE) tools and repository managers
- Data quality management processes (data staging, replication, cleanup, rehabilitation, certification management process, and data stewardship)
- How to manage and cope with data standards/regulatory considerations across the various forms of data (text, multimedia, electronic, fiche, paper, disk, tape . . .)

DATA WAREHOUSE CORE FUNCTIONAL REQUIREMENTS

All levels of data management maturity require the deployment of a set of core data warehouse functions that include

1. Decision support/management reporting and information access
2. Data warehouse database management
3. Technical infrastructure services for hardware, software, and network administration

DECISION SUPPORT/MANAGEMENT REPORTING, AND INFORMATION ACCESS FUNCTIONAL REQUIREMENTS

Our decision support organization(s) have a wide range of functional responsibilities that depend on the level of maturity and sophistication of the end users. Our decision support team(s) provides support for:

- Operational and decision support report writing (for report writers, ROLAP, and MOLAP tools)

- Data mining and predictive modeling
- Product and service campaign management and promotion tools
- Customer service and customer care tools
- Database marketing tools
- Software evaluation, selection, implementation, and end user training
- Providing help desk support

DATA WAREHOUSE DATABASE MANAGEMENT FUNCTIONAL REQUIREMENTS

The most familiar function(s) of our data warehouse remains the data repository. As is with the decision support function, the data warehouse database management organization is tasked with a range of functional responsibilities incorporating

- Data staging and replication
- Physical data cleanup, repair, and aggregation
- Database design, monitoring, and tuning
- Database backup, recovery, and archiving
- Physical data security
- Database capacity management
- Required decision support data access functions enablement
- Database management tools and technology certification and deployment decisions.

DATA WAREHOUSE TECHNICAL INFRASTRUCTURE FUNCTIONAL REQUIREMENTS

The hidden, but essential dimension from a data warehouse organizational perspective is the technical infrastructure organization(s). This functional organization(s) provides the essential functions of

- Defining and managing the mainframe and miniserver architectures and their physical and logical identification

- Defining and managing the physical and logical network
- Managing the physical architecture design and capacity (one, two, or three tier)
- Implementing hardware and network product and service selection and certification

THE PROCESS OF ORGANIZATIONAL DESIGN

Different methodologies exist that deal with IS organizational design and implementation. These can be readily adopted for our purpose in implementing the data management (data warehouse) organization. When evaluating and selecting a preferred vendor or service, address the following steps and/or sequence.

DATA WAREHOUSE FUNCTION AND ORGANIZATION DESIGN PROCESS

Process	Expected Outcome
1. Data Management Vision	Mission statement*
2. Data Management Strategy	Phased functional requirements, resources, and expected benefits*
3. Organizational Analysis	Change readiness assessment (Chapter 6)
4. IS Survey	Skills and culture survey (Chapter 6)
5. Data Management Functional Design	Workflow process and function design*
6. Data Management Organization Design	DW roles and responsibilities, job descriptions, and organization chart*
7. Recruiting and Resource Planning	Planning process and chart
8. Training and Education Planning	Training curriculum
9. Career Planning and Mentoring	Career planning process, compensation and rewards program, incentive program, mentoring process, and career path chart

*Content is provided for publication and review in the form of a data warehouse program management mandate or charter. (For a sample template document, consult the Data Warehouse Assistant on the CD ROM disk.)

DATA WAREHOUSE ORGANIZATION ROLES AND RESPONSIBILITIES

The organizational structure for the data warehousing function can be

- Developed during an initial pilot role out
- Extended to provide coverage for an initial production implementation or iteration
- Developed as the next stage of data warehousing evolution (i.e., operational to line of business)
- Determined as part of an IS organizational redesign

Once you determine this organizational scope the requisite roles and responsibilities are established (as stated here) under data management organizational design. Recruiting and mapping of available job skills occurs next, with pilot projects often being supported by significant consulting assistance to facilitate the quick delivery of this new functionality and technology. Over time the data warehouse organization can limit the role of consulting to product (vendor) support and new core competency based development (such as predictive modeling, neural networks, customer relationship, and management) once the essential core services are deployed within the organization.

ORGANIZATION ROLES[2]

The following key roles enable the data management (data warehouse organization) to perform the aforementioned functional requirements.

1. Data resource/data warehouse project manager
2. Data warehouse marketing business analyst
3. Metadata administrator
4. Data administrator/data architect
5. Data warehouse database administrator

---

[2] For a detailed description of each role, consult the Data Warehouse Assistant on the CD ROM disk and look up "Data Warehouse Organization Descriptions" document.

6. Decision support analyst
7. Data warehouse technical infrastructure architect
8. Data quality administrator
9. Data warehouse systems analyst

EXTERNAL ROLES

The following three external roles from the business and IT community provide liaison and project/program management functions.

1. Program/project champion
2. Program/project steering committee
3. Quality control council

ROLE DESCRIPTION

Each role is described by six key properties that define the required business, technical, analytic, and communication skills required to perform each aforementioned role.

Role Criteria	Role Properties
Responsibilities	Define the key job duties and responsibilities for this particular job function
Accountabilities	Identify direct and dotted line reporting relationships within and external to the data warehouse management organization
Authorities	Describe the supervisory, peer, and subordinate data management responsibilities and decision making mandate
Who	The type of individual (or group) required to successfully fulfill this job role
Skills Inventory	Required skills to perform the data management job role on an ongoing basis

DATA WAREHOUSE ORGANIZATION
CRITICAL SUCCESS FACTORS

Data management (data warehouse) must be seen as a key function within the overall information services technology delivery. Its successful operation is dependent upon several factors that are not directly under its control. These factors apply to the overseeing, or umbrella, data management function, of which the data warehouse organization forms one part. Success in the data management function will contribute greatly to success in data warehousing (with the converse being equally true).

1. COMMITMENT—the support of high level management to the concept of data resource management and information access.

2. TECHNOLOGY—the degree to which the data management functions are automated (e.g., a DBMS supporting automated data staging to ensure the timely and accurate integration and deployment of data across operational and information databases).

3. INTEGRATION—the degree to which data management functions are integrated within other information technology processes (data management is not viable as an add on or documentation do last task).

4. AUTHORITY—the degree of authority data management has over the development and management of metadata (e.g., authority to accept or reject models).

5. STAFFING—the number and the skill level of data management staff.

6. RESPONSIBILITY—data warehouse's placement within the organization and the perceptions of its responsibilities.

7. CULTURE—the rate at which change can be absorbed and the degree to which data management is accepted.

DATA WAREHOUSE ORGANIZATION
MANAGEMENT CHARTER

Data warehouse organizational design, much like many other internal or infrastructure tasks, is often relegated to a back room or "do as you go or need" status. This method may work in smaller installations, but major data warehousing initiatives at the line of business or enterprise level require proper planning, staffing, and coordination. Defining our organization and acquiring the right skills and technology to run it is a project in itself. Therefore, to ensure the appropriate amount of visibility and commitment by both the business and the information technology organization, we publish and maintain a program charter or mandate as a key deliverable. Since our data warehouse organization will grow and change as the business needs for decision support information change, we need to maintain an ongoing organization change management process to monitor or progress. All this information is collected and communicated via our program charter.

The data warehouse program charter contains a work plan describing our organizational development plan, budget, critical success factors, and program interdependencies and staffing requirements. The program charter for data warehouse management contains the following types of information[3]:

- Context
- Stakeholders
- Background
- Purpose
- Project objectives
- Project team structure
- Project management and sponsorship structure
- Project strategy or approach
- Project success factors and measures
- Project plan and proposed budget

Update the program charter for the data warehouse organization on an ongoing basis and use it as a planning and organization aid in developing future extensions or changes.

---

[3] Consult the Data Warehouse Assistant on the CD ROM disk for a template "DW Program Charter" document.

◆

CHAPTER EIGHT

Selecting the Data Warehouse Development Life Cycle

The key to long term success in growing the data warehouse lies in establishing a project delivery rhythm. The various project expectations can be defined and managed based on a life cycle perspective that can include, but is not limited to

- Piloting data mart or data warehouse delivery
- Developing full blown data warehouse architecture increments
- Certifying software and hardware upgrades
- Delivering training, education, and support to operational support personnel and to the end users
- Delivering, or enhancing, data quality management and data staging services
- Maintaining current data warehouse applications and database engines along with their supporting infrastructure
- Enhancing current decision support products or services

With overlapping, and in some cases conflicting delivery priorities, a mature data warehousing environment copes with contending project objectives in order to succeed. By establishing the priorities and boundaries for each type of project effort, these initiatives are then managed, measured, and adjusted to resource and cost thresholds on an ongoing basis. The perception and reality to business users is that despite the growing and disparate demands placed on the data warehouse, it is continuing to meet and, it is hoped, exceed expectations.

To appreciate the complexity of the task at hand, we must be able to determine the functional scope of our project effort and then overlay it with a project development process. The functional scope is determined from our description of the layers of the data warehousing architecture. The data warehouse architecture consists of five major layers (or properties) as described in Chapter 2.

1. Data staging
2. Data management
3. Data access
4. Infrastructure
5. Information directory

From this framework we determine the functional scope of our implementation (e.g., a pilot project is undertaken to develop segments of the data staging, data management, and data access layers of our architecture).

We then determine what development route to follow to complete the project, since our effort can be

- Development focused
- Enhancement enabled
- Maintenance directed

SIZING THE DATA WAREHOUSE DEVELOPMENT EFFORT

In terms of overall effort, a data warehousing project can be categorized for sizing and costing in terms of being small, medium, or large.

SMALL DATA WAREHOUSE PROJECT CRITERIA

A project can be considered small if

1. Data resource management resource days required are greater than or equal to five days and less than 21 days.

2. Duration is greater than or equal to three days and less than or equal to one month
3. Number of resources is less than or equal to three
4. Not more than one subject area or part of one subject area is affected

MEDIUM DATA WAREHOUSE PROJECT CRITERIA

A project can be considered of medium complexity if it

1. Meets and exceeds the criteria for a small project
2. Data resource management resource days are greater than or equal to 21 days
3. The duration is less than or equal to three months
4. The number of resources is less than or equal to six full time equivalents
5. The number of subject areas affected are less than or equal to two

LARGE DATA WAREHOUSE PROJECT CRITERIA

A project can be considered major or having large complexity if it

1. Meets and exceeds the criteria for a medium project
2. Data resource management resource days are greater than 21
3. The duration is greater than three months
4. The number of resources is greater than six full time equivalents
5. The number of subject areas affected is two or more

DATA WAREHOUSE DEVELOPMENT ROUTE

Data warehouse development initiatives focus on the delivery of new data management and data access services to one or more business units. The delivery mechanism follows either an iterative rapid life cycle analysis/design process or a proof of concept/pilot process for first time use or application of this technology within a business area. The criteria for establishing a development project involve

1. If the scope of effort involves identifying new decision support or data management business processes or reengineering current processes, then we consider this to be a data warehouse development project.

   - *For example:* Your company implements a customer relationship management process requiring closed loop data warehousing where historical customer information is sent to the customer service representatives for customer care management.

2. If the scope of effort involves capturing new data, then we are undertaking data warehouse development.

   - *For example:* External organization and internal firm a graphic data are required by your marketing and sales organization to develop competitive analysis assessments.

3. If the scope of effort involves supporting the reorganizing of existing business units or involves reassigning staff then we are initiating a data warehouse development project.

   - *For example:* A newly developed customer relationship management process requires the deployment of a customer subject area (data mart) containing campaign and promotional information technology for database marketing.

Once we understand that our project is new development and understand its potential scope in terms of complexity and cost (it is either small, medium, or large) we can then select the data warehouse technology and infrastructure requirements focus. The data warehouse technology and infrastructure requirements focus can be either minor or major. By selecting our focus we further refine the required resources, costs, and potential impact on the data resource management group and information services organization.

MINOR DATA WAREHOUSE DEVELOPMENT

Minor data warehouse development projects are those that

- Meet all the criteria of a small data warehouse project
- Do not require a vendor selection process to acquire new software or support services

- Do not require significant training in procedures and tools
- Do not involve more than one nonelementary business process or subject area

MAJOR DATA WAREHOUSE DEVELOPMENT

Major data warehouse development projects are those that

- Meet all the criteria of minor data warehouse development
- Meet all the criteria of medium or large data warehouse
- May require a vendor selection process for products or services
- Require significant training in new procedures and tools

In summary, major data warehouse development involves

- Package searches and vendor selection
- New/reengineered business data or process analysis covering more than one business process or subject area
- New/refined technology analysis for software, hardware, or network platform selection
- Business case preparation

If the proposed effort does not fall within the scope of development, then it is either a maintenance or an enhancement data warehouse project.

DATA WAREHOUSE ENHANCEMENT ROUTE

Data warehouse enhancement initiatives focus on the delivery of new data management and data access services within the context of existing decision support applications or data management procedures. The delivery mechanism follows either an iterative rapid life cycle analysis/design process or a design, test, and implementation process. The criteria for establishing an enhancement project include

1. The scope of effort involves augmenting current decision support or data staging/database management procedures then this is data warehouse enhancement project.

   - *For example:* The deployment of a data mining tool set to access an already in place data mart.

2. The data warehouse change involves restructuring existing data; we consider this to be data warehouse enhancement.

   - *For example:* New columns are added to an existing dimension requiring reloading and reindexing of the data.

3. If the effort involves implementing a new policy or procedure in support of an existing data access or data management process we consider this to be data warehouse enhancement.

   - *For example:* An additional data quality checkpoint is inserted into the existing data staging process to improve the accuracy of data being staged into the warehouse.

Once we understand that our project is enhancement and understand its potential scope in terms of complexity and cost (it is either small, medium, or large), we then select the data warehouse enhancement focus. The data warehouse enhancement focus can be either minor or major. By selecting our focus we further refine the required resources, costs, and potential impact on the data resource management group and information services organization.

Minor Data Warehouse Enhancement

Minor data warehouse enhancement projects are those that

- Meet all the criteria of small data warehouse
- Do not require a vendor service or support contract
- Do not entail significant end user or data resource management group training
- Do not involve more than one nonelementary business process or subject area

MAJOR DATA WAREHOUSE ENHANCEMENT

Major data warehouse enhancement projects are those that

- Meet all the criteria of minor data warehouse enhancement
- Meet all the criteria of medium or large* data warehouse
- May require significant end user or data resource management group training
- May require a vendor services or support contract

If the proposed effort does not fall within the scope of enhancement, consult either the maintenance or development routes for further assistance.

DATA WAREHOUSE MAINTENANCE ROUTE

Data warehouse maintenance initiatives focus on correcting and tuning existing data management and data access procedures and services within the context of existing decision support applications or databases. These projects are usually created by a problem investigation or performance threshold condition that triggers a problem analysis/resolution/closure process. The criteria for establishing a data warehouse maintenance project include

1. The focus of the effort involves reorganizing existing data. If so we consider this to be data warehouse maintenance.
   - *For example:* An index table space requires an unload/reload to improve performance for a fact table or dimension in the data warehouse.

2. The effort involves installing a program patch or applying a code fix. We would consider this to be data warehouse maintenance.
   - *For example:* Customer account rollups are not totaling properly so a change to the calculation algorithm is applied to the decision support program.

3. The effort involves verifying that a manual procedure requires correction. We would consider this to be a data warehouse maintenance requirement.

- *For example:* A manual checkpoint is audited to ensure that the records to be loaded into the warehouse from the staging area do not contain invalid company name formats.

Once we understand that our project is maintenance and understand its potential scope in terms of complexity and cost (it is either small, medium, or large), we then select the data warehouse maintenance focus. The data warehouse maintenance focus can be either minor or major. By selecting our focus we further refine the required resources, costs, and potential impact on the data resource management group and information services organization.

MINOR DATA WAREHOUSE MAINTENANCE

Minor data warehouse maintenance projects are those that

- Meet all the criteria of small data warehouse
- Do not require a vendor service or support contract
- Do not involve more than one subject area
- Do not require any new or additional training
- Do not require problem solving, constructing, and testing activity beyond correcting data warehouse application system components and procedures
- Do not require implementation procedures beyond migrating corrected application system components and procedures to production or filing completing problem investigations

MAJOR DATA WAREHOUSE MAINTENANCE

Major data warehouse maintenance projects are those that

- Meet all the criteria of minor data warehouse maintenance
- Meet all the criteria of medium or large data warehouse
- May require a vendor services or product contract
- Do not require any new or additional training
- Require construction or testing/problem solving activity involving correcting data warehouse components and maintenance procedures

- Require implementation and monitoring activity involving the migrating and correcting of data warehouse components and procedures

If the proposed effort does not fall within the scope of maintenance, consult either the enhancement or development routes for further assistance.

PARTICIPANT GUIDELINES

In Chapter 7 a series of organizational roles and responsibilities were described in terms of enabling the data warehousing environment. These roles perform various functions when applied in a project context (e.g., data warehouse marketing analyst could be a participant during requirement development and act as a validator during acceptance testing). Both project management and project delivery team roles are required to develop, enhance and maintain our data warehouse.

Project Management Team Roles[4]
- Project Steering Committee (SCM)
- Project Champion/Sponsor (PSC)
- Data Warehouse Project Manager (WPM)

Project Delivery Team Roles
- Data Warehouse Marketing Business Analyst (DWM)
- Metadata Administrator (MDA)
- Data Administrator/Data Architect (DAC)
- Data Warehouse Database Administrator (DBA)
- Decision Support Analyst (DSS)
- Data Warehouse Systems Analyst (DSA)
- Data Warehouse Technical Infrastructure Architect (DWT)
- Data Quality Administrator (DQA)
- Data Warehouse Organizational Analyst (DOA)

---

[4] For a definition of roles, consult the Data Warehouse Assistant on the CD ROM disk and look up the document titled "Data Warehouse Organization Team Roles."

Data Warehouse Product and Service Development Participation Guidelines

Each role performs one or more of the following duties during the project. These actions include

> A = Accepts data warehouse products and services
>
> V = Validates and reviews data warehouse products and services
>
> P = Produces a product or service
>
> S = Supports and/or provides additional input into the production of a product or service

Each action performed by a role is accountable for the development or delivery of a data warehouse product or service.

Acceptors (A)

Acceptors fulfill the following criteria:

- They are empowered to approve the product or service on behalf of the corporation.
- They are empowered to recommend changes to the business practice(s) as a result of the introduction of this new or enhanced product or service.

Validators (V)

Validators fulfill the following criteria:

- They are empowered to review/test the product or service.
- They possess the required technical or business expertise to adequately review/test the product or service.
- Their comments or feedback are used to shape the final form of the product or service.

PRODUCERS (P)

Producers fulfill the following criteria:

- They are empowered to develop the product or service.
- They have the required technical or business knowledge to produce the product or service.

SUPPORTERS (S)

Supporters fulfill the following criteria:

- They are empowered to provide additional input into the production of the product or service.
- They can assist in the resolution of issues related to the development of the product or service.
- They can provide human resources and facilities that will assist in the development and delivery of the product or service.

DATA WAREHOUSE COMPONENT
RESOURCE PLANNING

The following charts describe the data warehouse life cycle resource type requirements by components across the various states of development. The various life cycle stages include:

- Planning and evaluation
- Piloting
- Iterative design
- Testing and implementation
- Maintenance and support
- Evolution analysis

The following charts map these stages of evolution against the three data warehouse project types (development, enhancement, and maintenance). These project types and life cycle stages are mapped against the 11 major features or components described in Chapter 2 and are cross referenced against the aforementioned required resource roles. The data warehouse components that make up the five major layers of the data warehouse architecture include

1. Data staging
2. Data access
3. Data management
4. Information directory
5. Infrastructure (consists of seven components)
   a. Technology
   b. Organizational
   c. Procedural
   d. Project management
   e. Vendor
   f. Data stewardship
   g. Data security

The following chart illustrates the life cycle resource requirements of this component.

Data Warehouse Project Activity & Resource Planning Worksheet — Role Descriptions

Data Warehouse Functions	Life Cycle Activity	Management			Delivery								
		SCM	PSC	WPM	DWM	MDA	DAC	DBA	DSS	DSA	DWT	DQA	DOA
Data Staging	Planning & Evaluation	SA	S	SV	S	SV	SV	P	S	S	S	SV	S
	Piloting	SA	S	SV	S	SV	SV	P	SV	S	S	SV	S
	Iterative Design	SA	S	SV		SV	SV	P	SV	S	S	SV	
	Testing & Implementation	SA	S	SV		SV	SV	P	SV	S	S	SV	
	Maintenance & Support	SA	S	SV		SV	SV	P	S	S	S	SV	
	Evolution Analysis	SA	S	SV	S	SV	SV	P	S	S	S	SV	S

Role key column headers:
- SCM = Project Steering Committee (SCM)
- PSC = Project Champion/Sponsor (PSC)
- WPM = Data Warehouse Project Manager (WPM)
- DWM = Data Warehouse Marketing Business Analyst (DWM)
- MDA = Metadata Administrator (MDA)
- DAC = Data Administrator/Data Architect (DAC)
- DBA = Data Warehouse Database Administrator (DBA)
- DSS = Decision Support Analyst (DSS)
- DSA = Data Warehouse Systems Analyst (DSA)
- DWT = Data Warehouse Technical Infrastructure Architect (DWT)
- DQA = Data Quality Administrator (DQA)
- DOA = Data Warehouse Organizational Analyst (DOA)

Role Key

(A)ccepts
(P)roduces
(S)upports
(V)alidates

Data Staging — Data Warehouse Route to Life Cycle Activity Coverage

Data Staging	Development			Enhancement			Maintenance		
	Small	Medium	Large	Small	Medium	Large	Small	Medium	Large
Planning & Evaluation	✓	✓	✓	✓	✓	✓			
Analysis	✓	✓	✓	✓	✓	✓			
Iterative Design	✓	✓	✓	✓	✓	✓	✓	✓	✓
Testing & Implementation	✓	✓	✓	✓	✓	✓	✓	✓	✓
Maintenance & Support									
Evolution Analysis	✓	✓		✓					

DATA ACCESS RESOURCE REQUIREMENTS

The following chart illustrates the life cycle resource requirements of this component.

Data Warehouse Project Activity & Resource Planning Worksheet

Role Descriptions

Data Warehouse Functions	Life Cycle Activity	Management			Delivery									
		Project Steering Committee (SCM)	Project Champion/Sponsor (PSC)	Data Warehouse Project Manager (WPM)	Data Warehouse Marketing Business Analyst (DWM)	Metadata Administrator (MDA)	Data Administrator/Data Architect (DAC)	Data Warehouse Database Administrator (DBA)	Decision Support Analyst (DSS)	Data Warehouse Systems Analyst (DSA)	Data Warehouse Technical Infrastructure Architect (DWT)	Data Quality Administrator (DQA)	Data Warehouse Organizational Analyst (DOA)
		SCM	PSC	WPM	DWM	MDA	DAC	DBA	DSS	DSA	DWT	DQA	DOA
Data Access	Planning & Evaluation	SA	S	SV	S	SV	SV	P	S	S	S	SV	S
	Piloting	SA	S	SV	S	SV	SV	P	SV	S	S	SV	S
	Iterative Design	SA	S	SV		SV	SV	P	SV	S	S	SV	
	Testing & Implementation	SA	S	SV		SV	SV	P	SV	S	S	SV	
	Maintenance & Support	SA	S	SV		SV	SV	P	S	S	S	SV	
	Evolution Analysis	SA	S	SV	S	SV	SV	P	S	S	S	SV	S

Role Key

(A)ccepts
(P)roduces
(S)upports
(V)alidates

Data Warehouse Route to Life Cycle Activity Coverage

Data Staging

Life Cycle Activity	Development			Enhancement			Maintenance		
	Small	Medium	Large	Small	Medium	Large	Small	Medium	Large
Planning & Evaluation	✓	✓	✓		✓	✓			
Analysis	✓	✓	✓		✓	✓		✓	✓
Iterative Design	✓	✓	✓	✓	✓	✓	✓	✓	✓
Testing & Implementation	✓	✓	✓		✓	✓		✓	✓
Maintenance & Support									
Evolution Analysis	✓		✓		✓	✓			✓

Data Management Resource Requirements

The following chart illustrates the life cycle resource requirements of this component.

Data Warehouse Project Activity & Resource Planning Worksheet

Role Descriptions

Data Warehouse Functions	Life Cycle Activity	Management			Delivery								
		Project Steering Committee (SCM)	Project Champion/Sponsor (PSC)	Data Warehouse Project Manager (WPM)	Data Warehouse Marketing Business Analyst (DWM)	Metadata Administrator (MDA)	Data Administrator/Data Architect (DAC)	Data Warehouse Database Administrator (DBA)	Decision Support Analyst (DSS)	Data Warehouse Systems Analyst (DSA)	Data Warehouse Technical Infrastructure Architect (DWT)	Data Quality Administrator (DQA)	Data Warehouse Organizational Analyst (DOA)
		SCM	PSC	WPM	DWM	MDA	DAC	DBA	DSS	DSA	DWT	DQA	DOA
Data Management	Planning & Evaluation	SA	S	SV	S	SV	SV	P	S	S	S	SV	S
	Piloting	SA	S	SV	S	SV	SV	P	SV	S	S	SV	S
	Iterative Design	SA	S	SV		SV	SV	P	SV	S	S	SV	
	Testing & Implementation	SA	S	SV		SV	SV	P	SV	S	S	SV	
	Maintenance & Support	SA	S	SV		SV	SV	P	S	S	S	SV	
	Evolution Analysis	SA	S	SV	S	SV	SV	P	S	S	S	SV	S

Role Key

(A)ccepts
(P)roduces
(S)upports
(V)alidates

Data Staging

Data Warehouse Route to Life Cycle Activity Coverage	Development			Enhancement			Maintenance		
	Small	Medium	Large	Small	Medium	Large	Small	Medium	Large
Planning & Evaluation	✓	✓	✓		✓	✓			
Analysis	✓	✓	✓	✓	✓	✓			
Iterative Design	✓	✓	✓	✓	✓	✓	✓	✓	✓
Testing & Implementation	✓	✓	✓	✓	✓	✓	✓	✓	✓
Maintenance & Support							✓	✓	✓
Evolution Analysis	✓	✓	✓		✓				

INFORMATION DIRECTORY RESOURCE REQUIREMENTS

The following chart illustrates the life cycle resource requirements of this component.

Data Warehouse Project Activity & Resource Planning Worksheet

Role Descriptions

Data Warehouse Functions	Life Cycle Activity	Management						Delivery					
		SCM	PSC	WPM	DWM	MDA	DAC	DBA	DSS	DSA	DWT	DQA	DOA
Information Directory	Planning & Evaluation	SA	S	SV	S	SV	SV	P	S	S	S	SV	S
	Piloting	SA	S	SV	S	SV	SV	P	SV	S	S	SV	S
	Iterative Design	SA	S	SV		SV	SV	P	SV	S	S	SV	
	Testing & Implementation	SA	S	SV		SV	SV	P	SV	S	S	SV	
	Maintenance & Support	SA	S	SV		SV	SV	P	S	S	S	SV	
	Evolution Analysis	SA	S	SV	S	SV	SV	P	S	S	S	SV	S

Role Key:
- (A)ccepts
- (P)roduces
- (S)upports
- (V)alidates

Column legend:
- SCM — Project Steering Committee
- PSC — Project Champion/Sponsor
- WPM — Data Warehouse Project Manager
- DWM — Data Warehouse Marketing Business Analyst
- MDA — Metadata Administrator
- DAC — Data Administrator/Data Architect
- DBA — Data Warehouse Database Administrator
- DSS — Decision Support Analyst
- DSA — Data Warehouse Systems Analyst
- DWT — Data Warehouse Technical Infrastructure Architect
- DQA — Data Quality Administrator
- DOA — Data Warehouse Organizational Analyst

Data Staging

Data Warehouse Route to Life Cycle Activity Coverage

Life Cycle Activity	Development			Enhancement			Maintenance		
	Small	Medium	Large	Small	Medium	Large	Small	Medium	Large
Planning & Evaluation	✓	✓	✓	✓	✓	✓			
Analysis	✓	✓	✓	✓	✓	✓	✓	✓	✓
Iterative Design	✓	✓	✓	✓	✓	✓	✓	✓	✓
Testing & Implementation	✓	✓	✓	✓	✓	✓	✓	✓	✓
Maintenance & Support									
Evolution Analysis	✓	✓	✓	✓	✓	✓			

The following chart illustrates the life cycle resource requirements of this component.

Data Warehouse Project Activity & Resource Planning Worksheet — Role Descriptions

Data Warehouse Functions	Life Cycle Activity	Management			Delivery									
		SCM	PSC	WPM	DWM	MDA	DAC	DBA	DSS	DSA	DWT	DQA	DOA
Infrastructure Management (Technology)	Planning & Evaluation	SA	S	SV	S	SV	SV	P	S	S	S	SV	S
	Piloting	SA	S	SV	S	SV	SV	P	SV	S	S	SV	S
	Iterative Design	SA	S	SV		SV	SV	P	SV	S	S	SV	
	Testing & Implementation	SA	S	SV		SV	SV	P	SV	S	S	SV	
	Maintenance & Support	SA	S	SV		SV	SV	P	S	S	S	SV	
	Evolution Analysis	SA	S	SV	S	SV	SV	P	S	S	S	SV	S

Role Key:
- (A)ccepts
- (P)roduces
- (S)upports
- (V)alidates

Roles:
- Project Steering Committee (SCM)
- Project Champion/Sponsor (PSC)
- Data Warehouse Project Manager (WPM)
- Data Warehouse Marketing Business Analyst (DWM)
- Metadata Administrator (MDA)
- Data Administrator/Data Architect (DAC)
- Data Warehouse Database Administrator (DBA)
- Decision Support Analyst (DSS)
- Data Warehouse Systems Analyst (DSA)
- Data Warehouse Technical Infrastructure Architect (DWT)
- Data Quality Administrator (DQA)
- Data Warehouse Organizational Analyst (DOA)

Data Staging — Data Warehouse Route to Life Cycle Activity Coverage

Life Cycle Activity	Development			Enhancement			Maintenance		
	Small	Medium	Large	Small	Medium	Large	Small	Medium	Large
Planning & Evaluation	✓	✓	✓			✓			
Analysis	✓	✓	✓	✓	✓	✓	✓	✓	✓
Iterative Design	✓	✓	✓	✓	✓	✓	✓	✓	✓
Testing & Implementation	✓	✓	✓	✓	✓	✓	✓	✓	✓
Maintenance & Support				✓	✓	✓			
Evolution Analysis	✓	✓	✓	✓	✓				

ORGANIZATIONAL RESOURCE REQUIREMENTS

The following chart illustrates the life cycle resource requirements of this component.

Data Warehouse Project Activity & Resource Planning Worksheet

Role Descriptions

Data Warehouse Functions	Life Cycle Activity	Management				Delivery							
		Project Steering Committee (SCM)	Project Champion/Sponsor (PSC)	Data Warehouse Project Manager (WPM)	Data Warehouse Marketing Business Analyst (DWM)	Metadata Administrator (MDA)	Data Administrator/Data Architect (DAC)	Data Warehouse Database Administrator (DBA)	Decision Support Analyst (DSS)	Data Warehouse Systems Analyst (DSA)	Data Warehouse Technical Infrastructure Architect (DWT)	Data Quality Administrator (DQA)	Data Warehouse Organizational Analyst (DOA)
		SCM	PSC	WPM	DWM	MDA	DAC	DBA	DSS	DSA	DWT	DQA	DOA
Infrastructure Management (Organizational Change Management)	Planning & Evaluation	SA	S	SV	S	SV	SV	P	S	S	S	SV	S
	Piloting	SA	S	SV	S	SV	SV	P	SV	S	S	SV	S
	Iterative Design	SA	S	SV		SV	SV	P	SV	S	S	SV	
	Testing & Implementation	SA	S	SV		SV	SV	P	SV	S	S	SV	
	Maintenance & Support	SA	S	SV		SV	SV	P	S	S	S	SV	
	Evolution Analysis	SA	S	SV	S	SV	SV	P	S	S	S	SV	S

Role Key

(A)ccepts
(P)roduces
(S)upports
(V)alidates

Data Staging

Data Warehouse Route to Life Cycle Activity Coverage

	Development			Enhancement			Maintenance		
	Small	Medium	Large	Small	Medium	Large	Small	Medium	Large
Planning & Evaluation	✓	✓	✓	✓	✓	✓			
Analysis	✓	✓	✓	✓	✓	✓	✓	✓	✓
Iterative Design	✓	✓	✓	✓	✓	✓	✓	✓	✓
Testing & Implementation	✓			✓	✓	✓	✓	✓	✓
Maintenance & Support									
Evolution Analysis	✓		✓	✓	✓	✓			

The following chart illustrates the life cycle resource requirements of this component.

Data Warehouse Project Activity & Resource Planning Worksheet — Role Descriptions

Data Warehouse Functions	Life Cycle Activity	Management			Delivery								
		Project Steering Committee (SCM)	Project Champion/Sponsor (PSC)	Data Warehouse Project Manager (WPM)	Data Warehouse Marketing Business Analyst (DWM)	Metadata Administrator (MDA)	Data Administrator/Data Architect (DAC)	Data Warehouse Database Administrator (DBA)	Decision Support Analyst (DSS)	Data Warehouse Systems Analyst (DSA)	Data Warehouse Technical Infrastructure Architect (DWT)	Data Quality Administrator (DQA)	Data Warehouse Organizational Analyst (DOA)
		SCM	PSC	WPM	DWM	MDA	DAC	DBA	DSS	DSA	DWT	DQA	DOA
Infrastructure Management (Policies & Procedures)	Planning & Evaluation	SA	S	SV	S	SV	SV	P	S	S	S	SV	S
	Piloting	SA	S	SV	S	SV	SV	P	SV	S	S	SV	S
	Iterative Design	SA	S	SV		SV	SV	P	SV	S	S	SV	
	Testing & Implementation	SA	S	SV		SV	SV	P	SV	S	S	SV	
	Maintenance & Support	SA	S	SV		SV	SV	P	S	S	S	SV	
	Evolution Analysis	SA	S	SV	S	SV	SV	P	S	S	S	SV	S

Role Key

(A)ccepts
(P)roduces
(S)upports
(V)alidates

Data Staging Data Warehouse Route to Life Cycle Activity Coverage

	Development			Enhancement			Maintenance		
	Small	Medium	Large	Small	Medium	Large	Small	Medium	Large
Planning & Evaluation	✓	✓	✓	✓	✓	✓			
Analysis	✓	✓	✓	✓	✓	✓			
Iterative Design	✓	✓	✓	✓	✓	✓	✓	✓	✓
Testing & Implementation	✓	✓	✓	✓	✓	✓	✓	✓	✓
Maintenance & Support				✓	✓	✓	✓	✓	✓
Evolution Analysis	✓	✓	✓		✓	✓			

Project Management Resource Requirements

The following chart illustrates the life cycle resource requirements of this component.

Data Warehouse Project Activity & Resource Planning Worksheet — Role Descriptions

Data Warehouse Functions	Life Cycle Activity	Management			Delivery								
		SCM	PSC	WPM	DWM	MDA	DAC	DBA	DSS	DSA	DWT	DQA	DOA
Infrastructure Management (Project Management)	Planning & Evaluation	SA	S	SV	S	SV	SV	P	SV	S	S	SV	S
	Piloting	SA	S	SV		SV	SV	P	SV	S	S	SV	S
	Iterative Design	SA	S	SV		SV	SV	P	SV	S	S	SV	
	Testing & Implementation	SA	S	SV		SV	SV	P	SV	S	S	SV	
	Maintenance & Support	SA	S	SV		SV	SV	P	S	S	S	SV	
	Evolution Analysis	SA	S	SV	S	SV	SV	P	S	S	S	SV	S

Role abbreviations:
- SCM — Project Steering Committee
- PSC — Project Champion/Sponsor
- WPM — Data Warehouse Project Manager
- DWM — Data Warehouse Marketing Business Analyst
- MDA — Metadata Administrator
- DAC — Data Administrator/Data Architect
- DBA — Data Warehouse Database Administrator
- DSS — Decision Support Analyst
- DSA — Data Warehouse Systems Analyst
- DWT — Data Warehouse Technical Infrastructure Architect
- DQA — Data Quality Administrator
- DOA — Data Warehouse Organizational Analyst

Role Key
- (A)ccepts
- (P)roduces
- (S)upports
- (V)alidates

Data Staging — Data Warehouse Route to Life Cycle Activity Coverage

Data Warehouse Route to Life Cycle Activity Coverage	Development			Enhancement			Maintenance		
	Small	Medium	Large	Small	Medium	Large	Small	Medium	Large
Planning & Evaluation	✓	✓	✓	✓	✓	✓			
Analysis	✓	✓	✓	✓	✓	✓	✓	✓	✓
Iterative Design	✓	✓	✓	✓	✓	✓	✓	✓	✓
Testing & Implementation	✓	✓	✓			✓	✓	✓	✓
Maintenance & Support					✓	✓			
Evolution Analysis		✓				✓			✓

VENDOR RESOURCE REQUIREMENTS

The following chart illustrates the life cycle resource requirements of this component.

Data Warehouse Project Activity & Resource Planning Worksheet

Role Descriptions

Data Warehouse Functions	Life Cycle Activity	Management			Delivery								
		Project Steering Committee (SCM)	Project Champion/Sponsor (PSC)	Data Warehouse Project Manager (WPM)	Data Warehouse Marketing Business Analyst (DWM)	Metadata Administrator (MDA)	Data Administrator/Data Architect (DAC)	Data Warehouse Database Administrator (DBA)	Decision Support Analyst (DSS)	Data Warehouse Systems Analyst (DSA)	Data Warehouse Technical Infrastructure Architect (DWT)	Data Quality Administrator (DQA)	Data Warehouse Organizational Analyst (DOA)
		SCM	PSC	WPM	DWM	MDA	DAC	DBA	DSS	DSA	DWT	DQA	DOA
Infrastructure Management (Vendor & Contract)	Planning & Evaluation	SA	S	SV	S	SV	SV	P	S	S	S	SV	S
	Piloting	SA	S	SV	S	SV	SV	P	SV	S	S	SV	S
	Iterative Design	SA	S	SV		SV	SV	P	SV	S	S	SV	
	Testing & Implementation	SA	S	SV		SV	SV	P	SV	S	S	SV	
	Maintenance & Support	SA	S	SV		SV	SV	P	S	S	S	SV	
	Evolution Analysis	SA	S	SV	S	SV	SV	P	S	S	S	SV	S

Role Key

(A)ccepts
(P)roduces
(S)upports
(V)alidates

Data Staging

Data Warehouse Route to Life Cycle Activity Coverage	Development			Enhancement			Maintenance		
	Small	Medium	Large	Small	Medium	Large	Small	Medium	Large
Planning & Evaluation	✓	✓	✓	✓	✓	✓			
Analysis	✓	✓	✓	✓	✓	✓			
Iterative Design	✓	✓	✓	✓	✓	✓	✓	✓	✓
Testing & Implementation	✓	✓	✓	✓	✓	✓	✓	✓	✓
Maintenance & Support									
Evolution Analysis	✓	✓	✓	✓	✓				

DATA STEWARDSHIP RESOURCE REQUIREMENTS

The following chart illustrates the life cycle resource requirements of this component.

Data Warehouse Project Activity & Resource Planning Worksheet — Role Descriptions

Data Warehouse Functions	Life Cycle Activity	Management			Delivery								
		SCM	PSC	WPM	DWM	MDA	DAC	DBA	DSS	DSA	DWT	DQA	DOA
Infrastructure Management (Data Stewardship)	Planning & Evaluation	SA	S	SV	S	SV	SV	P	S	S	S	SV	S
	Piloting	SA	S	SV	S	SV	SV	P	SV	S	S	SV	S
	Iterative Design	SA	S	SV		SV	SV	P	SV	S	S	SV	
	Testing & Implementation	SA	S	SV		SV	SV	P	SV	S	S	SV	
	Maintenance & Support	SA	S	SV		SV	SV	P	S	S	S	SV	
	Evolution Analysis	SA	S	SV	S	SV	SV	P	S	S	S	SV	S

Role Descriptions:
- SCM — Project Steering Committee
- PSC — Project Champion/Sponsor
- WPM — Data Warehouse Project Manager
- DWM — Data Warehouse Marketing Business Analyst
- MDA — Metadata Administrator
- DAC — Data Administrator/Data Architect
- DBA — Data Warehouse Database Administrator
- DSS — Decision Support Analyst (DSS)
- DSA — Data Warehouse Systems Analyst
- DWT — Data Warehouse Technical Infrastructure Architect
- DQA — Data Quality Administrator
- DOA — Data Warehouse Organizational Analyst

Role Key
- (A)ccepts
- (P)roduces
- (S)upports
- (V)alidates

Data Staging — Data Warehouse Route to Life Cycle Activity Coverage

Data Warehouse Route to Life Cycle Activity Coverage	Development			Enhancement			Maintenance		
	Small	Medium	Large	Small	Medium	Large	Small	Medium	Large
Planning & Evaluation	✓	✓	✓	✓	✓	✓			
Analysis	✓	✓	✓	✓	✓	✓		✓	✓
Iterative Design	✓	✓	✓	✓	✓	✓	✓	✓	✓
Testing & Implementation	✓	✓	✓	✓	✓	✓	✓	✓	✓
Maintenance & Support									
Evolution Analysis	✓	✓	✓		✓	✓			

DATA SECURITY RESOURCE REQUIREMENTS

The following chart illustrates the life cycle resource requirements of this component.

Data Warehouse Project Activity & Resource Planning Worksheet

Role Descriptions

Role Code	Role Name
SCM	Project Steering Committee (SCM)
PSC	Project Champion/Sponsor (PSC)
WPM	Data Warehouse Project Manager (WPM)
DWM	Data Warehouse Marketing Business Analyst (DWM)
MDA	Metadata Administrator (MDA)
DAC	Data Administrator/Data Architect (DAC)
DBA	Data Warehouse Database Administrator (DBA)
DSS	Decision Support Analyst (DSS)
DSA	Data Warehouse Systems Analyst (DSA)
DWT	Data Warehouse Technical Infrastructure Architect (DWT)
DQA	Data Quality Administrator (DQA)
DOA	Data Warehouse Organizational Analyst (DOA)

Data Warehouse Functions

Infrastructure Management (Data Security) — Life Cycle Activity	Management			Delivery								
	SCM	PSC	WPM	DWM	MDA	DAC	DBA	DSS	DSA	DWT	DQA	DOA
Planning & Evaluation	SA	S	SV	S	SV	SV	P	S	S	S	SV	S
Piloting	SA	S	SV	S	SV	SV	P	SV	S	S	SV	S
Iterative Design	SA	S	SV		SV	SV	P	SV	S	S	SV	
Testing & Implementation	SA	S	SV		SV	SV	P	SV	S	S	SV	
Maintenance & Support	SA	S	SV		SV	SV	P	S	S	S	SV	
Evolution Analysis	SA	S	SV	S	SV	SV	P	S	S	S	SV	S

Role Key

- (A)ccepts
- (P)roduces
- (S)upports
- (V)alidates

Data Staging — Data Warehouse Route to Life Cycle Activity Coverage

Life Cycle Activity	Development			Enhancement			Maintenance		
	Small	Medium	Large	Small	Medium	Large	Small	Medium	Large
Planning & Evaluation	✓	✓	✓		✓	✓			
Analysis	✓	✓	✓		✓	✓	✓	✓	✓
Iterative Design	✓	✓	✓		✓	✓	✓	✓	✓
Testing & Implementation	✓	✓	✓		✓		✓	✓	✓
Maintenance & Support									
Evolution Analysis	✓	✓			✓				

ESTIMATING RESOURCE COSTS FOR
DATA WAREHOUSE DEVELOPMENT

Once the number of roles and their participation on the project have been decided, the final step is to determine, from a project planning and budgeting perspective, an estimated cost. The following chart acts as a guideline in determining the cost profile of a perspective project type.

Data Warehouse Development Life Cycle Reference Sheet

This sheet describes where effort can be determined as well as estimate a potential per day cost which can be used as a project planning measure.

	Development			Enhancement			Maintenance		
	Small	Medium	Large	Small	Medium	Large	Small	Medium	Large
Data Warehouse Functions									
Data Staging	B	I	I		B	I	B	B	I
Data Management	B	I	I	B	B	I	B	B	B
Data Access	I	C	C	B	I	C	B	B	I
Information Directory	B	I	I	B	B	I	B	B	B
Infrastructure Management	I	C	C	I	I	C	B	I	I
Infrastructure Management									
Organizational Change Management	I	C	C	I	I	C	B	I	I
Policies & Procedures Control	B	B	B	B	B	B	B	B	B
Project Management	B	I	I	B	B	I	B	B	B
Vendor & Contract Management	B	B	I	B	B	B	B	B	B
Data Stewardship	B	I	I	B	B	I	B	B	B
Data Security	B	I	I	B	B	I	B	B	B
Technology Management	I	C	C	I	I	C	B	I	I

Human Resource Requirements Key*

	Per Day Costs	
(B)asic	$3K	(One to three people with up to one half resources supplied by consulting firms)
(I)ntensive	$6K	(Three to six people with up to one half resources supplied by consulting firms)
(C)omplex	$12K	(Six to eight people with up to one half resources supplied by consulting firms)

*Please note these costs do not include Business End user or (non data warehouse). It is assumed that consulting costs will be at least double, internal staff costs.

CHAPTER NINE

Adopting a Guideline for Success: Methods and Tools

A critical, yet often overlooked task in developing the necessary infrastructure for data warehousing is deployment of methods and tool suites for data warehouse development. The routes one can adopt are

- Development of a home grown approach
- Augmenting your current OLTP (S)ystems (D)evelopment (L)ife (C)ycle methodology
- Purchasing a methodology and tool suite from a vendor geared toward data warehousing

The route you select also depends upon the nature of the data warehousing development effort. If you are deploying an operational data store or data warehouse as a normalized database design with typical transaction based data access, then your current OLTP methodology and tool suite will suffice. If you are looking at a rapid deployment of a data mart or data warehouse, however, with all of the required infrastructure components such as data access, data management, and metadata management then a departure from the standard OLTP SDLC should be considered.

DATA WAREHOUSE METHODOLOGY PRINCIPLES

Data warehouse development is radically different from traditional OLTP systems. A number of principles apply when considering which development

143

route to adopt. These principles are central to the development of any data warehouse.

DATA CONVERSION AND MOVEMENT IS AN ONGOING PROCESS

OLTP systems deal with data conversion and restaging as a one time event. Data warehouses deal with it as an ongoing activity. Data warehouses must also address consolidating and selecting the best source or system of record data as an ongoing event. The data warehouse DBA must keep a wary eye on events occurring within the OLTP world as data reengineering, ERP, and new systems development projects provide new options to consider and change as the nature of the business changes.

DATA QUALITY MANAGEMENT IS KEY

Because of the cross systems nature of the data warehouse, how data are combined and where and how external or third party data are added to the mix can result in severe data quality issues. A data quality management process is critical to success. OLTP systems usually focus on transaction based data quality. In data warehousing we focus on subject area data quality, where the key dimensions of the business are quality assured across lines of business. This new dimension can and will cause change in how the business views its information assets and how best to manage those assets. Whether we consider a data mart or data warehouse implementation, data quality verification of the system of record feeds must be considered and managed as part of the overall implementation effort.

DATABASE DESIGN IS CENTRALIZED

Data warehouse databases collect data across internal systems and augment them with external data from outside the business. The combination of these data results in the creation of new data that do not exist anywhere else in the business. (This is a key consideration, as a data warehouse is not just a historical repository of data, but will actually contain new information when the data are aggregated and summarized.)

Database Design Is Time Variant

OLTP databases are designed with current state business rules in mind. Each time a business rule changes the database must be redesigned and affected data reloaded. This works well with a normalized (or current state dependent) database management process. Due to the nature of the data warehouse this process fails in that

- The size of the data warehouse precludes ongoing database redesign
- The cross systems nature and dependencies that exist in the warehouse inhibit current state business rule changes
- The time variant nature of the data warehouse precludes a normalized design process, since each change causes the warehouse to lose history

Requirements Are Not Fixed

Unlike OLTP systems design where requirements are signed off before coding and testing commence, data warehouse data access design changes radically through the piloting and implementation process. Success with such an approach often requires the deployment of two data staging areas. The first addresses the core data extraction, repair, and aggregation process while the second is used to facilitate data access design by providing a test repository of data.

Metadata Management Is Critical

Again, unlike OLTP systems that deal with only internal and external schema metadata as they apply to database DDL or application library code, data warehouses rely on metadata to understand the content, viability, and nature of the warehouse and its access mechanisms. Therefore it is important to consider how your metadata tool will

- Communicate with the database(s) and front end DSS tools
- Provide access to the end user community so that they can understand the data and how to make use of it

SELECTING AN OFF THE SHELF APPROACH OR DEVELOPING A CUSTOM METHOD

The seven steps for selecting an off the shelf approach or customizing your current SDLC include

1. Develop a functional model of the proposed architecture.
    1.1 Define each component of the data warehouse architecture.
    1.2. Determine and define the links between each component.
    1.3. Determine and define the development and maintenance responsibilities for each component.
    1.4. Determine what is already in place and what must be developed to support each data warehousing project.
    1.5. Publish and approve the proposed architectural approach.

2. Determine the scope and nature of the development effort to be supported.
    2.1. Determine the level of required decision support functionality (e.g., management reporting, executive information systems, Internet/intranet data access, data mining).
    2.2. Determine what data security and charge back measures are required.
    2.3. Determine and define what data quality measures are required.

3. Determine the scope and nature of the available in house SDLC.
    3.1. Review data staging methods, tools, and procedures.
    3.2. Review data management methods, tools, and procedures.
    3.3. Review data access (systems development) methods, tools, and procedures.
    3.4. Review infrastructure methods, tools and procedures (for technology, metadata, project management, vendor management, etc.).

4. Develop a three schema meta model of the proposed architecture.
    4.1. Develop the database or internal schema view.
    4.2. Develop the decision support or external schema view.
    4.3. Develop the conceptual or business rules layer view.

5. Determine a gap analysis.
    5.1. Map three schema requirements to existing architecture.
    5.2. Determine SDLC life cycle gaps and closure strategy.
    5.3. Augment SDLC with required methods and tools or develop an RFI.
    5.4. Research and distribute RFI to available vendors, or
    5.5. Distribute RFI to current technology business partners.

6. Recommend methods and tools adoption.
    6.1. Implement SDLC changes in pilot mode as part of the next data warehouse or data mart development process, or
    6.2. Short list and pilot a vendor solution.

7. Implement methods and tools processes in production.
    7.1. Adopt the augmented SDLC or vendor solution upon conclusion of a data warehousing project and recommend further changes or additions.
    7.2. Create or augment current education and training material for distribution and publication across the information technology organization.

DEVELOPING A LIFE CYCLE METHOD

If it is your intention to develop a home grown approach or to augment your current SDLC, there are six key points to include.

DEVELOP THE WORKPLAN STAGE BY STAGE THROUGH THE PROCESS

A six to nine month plan developed for the first time will not prove accurate or complete. Best practices in project management suggest a detailed two month plan with broad place holders for the balance of the activities. As you complete your project, check back against the standard timeline and adjust each phase according to what you have learned.

As an example, the sample high level activity plan shown on the following page can be used/adjusted to reflect the initial scope/nature of your data warehousing effort.

Figure 9–1
Data Warehouse Initiation Plan

Activity Id	Activity Description	Measure	Quantity	Effort Per Activity	Days Duration Est.	% of Total
1	Review the Business Case and Industry Research	Persons	2.0	2.0	2	5%
2	Determine the type of Data Warehouse Requested	Interviews	2.0	1.0	2	5%
3	Determine Data Warehouse Architecture	Architecture	4.0	3.0	12	30%
4	Determine DW Project Life Cycle	Plan	2.0	5.0	2	5%
5	Describe the Proposed DW Project Management Approach	Interviews	1.0	1.0	2	5%
6	Determine the required IT and business resources and training	Persons	1.0	2.0	3	8%
7	Determine required consulting services	Persons	1.0	2.0	2	5%
8	Determine the initial data access environment requirements	Interviews	4.0	3.0	15	38%
	Totals:				40	100%

LIMIT THE SCOPE OF IMPLEMENTATION TO PART OF ONE SUBJECT AREA

This subject area should not access more than three critical business systems and/or one line of business. Politics will inhibit success in data warehousing, so unless you have undertaken a detailed organizational maturity assessment as suggested in Section One, it is best to limit the data management issues you will face.

AUTOMATE YOUR PROJECT PLANNING AND BUDGETING PROCESS

Wherever possible think "reuse" in your selection of project planning, budgeting, and analysis tools. A number of effective project management tools exist in the market. Some can be accessed or interfaced to planning and analysis CASE based development tools to provide a more complete picture.

OBTAIN SIGNOFF AND APPROVAL AT EACH STAGE

As you develop your workplan and process, obtain a signoff of the work accomplished and deliverables produced at each stage, especially for the scope and content of the data staging environment.

OVERSTAFF THE DEVELOPMENT TEAM

Where possible, overstaff or allow for backups of each critical role in the development process discussed in Chapter 8. A major consideration for most data warehousing projects is maintaining the level of effort, especially in an environment where some or all of the work must be provided by the internal information technology organization, which may be stretched to provide the required resources due to other project commitments.

DESCRIBE DELIVERABLES AND MILESTONES

Whether developing a home grown approach or adopting a vendor's method, two key project management principles apply.

1. Keep the workplan tight by detailing activities at no more than two month intervals. Timeframes longer than two months require the plan to change, requiring rework of any subsequent or parallel work activities.

2. Ensure that each workstep or task listed is either a:

   - A label or place holder for a lower level task
   - A milestone with a time period focusing on review or validation of work completed to date
   - An activity that will result in the production of a work product or deliverable

Any other activities should be treated as superfluous and removed from your work plan.

DOCUMENT MEASURES AND MECHANISMS

Measures to be developed for your project include

1. Project management and reporting guidelines and measurement mechanisms

2. Performance management guidelines

3. Communication guidelines, internal (team) and external (user), in terms of

   a. Customer surveys and feedback mechanisms for team members
   b. Inter and intraproject communication
   c. Vendor communication and performance measurement
   d. Industry or business partner input or review

4. Mechanisms for managing issues and change management

5. Issue resolution procedures

6. Deliverable quality assurance guidelines and review processes, including

   a. Test procedures and scripts
   b. Data quality management procedures and auditing

7. Development to production vendor tool and data warehouse application certification

8. End user participation in DSS application development

9. Infrastructure development and implementation in terms of
   a. Hardware and software
   b. Network and facilities
   c. Maintenance and support
   d. Help desk
   e. Metadata management

10. Education and training measures for team members, support personnel, and the end users

DATA WAREHOUSE METHODOLOGIES AND TOOL SETS

The following chart illustrates sample data warehousing methodologies and tool sets and vendors who provide product or consulting services expertise to assist you in your data warehousing efforts. The data warehousing methodologies have been mapped against our generic life cycle process and illustrate the strength areas of each approach. The tool set section focuses on specific as well as generic tool sets from a selection of vendors who can assist in the automation of various parts of the data warehouse life cycle. Consult the companion CD under Chapter 9 for the electronic version of this table, which contains hot links to the various vendor sites.

Figure 9–2
Data Warehouse Methods and Tools Selection Worksheet

Sample Methodologies and Tools Summary   Last Updated On:

Methodologies	Company Name (Consulting & Product Vendor)	URL/Web Page Address	Scope of Services Provided					
			Planning & Evaluation	Piloting	Iterative Design	Testing & Implementation	Maintenance & Support	Evolution Analysis
Data Warehouse Methodology	Relational Solutions, Inc.	www.relationalsolutions.com/Methodology.htm					✓	
Sysix - Data Warehouse Methodology	Sysix	www.xsite.net/~dante/sysix/dataware/method.htm	✓	✓	✓	✓	✓	
Data Warehouse Methodology: Implementation	SAGA Software AG	URL: 157.189.11.40/services/educ/courses/dwi-001.htm		✓	✓	✓	✓	✓
Intro to Data Warehousing: Concept to Creation	Barnett Data Systems	www.barnettdata.com/html/sems/sem02.htm		✓	✓	✓	✓	✓
Solutions : KMS Data Warehousing	inforte corporation	www.infortecorp.com/Solutions/KMS_DataWarehousing.as	✓	✓	✓	✓	✓	
NCR's Scalable Data Warehousing - Services	NCR	www3.ncr.com/data_warehouse/services.htm	✓	✓	✓	✓	✓	✓
EAI Implementation Services	Enterprise Architects, Inc	www.enterprise-architects.com/implementationservices.htm		✓	✓	✓	✓	
Millennia Vision Corporation Data Warehousing and Decision Support Services	Millennia Vision Corporation	www.mvsn.com/Practice DW-DSS.html	✓		✓	✓		
Informix Consulting: The Data Warehousing Practice	Informix	www.informix.com/informix/services/consulting/dwcons.htm	✓	✓	✓	✓	✓	
Oracle Warehouse	Oracle	www.oracle.com	✓	✓	✓	✓	✓	✓
DecisionEdge	IBM	http://direct.boulder.ibm.com/bi/decisionedge/index.htm	✓	✓	✓	✓	✓	✓

Sample DW Vendor Tools	Company Name (Consulting & Product Vendor)	URL/Web Page Address
Constructa	Anubis	www.anubis.com
Applied Data Resource Environment	Applied Data Resource Management	www.adrm.com
AppsMart	AppsCo	www.apsco.com
Modeler	CASEwise Systems	www.casewise.com
Terrain	Cayenne Software, Inc.	www.cayennesoft.com

ER Studio 2.0	Embarcadero Technologies	www.embarcadero.com
Visual Warehouse	IBM	www.ibm.com
ERWin, ModelMart, Universal Directory	LogicWorks (PLATINUM)	www.logicworks.com
MQP - Iterative Data Warehousing Methodology	Metamor Technologies, Ltd.	www.metamortech.com
AnswerSets	Metamor Technologies, Ltd.	www.answersets.com
Designer/2000	Oracle Corporation	www.oracle.com
DB XL, Open Edition Environment	PLATINUM technology, inc.	www.platinum.com
System Architect, SA/Data Architect	Popkin Software & Systems, Inc.	www.popkin.com/
PowerDesigner WarehouseArchitect	Powersoft	www.powersoft.com
Warehouse Executive, Iteration	Prism Solutions	www.prismsolutions.com
META EXCHANGE, USAGE TRACKER, ACTIVATOR, CONTENT TRACKER, COST TRACKER, REFRESHMENT TRACKER	PineCone	www.pine-cone.com
SELECT SE	SELECT Software	www.select.st.com
SILVERRUN	SILVERRUN Technologies, Inc.	www.silverrun.co
SQL Mill	IronBridge Software	www.ibsw.com
PowerDesigner		
Early Harvest	Sybase, Inc.	www.sybase.com
Visible Advantage Data Warehouse Edition, Visible Analyst	Tessera Enterprise Systems, Inc.	www.tesent.com
	Visible Systems Corporation	www.visible.com
InfoModeler, Visio Professional,	Visio Corporation	www.visio.com
4Keeps		
WareAbouts	Métier	www.metier.com
Component Engineering Methodology	Zyga Corporation	www.zyga.com

◆

CHAPTER TEN

Architecture Design and Implementation Strategy

INTRODUCTION TO DATA WAREHOUSE ARCHITECTURE PLANNING

To design our data warehousing architecture three factors must be considered.

1. The maturity of our IT organization
2. The nature of the business request for decision support services
3. The chosen technology path

IT Maturity

The current maturity level within our IT organization will largely dictate what is possible for our initial and subsequent data warehousing iterations. Picking an architecture strategy that will work with, and not against our IT culture will go a long way toward ensuring the success of our data warehousing strategy. Conducting a maturity assessment of our IT organization (Section One) should be considered as a necessary first step in developing our approach. A number of other factors to consider include

- The level of data management maturity (Does our IT organization support a data architecture/data administration function?) or does the organization consider data management as a solely physical database administration role? If such an organization exists, where is it placed in

155

the IT organization? (A data management group buried under systems development will not provide the necessary level of support.)

- Data stewardship, in terms of active data ownership within the business, where data is reviewed and certified by an end user council before being released to IT for systems engineering

- The existence of a program management office that coordinates systems projects across multiple departments or lines of business

- An active, current, and up to date systems development life cycle methodology, fully supported by automated tools, workbenches, repositories, and facilities

BUSINESS DECISION SUPPORT REQUIREMENTS

As in most things, we learn by doing. This holds true for businesses as well that are venturing into these new and often unchartered waters. In most cases, the user starts with requests for operational management reporting based information before becoming more sophisticated and aware of what is truly possible. Finance and supply chain departments focus on near or current state data only, while marketing, customer relationship management, and product planning groups require more forward looking business intelligence systems. Depending upon the source of our first major request, we look toward building our architecture in an evolutionary manner, starting with an initial or core data staging environment and feeding an operational data store. In such cases report writing tools should be considered over decision support tools, and relational databases over multidimensional. Again, we should engineer for what is required, and not what we would like the user to have.

Politics has a large part to play in the development and evolution of our data management layer. Sharing information about our customers, products, locations, and vendors (the core subject areas of our business) may prove to be a Herculean task if not approached in a rational, realistic manner. If lines of business do not talk to one another and share data, the data warehousing strategy will have to be adjusted to suit. In these situations, a central data warehouse may not be developed at all. Instead, data is moved from the data staging area directly into the line of business data marts. The data staging area in effect becomes the data warehouse until cross line of business sharing of corporate data is supported in the business through its OLTP systems.

THE TECHNOLOGY PATH

Our architecture for the data warehouse will be heavily influenced and steered down a certain path once a technology is selected. This becomes even truer in the case of ERP vendors, where the data warehousing environment is seen as an operational data store extension to OLTP processing. Therefore, we must choose as open an architecture as possible, which allows for staged growth without inhibiting business performance due to our inability to change rapidly with the changing business landscape.

In preparing for the delivery of our data warehouse architecture, we must consider the immediate needs of our business client while keeping the long term picture in mind. In preparing our strategic direction for the data warehouse environment we focus on

- Scalability
- Data management
- Metadata management
- Information access (decision support)
- Infrastructure

SCALING THE DATA WAREHOUSE ARCHITECTURE

No matter how carefully we plan for growth, we often grossly underestimate what is required to meet demand due to

- Large memory access requirements against terabytes of data
- Ad hoc requirements for data against the data warehouse. (However, the ability to access large blocks of data is a big advantage in solving this problem.)
- Architecture support for 1 to N tier architecture design in thinning out the client or DSS layer while moving applications and data onto separate servers
- Moving the extraction, transformation, repair, and aggregation process into a separate data staging environment
- Obtaining fat pipes for moving data through the server environment quickly and efficiently

- Robust and extensible data storage devices that can grow with our needs without having to undergo reengineering or the adoption of new processor technology

- Employing 64 bit VLM technology that moves beyond the 32 bit 2GB memory range limitation and will support up to 14GB of memory usage and more and with no migration issues (the way of the future)

Current server configuration options include

1. Clustering. This is the most mature environment, but the least scalable This environment is also limited by its processor architecture to primarily 32 bit systems.

2. SMP. This mature processor architecture reaches performance thresholds when parallel processing becomes critical to satisfying demand when running large numbers of queries all requiring significant volumes of data. SMP systems reach performance thresholds when managing data warehouse databases of 500 or more gigabytes of data. This still remains the architecture type of choice for the majority of data warehouses in use today.

3. MPP. This is one of the newest architectures. MPP reaches performance thresholds in processing large transactions in a VLDB environment due to its limited memory sharing capability (this results in excessive paging due to the inability to acquire as much memory as is required for caching the transaction).

4. Numa. This is the newest architecture. Numa technology solves the memory sharing problem but is the least mature of all the technologies currently available on the market today. Because of its extensibility it will become the preferred processor architecture of the future.

ADOPTING A DATA MANAGEMENT STRATEGY

A number of data management considerations come into play when devising our data management strategy. We need to plan for

1. The number of database instances installed and how to keep the database software in sync for version control and software releases

2. Data warehouse database design versus data mart database design (Our choices are normalizing or denormalizing the data.)

   - Normalized design involves creating a large number of tables to eliminate data redundancy. However, this process inhibits the understanding of the data structures by the end user and the coding of queries. These types of designs are usually employed only at the data warehouse or operational data store level and use relational technology. Disadvantages of this approach are the database structures between the layers of the data warehouse architecture may be different, requiring us to build an additional extraction transformation layer to move the data from the warehouse to the marts. The second major drawback of this approach is that the data in the data warehouse are not in a user friendly format and will cause the usual performance issues associated with OLTP systems when querying significant amounts of data across a large number of tables.

   - Denormalized design involves star schema design of the dimensions and facts of the business in subject areas (business processes). These types of designs can be employed either at the data warehouse or data mart level and can employ either relational or multidimensional DBMS technology. The star schema approach remains the best design for the data warehouse/mart layer. Dimensional (star schema model) promote easier integration and synchronization of data through the employment of compatible data structures across the warehouse to the mart. It also allows the end users to drill through the aggregated and summarized data of the marts to the detail data held in the data warehouse. Creating a compatible denormalized design for the warehouse and the marts eliminates the need for an additional data staging area and also permits easier drill through by DSS tools from the mart to the warehouse.

3. Database design approach in terms of deciding upon the grain (level of granularity) of the fact and dimension tables of the data warehouse. Along with this we need to consider how queries will be analyzed in terms of accessing the detail or leaf level tables of our warehouse (and our summary or aggregate tables). These types of ad hoc queries are usually managed by the employment of a query navigator. Predefined decision support routines and precanned reports can be set up to view

the appropriate level of detail and to allow for drill through to the leaf level fact tables. This is managed through the definition of views or a related mechanism, which insulates the base tables from direct access (consult your DSS vendor and ask them how they insulate database schemas from direct access).

4. Distribution of data across multiple databases across diverse geographic locations. Key considerations include:

   • Replication strategy of shared or summarized dimension data moving from the data warehouse to the data mart.

   • Synchronization strategy for dimension table updates to the distributed data warehouse/mart servers and the aggregation or roll up of fact table data to a central data warehouse for executive management analysis and reporting.

5. Synchronization of data across the layers of the data warehouse architecture (data warehouse(s) and associated data marts. We need to consider whether or not to centralize the data through the data warehouse or distribute them through data marts (this is not the same type of architecture as distributed data warehouse databases as discussed earlier). Data distribution of the data warehouse across the marts can be set up as either

   • All dimension and fact table data controlled at the data warehouse level and replicated for performance to the mart level or to a distributed data warehouse.

   • All dimension and fact table data controlled at the data warehouse with only a portion of the dimension and fact table detail and summary level data replicated to the marts.

   • All dimension detail and summary data and only summary fact table data managed at the warehouse level with only summary and/or a portion of the dimension data and all the detail fact table data controlled at the mart level. In this type of environment, each mart controls a different family of fact tables based on their line of business.

   • All dimension and fact table detail data controlled at the warehouse level with only a portion of the dimension and fact table data (lightly summarized) managed at the mart level (this is the preferred option) in most cases.

6. Structure of data to support a growth in the number and size of queries. Can our architecture support a growing number of queries and eventually move to parallel processing?

7. Parallelization of storage threads and building of indexes.

8. Large memory caches to store temporary data sets and a fast I/O subsystem.

9. Employment and use of message based interfaces.

Other data management considerations include

1. Load performance

   a. How many rows can we insert into our warehouse over a given timeframe and will this window decrease over time? What strategy should we consider in working within a 7 x 24 environment in terms of mirroring our production data warehousing environment to deal with data loading?

   b. How will we plan for new data extracts, and how they can be integrated within our load window? A number of options exist here.

      I. *Direct read and write from the source system into the data warehouse. (This option is provided by a number of vendors. It is not recommended due to the severe performance problems it will cause, not only to the source environment, but also to the data warehouse environment).*

      II. *Amending our production systems to log transaction changes as they occur. This is not recommended due to the impact on the production environment and impact on its performance due to the fact that a new I/O routine will have to be written to log changes.*

      III. *Reading transactions from the DBMS log or journal files. This option may or may not be available based on the DBMS used as not all journal/log files are "open."*

      IV. *Reading the entire source file and comparing it to the last data warehouse data staging load file for changes. In most instances this is the only viable (and recommended) strategy, especially if we will be accessing our load files from multiple changing DBMS and other nonrelational environments (such as IDMS or IMS files).*

    c. How we load multiple tables simultaneously into our warehouse. This process is usually managed through a data staging environment that serves three purposes.

> *I. Serves as an insulated data preparation environment, where data from disparate source systems can be combined and checked prior to loading*
>
> *II. Acts as a data backup and verification environment, where data warehouse versions can be recovered from previous backups and reloaded as required*
>
> *III. Provides snapshot verification in that new data loads can be compared to previous load files to extract all delta or change records*

2. How we plan to manage updates to our changing dimensions (the addition of new columns) to manage context and content changes to our frames of reference (our dimensions) across time. Changes to dimension data can be managed by

    a. Overwriting existing data with the new data

    b. Creating a new column to manage the old and the new data

    c. Allowing for changing data by creating a generic code and description column for each possible column that could change, allowing it to grow without having to physically change the dimension table

    d. Date time stamping and or adding version control numbers to each dimension table

3. Does the DBMS we select have an optimizer that will recognize the STAR, or will it employ plain math to optimize the query? Does our DBMS support the parallel features of our processor or is some other approach utilized? Ensure that the processor and DBMS you select support the same data management and data access technology. Does the optimizer utilize a query governor to determine if the ad hoc request for data should be run against the aggregate or summary tables instead of the leaf level or base tables?

4. How will data be partitioned in our warehouse, does our DBMS allow for horizontal, vertical, and union partitioning? Partitioning of data across multiple disks for large data warehouse databases is a given criteria; therefore, we should select a DBMS and processor architecture

that allows us to either partition the data automatically and/or allow us to do the partitioning ourselves.

5. How easy is it for our DBMS to archive and recover space from our warehouse? We need to consider what sort of data warehouse DBMS monitoring tool set to select to monitor the performance of our warehouse and to identify stale data that have not been accessed for some predetermined timeframe and that should be placed in archive.

SELECTING A METADATA MANAGEMENT APPROACH

Metadata management is critical to success in understanding the data to be stored in the warehouse and the rules governing how they are to be accessed and used by the end users.

Strategies for metadata management need to be developed for considering how the conceptual (business rules, procedures, and models) will be mapped and synchronized with the internal (technical DBMS level) and the external (end user presentation layers). Key considerations include

1. How mature is our data management culture and what is the business willing to pay for metadata management? Is the business willing to institute a data certification process to manage the definition and use of metadata across the lines of business? This additional cost needs to be considered as part of the data warehousing environment budget and/or the overall data resource management budget.

The data warehouse will also create new data that are not captured anywhere else in the organization due to the nature of their being, in most cases, the only true integration point for dimension data. New data created by the data warehouse should also be subject to the same rules of data certification. Some thought should also be given toward metadata support. Will a help desk be sufficient or will it be necessary to provide support via some other group or function? Consideration should be given to these questions when setting up the necessary human resource support organization as discussed earlier in Section Two.

2. How important is it to provide good metadata to our end users through a user friendly interface so they can understand the data in the

warehouse? A best practice would be to consider using a Web browser as the user interface. This method can be used not only to access data in the warehouse but also to provide the necessary contextual frame of reference by providing both current and future multimedia support capability over the textual and fact related data stored in the warehousing environment.

3. How well do our vendors integrate metadata between the DBMS, extraction software, and information access software environments? Is this integration through marketing alliances or through proven interproduct performance? What level of metadata integration is sufficient for your needs? The combinations to consider include

- DBMS to data staging to information access to repository
- DBMS to data staging to information access
- DBMS to data staging
- DBMS to information access
- Data staging to information access to repository
- Data staging to information access
- Information access to repository

4. What library managers or data dictionaries for source code management that you currently use can be mapped to this overall architecture?

5. How shall we manage the data warehouse logical and physical data models? Should we allow the case tools to overlay the logical view with physical properties such as the definition of surrogate keys (which provide superior database performance and to better insulate business identifiers data from change by the end users)? Or, shall we select a data modeling case tool and repository manager that separates and manages the logical and physical models as two separate views?

- In considering a model management strategy, look at the available repository management tools and what data modeling tools they work with. The data modeling (or case tool) should allow for the translation of the logical data model into the logical database design, which can then be generated as DDL. In conjunction, both models should come under version control of a repository manager that is either part of the case tool or is part of another tool that shares meta-data with the case tool.

- Does the repository manager you select support the definition of multimedia objects as well as the more traditional text and fact based attributes? Will it allow us to define additional object types and manage them as part of the overall architecture? A growing number of tools on the market today allow for the definition and integration of user defined objects in their repositories.

6. What overall metadata industry standard will you follow? A number of options are currently emerging from the software industry. Based upon which one you choose, you may or may not be able to employ the data warehouse tools you prefer. Therefore, as part of your tool selection process, ensure that metadata management is integrated within your selection criteria; otherwise you may be in for some costly surprises if metadata management is left to a subsequent iteration of your warehousing environment to manage.

MANAGING THE INFORMATION ACCESS ENVIRONMENT

Some key considerations in designing the information access (DSS) layer include

1. Employing thin clients containing only local use desktop software for viewing and presentation of the data. In some instances, this may also necessitate reconfiguration of the user desktop by eliminating diskette and cd drives and or turning the desktop into a read only viewing environment with no local end user storage (except through a shared application/data server that can be monitored and controlled). Use of standard PC configurations for end user desktop computing will eventually become a thing of the past as more control is centralized at the server level, so that improved performance and better data management and software support can be provided.

2. Moving as much processing logic as possible to the application servers and away from the desktop to promote flexibility and maintenance of application software indicated here.

3. Identifying and separating the various layers of end users and appropriate tools and selecting software that address the functional requirements of the end user community without adversely impacting the architecture. These end user layers include

- Tactical operational reporting through the development and deployment of precanned reports using report writing software. These application components can be deployed against the production environment (not recommended due to the degradation it may cause in production processing), or this application software can access the data warehouse or, more preferably, one or more operational data stores.

- Executive summary or aggregate data presentation through EIS and Web desktop functionality. With these types of systems we usually create executive "dashboards" containing triggers to precanned routines, Web gophers (or agents), and/or predefined analysis queries.

- Analytical processing through the employment of OLAP tools, which allow for data to be presented and drilled into using different presentation formats. Depending upon the type of DSS tools selected, they can be used to interface with the Web, as well as being able to access the data warehouse, operational data store, and/or the data mart environment. The more open the tool is to these options the more you can easily adjust to the changing demands of your end users without having to go through the expensive and time consuming process of selecting and training your user environment in a new tool set.

- Data mining and predictive modeling, using preselected patterns that are validated by extracting data from either data warehouses or operational systems. These tools should be reserved for your business analysts and modelers only and restricted to the amount of data they can query from the operational systems at any one time.

- Database marketing functionality designed through the employment of campaign management and promotional software that analyzes customer retention, segmentation, and loyalty. If a customer relationship management systems is being designed in concert with or as a driver of the data warehouse, then this software layer must form part of the initial architecture. Again, tool selection and data access are the critical components to consider.

GROWING THE DATA WAREHOUSE INFRASTRUCTURE

Key infrastructure areas to consider are the compatibility across the various operating systems employed by the data warehouse architecture and include how we will manage

1. Distributed computing across diverse geographical areas.

2. Gateway integration.

3. Protocol compatibility such as TCP/IP (If we are using the mainframe environment as either data or application servers how will we manage the interface between EBCDIC and ASCII?).

4. Physical multimedia architectures (blobs) and how we intend to manage these diverse data types such as audio and video files.

5. Backup, recovery, and disaster planning. Since the data warehouse is a production system, we must put into place a backup, recovery, and disaster planning strategy. This disaster recovery strategy may involve building in redundant processors, additional network access, and disk. Or, we could set up an alternate site, running mirror images of our complete warehousing environment as part of our backup and recovery process.

We must decide how to manage release changes to software and hardware as they become available. Our options include

1. Developing a separate testing/staging environment for hardware and software certification. This verification must first be conducted at the unit or component level, then across the entire architecture.

2. Setting up a separate, but temporary testing and certification environment by redeploying production assets over a short timeframe to conduct the necessary evaluation and integration testing.

3. Integrating changes while our current production environment continues to run (not recommended due to the potential down time implications and impact on data and application assets (recoverability)).

What will our strategy be for the Program Management Office (PMO) layer? Options to consider include

1. Developing an in house PMO function and supporting procedures.

2. Adapting the currently available PMO functions and processes from our OLTP environment.

3. Acquiring a third party PMO process geared toward the data warehousing process.

The same three options exist for selecting a (S)ystems-(D)evelopment-(L)ife-(C)ycle methodology and supporting tool set (repository and case tools). Unfortunately, third party methodologies are not yet mature. A better option is to acquire experienced consulting support from firms or individuals who possess industry recognized core competency in one or more layers of the data warehousing environment as discussed in this book.

CHAPTER ELEVEN

Finding, Evaluating, and Contracting Vendors

INTRODUCTION TO VENDOR MANAGEMENT

In data warehousing, nothing is so critical to success yet fraught with more peril than the vendor selection process. Managing third parties is a political and a cultural process. The stakes are high. Data warehousing is a costly proposition and, if successful, can grow into a multimillion dollar investment. Dollars spent on consulting and technology resources for even the most modest undertaking can cause significant inroads into the information technology or line of business budget. Cost justification and monitoring can become as critical to the success of the data warehousing process as the efficiency and extensibility of the architecture. How then, can we manage this enormous risk, without adversely affecting the data warehousing process? In this chapter we review some concepts and processes that can be employed to manage this most difficult and potentially politically charged process.

SOME INITIAL CONSIDERATIONS FOR VENDOR MANAGEMENT

Most information technology professionals are not trained in purchase order management or the legalities of vendor management. From a negotiating and contracting standpoint IT professionals are often the worst equipped to deal with third party contracting. A best practice would be to adopt or involve the purchasing function and legal functions of the business in assisting you through this process by providing materials and procedures on what to do and how to go about completing the vendor selection and contracting process.

Other considerations include gauging your level of support for the data warehouse. Could a third party circumvent or undermine your authority before, during, or after the vendor selection process by consulting a higher authority? Are these higher authorities on board with the need to direct all such inquires or requests through you? If you do not have executive sponsorship and direct support (which should be stated up front, in writing, and agreed to by the executive sponsors), then you may end up having little or no control over the selection of your technology and consulting partners.

What direct access or influence do third party vendors have over your end users? Often the major cause of concern lies here, with vendors marketing their services to the group least able to cope or understand what is being presented to them. Again, a formal contract must be put in place with the business client (which forms part of your program or project charter) that states the rules of engagement with vendors. Without some hard assurances, you may become a victim of a carefully designed vendor strategy that forces you to implement an incompatible architecture, due to the vendors themselves not truly understanding or appreciating what is required. Vendors, whether consulting or product focused want to be successful and provide you with good support. The best way to accomplish this is to educate them to your proposed architecture and brief them on how the vendor selection process will be conducted. Throughout this process, it is also advisable to open a channel to them by encouraging their support and advice, but always under your control and supervision.

The surest way for your client, the vendor(s), and you to all work from the same page is to have a common frame of reference. To be successful in this endeavor we must

1. Lay out the vendor selection, evaluation, and contracting process in terms of procedures and work products and to educate all parties on these processes.

2. Put a communication process in place so that quick updates are pro-vided to the project sponsors while monitoring their compliance to the overall process.

3. Define a functional architecture that describes, in our words, each com-ponent of the data warehouse architecture. This architecture forms the requirements blueprint against which all vendors are measured.

4. Define the roles of each party in the vendor selection process (sponsor, client, vendor, and you).

5. Enable the rapid deployment of the short listed technology in support of the first or subsequent iteration of the data warehousing environ-ment (vendors can often be convinced to provide 30 to 90 evaluation periods for their hardware or software free of charge to you as part of this evaluation process).

EVALUATING VENDORS

The vendor evaluation process takes many forms; D&B reports, industry surveys, reviewing published benchmark studies, and conducting site visits to verify information along with vendor references. The timeframe avail-able and scope of the data warehousing initiative largely determines the focus and level of intensity to be devoted to these efforts. In data ware-housing, the technology evaluation process never ends. Our job is not done once a vendor(s) is selected as there is always the next iteration of our envi-ronment to consider. Whether we are adopting a new processor technology or functional capability (e.g., predictive modeling in our next project), this cycle will be repeated many times. Therefore, it is essential to not only to put a rigorous process in place, but to define and support it as part of the overall suite of infrastructure services provided by our data warehousing environment.

The following spreadsheet describes a sampling of Internet sites worth searching to obtain the necessary impartial background information other than consulting the vendors Web site directly.

Figure 11 1
Vendor Background Search List

This figure contains internet addresses for searching information about data warehousing product and consulting vendors. This is not an exhaustive list but is representative of the types of searches you may be required to conduct. This table is broken up into a number of sections each dealing with a specific research topic.

Financial and Business Stability Search URL's

Dun & Bradstreet Financial Analysis — http://www.dnbcorp.com/home.cfm

U.S. Financial Analysis EDGAR — http://www.sec.gov/cgi bin/srch edgar

U.S. Securities and Exchange Commission — http://www.sec.gov/(http://www.sec.gov/)

Industry Survey URL's

The Gartner Group — http://gartner3.gartnerweb.com/public/static/home/home.html

The Meta Group — http://www.metagroup.com/

Patricia Seybold Group — http://www.psgroup.com/

Technical and Other URL's

DAMA International (Data Management Assoc) — http://www.dama.org/damamore.htm

Data Warehousing on the Web — http://www.datawarehousing.com

DBMS Magazine — http://www.dbmsmagazine.com

The Data Warehouse Information Center — http://pwp.starnetinc.com/larryg/index.html

The Data Warehousing Institute — http://www.dw institute.com/confindex.htm

The Data Warehouse Network — http://indigo.ie/~dataware/dwnpag1.htm

DM Review Direct — http://www.dmreview.com/dmdirect/

DM Review Metadata Link — http://www.data warehouse.com/issues/_meta.htm

Zachman Framework — http://www.ozemail.com.au/~ieinfo/zachman.htm

SELECTING THE RIGHT VENDORS

If a formal process or processes are required to review and select vendor(s), then the following activities, deliverables, and milestones must become part of our overall data warehousing environment development plan. Description of a typical RFI, RFP process follows.

VENDOR SELECTION PROCESS ACTIVITY MAP

1. Select/evaluate data warehouse vendor
    1.1. Determine vendor selection method by developing (RFI/RFP's, reference checks, industry surveys or on site product evaluations)
        1.1.1. Conduct reference checks

        Obtain a list of install sites where the software or hardware has been in active production use for at least one year. Contact and evaluate each reference indicated under the vendor selection method described later.

        1.1.2. Check industry survey reports

        Review the list of industry web page addresses and contact or review material presented by each association or group.

        1.1.3. Conduct site visits

        From the results achieved from the reference checks and industry survey reports analysis, select a short list of sites to visit containing as many of the hardware and software vendors you are considering (closest match to your proposed or in place architecture).

    1.2. Build evaluation criteria
        1.2.1. Build business requirements criteria

        Generate a requirements list for business information and functionality as a result of business area analysis.

        1.2.2. Build systems requirements criteria

        Generate a technology requirements list in terms of

        a. Operating systems hardware and systems software it must run on

b. Applications systems software that it must be compatible to in the architecture

1.2.3. Create a weighted scoring method

Generate a list of weights to be applied against each requirement for vendor product scoring. For example: The product meets (2), partially meets with customization (1), does not meet even with customization (0) a specified requirement. Weighted scoring can be applied itteriively to the selection process and often involves the development of initial (or high level criteria and detail) or short listing criteria for more thorough evaluations. Weighted scoring can also include cost versus functionality (payback) assessments.

1.3. Solicit vendor responses

1.3.1. Solicit RFI responses

Review vendor software profiles and solicit information on products for consideration as input to an RFP process or to update the list of current vendor offerings. This step can start after the completion of *Build business requirements criteria* (1.2.1).

1.3.2. Compile an RFP

Format the list of evaluation requirements and include corporate response conditions and reply format. Include a timeframe for a response, solicit a list of vendor references, and request additional information to be forwarded such as financial statements. Request that the vendor conduct demos or permit site visits to clients currently utilizing the software. Note that this step can start after the completion of *Build systems requirements criteria* (1.2.2).

1.3.3. Score vendors and short list to a selected response

Prepare a list of suitable vendors and solicit responses by distributing an RFP. Optionally build a requirement's model of the vendor package, or request a copy from the vendor and compare against the current requirements.

1.3.4. Select vendor alternative

Score responses and notify short listed vendors. Screen short listed vendors and recommend one or more for contract negotiation.

2. Conduct contract negotiation with vendor

   2.1. Arrange for purchase after prototype is completed

   Contract the vendor to provide software and/or hardware free of charge to you during the evaluation period and ensure this period lasts for at least 30 to 90 days.

   2.2. Review Package Environment

   Prior to package installation, review the recommendations contained within the vendor selection report regarding the deployment and/or use of this software and/or hardware.

   2.3. Review package release/patch levels installation instructions

   Before planning the installation of the package, version check its release installation instructions and patch level.

   2.4. Check licensing agreements as they apply to the current production version

   Check licensing agreements as they apply to the package for installation and authorized license or site/seat copy counts.

3. Review and approve vendor selection results

   3.1.1. Document vendor selection results

   Prepare final vendor selection report for review by the project champion and/or the project steering committee.

   3.1.2. Integrate data warehouse project libraries

   Update the project repository with the latest version of vendor evaluation deliverables, working papers, and survey and selection information.

4. Obtain approval for vendor selection process

   4.1. Obtain approval for the final vendor selection report

   Prepare presentation material and distribute the final vendor selection report for preliminary review. Conduct a review session and make any necessary corrections and, if required, resubmit for approval.

   4.2. Review pilot results

   Review the results achieved from the 90 day evaluation period if a pilot was conducted as part of the approval process as embodied in the final vendor selection report.

4.3. Develop vendor support and maintenance process

Develop the necessary contract maintenance and vendor performance management benchmarks used in the ongoing evaluation/justification of the vendors' products and/or services. These benchmarks should be evaluated against recognized industry standards to ensure performance compliance by the vendor(s) in question.

DELIVERABLES

The following documents and procedures are produced out of this process:[1]

1. Vendor selection method
2. Vendor RFI (optional)
3. Vendor RFP
4. Final vendor selection recommendation report

VENDOR SELECTION METHODS AND TECHNIQUES

This section describes what information needs to be collected and managed to perform the necessary due diligence in the vendor selection process.

ESTABLISHING A VENDOR SELECTION METHOD

The Vendor Selection Method identifies the methods and techniques to be applied in selecting and evaluating one or more product or service providers. It includes procedures and criteria for vendor selection such as scoring and interviewing. Items to include are

1. Vendor approach details

We must describe the various approaches outside detailed scoring to be undertaken during the vendor selection process. These can include

• Format and completeness of vendor response

---

[1] Consult the Data Warehouse Assistant for a list of deliverable templates to be used in the vendor selection process.

- Financial statements
- Reference checks
- On site visits

2. Conducting a vendor background check

   Vendor Background Check describes where any additional information that was collected outside formal scoring is to be documented.

   A form that allows the following information to be logged should be developed. This form should document

   - Results of any site visits
   - Results of product demos
   - Results of vendor reference checks
   - Results of financial statement and accreditation checks and includes
     - Vendor name
     - Product name
     - Reviewer name
     - Comments
     - Recommendations

3. Developing vendor weights

   A strategy for scoring vendor responses is required. This method should cover

   - Vendor weights

     Weights to be applied and the numeric value for each criteria such as:

     - Mandatory (1)
     - Optional (0)

4. Determining vendor scores

   Scoring to be applied and the numeric value for each criteria such as

   - Fully meets (3)
   - Partially meets (2)
   - Does not meet (1) (requires customization)
   - Does not meet requirements at all (0) (customization is not possible)

5. Establishing vendor review methods

   We need to also describe how vendor reviews are to be conducted. Such a process should include

   - A recommended evaluation approach:
     - Vendor presentation and/or
     - Vendor interviews
   - A list of prepared questions as taken from scoring criteria
   - A grading method that evaluates the vendor presentation in terms of
     - Knowledge of the business requirements
     - Communication skills
     - Support of the proposal in terms of backup or additional resources
     - Knowledge of the proposed consultants or knowledge of their product
   - A vendor questionnaire describes short listing interview questions and response scores. The questionnaire includes
     - Vendor name
     - Interview date
     - Reviewer name
     - List of questions
     - Consultant names
     - Vendor response matrix:
       - *Strong*
       - *Acceptable*
       - *Weak*
       - *Unacceptable or could not reply*

6. Developing a Vendor Distribution List.

   This list itemizes all vendors who are to be issued RFPs and is used to track responses. This checklist contains

   - Vendor name
   - RFP sent flag
     - Response received flag

- Failed to respond flag
- Cost total

7. Business requirements evaluation scoring criteria

   For each criteria in the RFP, describe the weighted score to be used.

8. Information technology evaluation scoring criteria

   For each criteria in the RFP, describe the weighted score to be used.

9. Package evaluation scoring criteria

   For each criteria in the RFP, describe the weighted score to be used.

10. Vendor services evaluation scoring criteria

    For each criteria in the RFP, describe the weighted score to be used.

11. Package testing approach

    Describes a list of test procedures and sample test data that will exercise all of the unmodified package components in terms of

    - A test schedule and
    - A scoring sheet for each package function

12. Defining a Vendor Score Spreadsheet

    Vendor package score describes the weights and scores applied across package business and technology evaluation criteria. Failure to meet all mandatory requirements could result in a total score of zero.

    A spreadsheet containing the results of vendor scoring includes

    - Vendor name
    - Product name
    - Reviewer name
    - Review date
    - Requirement description
    - Requirement weighting score
    - Requirement evaluation score
    - Requirement total score
    - Requirement weighted total score
    - Section totals

13. Package test forms

Software evaluation testing involves determining overall package performance, reliability, data capture capability, and user interface scoring results based on a set of specified test conditions.

A test form containing package evaluation results includes

- Package name
- Package component identification
- Procedure to be tested
- Reviewer name
- Test date
- Test response criteria, which includes
  - Procedure requirements (met/not met)
  - Degree of accessibility/ease of use
  - Response time
  - Error conditions
  - Comments

DEVELOPING AN RFI PROCESS

The Request for Information (RFI) process defines criteria for gathering information about vendors. The RFI also provides vendors with a list of your expectations and a set of response instructions for information technology products or services. Information to be sent to the vendor about your business should include

- The purpose and expected outcomes of this process.
- A corporate profile describing business information relative to your company. It details general information concerning the size and future direction of the corporation. A corporate profile is used to convey this understanding to external organizations with which your company may wish to conduct business and will usually contain information about
  - A brief description of key corporate objectives as described in your corporate policy and procedure guides that relate to the business area under investigation

- A brief description of your company's market segment as a statement of its customer base and product and service offering
- A brief overview of your company's structure
- A technology overview describing the information technology profile of your organization containing
  - A list of the major hardware components applicable to the business system. This would include
    - *Mainframe and miniprocessors and controllers specifications*
    - *Direct Access Storage Devices (DASD) & tape backup facilities*
    - *Printers (local and remote)*
    - *Cabling*
    - *Terminals and workstations*
    - *Communications devices (bridges, routers, multiplexors . . .)*
  - A list of either preferred or standard software components to be used in in house development including
    - *Software development languages*
    - *Database platforms*
    - *GUI interface software (Windows)*
    - *Development support software (word processors, spreadsheets, diagramming tools, CASE)*
    - *Portfolio of customized package software*
    - *Archiving, security, and audit software (RACF)*
    - *Operating systems software (Unix, NT, VM, MVS)*
  - A list of the major communications hardware and software components.
- A business requirements overview describing the major data, process, and technology requirements of the proposed decision support business system in terms of
  - A brief description of the major business processes that require support, taken from the business area process detail model
  - A brief description of the major classes of information (subject areas or fundamental entity types) to be managed, as taken from the business area data detail model

- A list and brief outline of the technology requirements, as taken from the proposed system design, which includes
  - *Proposed user interface (graphical user interface, WYSIWYG)*
  - *Development environment (4GL, relational . . .)*
  - *Expected system interfaces (automated, manual, batch, external)*
  - *Communications environment (LAN, WAN, Token Ring)*
- Vendor Contact Instructions describing your company's requirements for vendor solicitation of products or services. Vendor response instructions indicate to whom and where in your company a contractor should forward his or her response and should include a statement describing where the response should be directed. This information includes
  - Your mailing address
  - Contact person name
  - Contact person department
  - Contact person phone number/Fax
  - Closing date
  - Format instructions stating how the vendor is to respond to the RFI
  - Statement of confidentiality describing any proprietary requirements regarding products or services that the vendor may wish to state in terms of their response
- A Request for Information Questionnaire that includes a cover sheet containing
  - Vendor address
  - Types of services offered
  - Price list
  - Contact names and phone numbers/fax
  - Authorizing signature
  - A questionnaire soliciting responses to a series of questions on topics, which include
    - *Corporate profile and financial background*
    - *Target market*

- *Corporate references (at least three where the product has been in use for more than one year)*
- *Background information on previous work that meets your business requirements*
- *Financial/legal requirements (federal and state tax regulations . . .)*
- *Functional requirements*
- *Technical requirements*
- *Data requirements*

DEVELOPING A VENDOR RFP PROCESS

The request for proposal process identifies a set of structured business system requirements for vendor response. This document is used as a mechanism to procure vendor services or products based on established evaluation criteria as stated under the vendor selection method. The Request for Proposal (RFP) is used to convey an understanding of the business situation to the stakeholders and vendors who would be involved in providing products or services in support of the decision support business systems design.

STATING THE RULES: THE IMPORTANCE OF A COVERING LETTER

An RFP should contain an instruction or covering letter of invitation from the client representative responsible for the Request for Proposal, soliciting vendor responses. The letter should contain:

- Date of issue
- Name of the person to respond to if different from the authorizing signature
- Address to respond to and phone number/Fax number
- RFP title/number and closing date and time
- A paragraph inviting the vendor to respond and a statement that identifies this as an RFP

- A concise description of what is being looked for
- Consulting services
- Authorizing corporate signature
- An attached form or statement for the vendor to sign agreeing that your company's RFP requirements should be treated as confidential information
- An introduction explaining the purpose of the Request for Proposal in a brief paragraph
- A corporate profile describing business information relative to your company. It details general information concerning the size, and future direction of the corporation. A corporate profile is used to convey this understanding to external organizations with which your company may wish to conduct business and contains
  - A brief description of key corporate objectives of your company as described in corporate policy and procedure guides that relate to the business area under investigation
  - A brief description of your company's market segment as a statement of its customer base and product and service offering
  - A brief overview of your company's company structure

The RFP should also include a technology overview describing the information technology profile of your company. A technology overview is used to convey an understanding of the information technology structure of your company to external organizations. Information to be provided includes

- A brief description of the content of this section covering your company's information technology profile
- A list of the major hardware components applicable to the business system. This would include
  - Mainframe and miniprocessors and controllers specifications
  - Direct Access Storage Devices (DASD) and tape backup facilities
  - Printers (local and remote)
  - Cabling

- Terminals and workstations
- Communications devices (bridges, routers, multiplexors, etc.)
- A list of either preferred or standard software components to be used in in house development including
  - Software development languages
  - Database platforms
  - GUI interface software (Windows)
  - Development support software (word Processors, spreadsheets, diagramming Tools, CASE)
  - Portfolio of customized package software
  - Archiving, security, and audit software (RACF)
  - Operating systems software (OS/2, DOS, VM, MVS)
  - A list of the major communications hardware and software components

The RFP should also discuss the current business requirements, describing the major data, process, and technology requirements of the decision support business system. Information to be included would be

- A brief introductory paragraph explaining the background of the proposed work and statement of requirements
- A brief description of the major business processes that require support, taken from the business area process detail model
- A brief description of the major classes of information (subject areas or fundamental entity types) to be managed, as taken from the business area data detail model
- A list and brief outline of the technology requirements, as taken from the proposed system design
  - Proposed user interface (Graphical User Interface, WYSIWYG)
  - Development environment (4GL, Relational . . .)
  - Expected system interfaces (Automated, Manual, Batch, External)
  - Communications environment (LAN, WAN, Token Ring, etc.)

The RFP should also include a set of vendor response instructions if not defined in sufficient detail in the covering letter. This information would include

- A brief description of the purpose and scope of this document, explaining what kinds of commitments your company is willing to make
- Instructions related to the RFP submission process that contains information on what must be returned to you to be considered a valid response, such as
  - Documents to be returned
  - Legal authorization
  - Commitment of the vendor to the RFP
- Your company's statement of exclusion to accept any or all RFP documents
- A brief description of how your company will manage vendor inquiries on the RFP and provide feedback

We need a description of the overall evaluation process, to provide an overview of the method that will be applied to evaluating and selecting a vendor. A number of different techniques can be used that will depend upon whether or not a vendor product or service is being evaluated. These can include

- Weighted scoring
- Interviewing
- Presentations
- Demos
- Reference searches and financial evaluations
- Describe how vendor contracting shall be conducted with the successful vendor as a statement of
  - The contracting process
  - Legal terms and conditions
  - Bonding
  - Company registration with the state

- Liability insurance
- Compensation or insurance coverage

Include vendor contact instructions describing your company's requirements for vendor solicitation of products or services. Vendor response instructions indicate to whom and where in your company a contractor should forward his or her response.

The RFP should also include a brief description of how the vendor is to respond to the RFP in terms of a documentation format. This information usually includes

- A cover sheet containing
  - Vendor address
  - Types of services offered
  - Price list
  - Contact names and phone numbers/Fax
  - Authorizing signature
- A documentation format that contains
  - Required table of contents
  - Instructions on how to respond to each mandatory and optional requirement
- A section on business requirements to respond to containing business system evaluation items taken from the vendor selection method
- A section containing a high level process model
- A section containing a subject area decomposition model and area entity relationship model(s) that fall within the scope of the proposed decision support business system along with definitions
- Audit and control requirements specifications for data management (backup, journaling, and recovery) as well as data security and auditing considerations
- Staging requirements (if considering an extraction transformation tool) that include a context model diagram or a table showing all staging systems from the analysis phase and provide a brief definition of how each system will be stage data to the proposed decision support business system

- Technology evaluation criteria that describe analysis phase technical infrastructure issues. This information should include
- A description of the technical specifications for hardware such as component types and processing platform
- Criteria for evaluating customization and release installs of vendor software including
  - Flexibility of the product to change over versions or releases
  - Availability of additional components or modules (via a third party or from the vendor)
  - Package modification procedures
- Criteria for evaluating the product in terms of network management and communications protocols
- A description of your company's documentation requirements across all media for vendor products or expected documentation if developing the decision support business system as part of vendor services. This includes documentation format requirements for
  - Voice
  - Image
  - Text/graphics
- Capacity, volumetric, and operational performance requirements, describing your company's expected transaction volumes and expected response times for vendor compliance
  - Operating environment considerations describing any environmental requirements of the hardware or software such as sensitivity to magnetic fields, heat, and moisture
- Vendor consultant evaluation criteria describing the evaluation criteria for consultants in terms of required skills and work experience
- Vendor package evaluation criteria describing package requirements in terms of
  - Technical profile
  - Licensing options
  - Package components and cost breakdown
  - Number of sites using product

- Vendor services evaluation criteria describing service or package requirements in terms of
  - Additional vendor services offered and cost
  - Help desk support and locations
- Statement of vendor responsibility from the primary contractor who will represent all vendors who are responding under this RFP (if more than one contractor is involved in the bid)
- A vendor marketing profile describing where additional information of interest to your company can be found in terms of
  - References
  - Financial statements
  - WEB sites
- A description of the vendor product management approach identifying criteria for vendor compliance with your corporation. Provides a section for the vendor to explain their staffing approach and equipment and space requirements.
- Vendor human resources profile provides a section where consultant resumes can be provided. This information can include
  - Resource matrices
  - References
  - Resumé structure

THE FINAL VENDOR SELECTION PROCESS

The final vendor selection process identifies the results of vendor short listing. It provides a summary of the methods and techniques used during this process and includes the vendor scoring results. The final vendor selection conveys an understanding of the evaluation process and recommends a specific vendor's services or products to the stakeholders who would be involved in sponsoring the decision support business system. Information that should be considered to form part of this process and document includes

- An executive summary describing the purpose of the document in a few paragraphs

- Background information summarizing the approach taken and results achieved
- Vendor recommendation identifying the approved vendor(s) and including a short list comparison table showing how the vendor(s) scored as compared to its closest rivals
- A vendor selection summary describing the purpose of this section in a brief paragraph that includes
  - A vendor selection approach that provides an introduction to the method taken in the evaluation in more detail
  - A vendor scoring results summary, providing a summarized result of all vendor scoring in terms of a section for each vendor, describing
    - *Pros*
    - *Cons*
    - *Summarized scoring results*
    - *Comments*
- An appendix where additional information referenced in the recommendation report can be found. This information can cover
  - Vendor distribution lists
  - Vendor package scores
  - Software evaluation tests
  - Vendor background checks
  - Vendor questionnaires

CONDUCTING VENDOR PERFORMANCE REVIEWS

Vendor performance reviews are conducted by consulting recognized performance benchmark studies described by the work plan illustrated earlier in this section. Recognized studies include TCP D benchmarks and those provided by industry special interest organizations such as Gartner, Seybold, and MetaGroup.

MONITORING AND MANAGING VENDORS AND CONTRACTS

To monitor contractual and product and/or service performance by vendor(s) requires that a procedure be established up front as part of the conditions of the overall contract. The vendor(s) will understand that their continued licensing or provision of services will be renewed or rescinded based upon their compliance to your company's legal and contracting standards as well as the performance standards you publish as part of the service agreement between the data warehousing organization and the business. Information for this review is usually gathered after six months and one year of the data warehousing environment component being in production as part of an overall assessment of the production system.

Design, Implementation, and Assessment

THE DATA WAREHOUSE DEVELOPMENT SPIRAL

OVERVIEW

In Section Two we reviewed the infrastructure activities necessary to establish the data warehousing environment. With these foundation setting activities in place we are now ready to proceed toward developing a data warehousing increment.

Section Three describes the heart of the data warehousing process by discussing the planning, analysis, design, and implementation process. In this section we review the iterative nature of data warehousing development, the unique data management requirements for in the deployment of a data staging area, and the unpredictable performance challenges it places on us as we gauge initial thresholds while also allowing for future growth.

In this section we also discuss various strategies dealing with how to manage a diminishing data loading time window, as new subject areas and business units are added to the mix. Challenges in data transformation and repair in terms of establishing the data quality thresholds are reviewed. In dealing with data transformation, we establish a set of measures to ensure that the data warehouse does not become corrupted with either missing or conflicting data. Finally, the unique features of the data warehouse monitoring process are discussed as are the requirements for archiving data in the warehouse that has fallen out of use.

CHAPTER TWELVE

Initiating a Data Warehouse Project

INTRODUCTION TO DATA WAREHOUSE PLANNING AND ANALYSIS

In starting our development and delivery of a data warehousing project increment, we must have a good idea of

1. What the client is asking for and its value to the business in terms of a business case with a predefined and approved scope

2. How we intend to clarify this scope for the purposes of the first phase of this project in the form of a project mandate document or charter

3. How we intend to run the project in terms of program management activities related to

   a. Interdependencies with other ongoing OLAP based efforts

   b. Methodology and tools we intend to employ to guide the effort

   c. Training and support the team will require throughout the process

   d. How we intend to provide communication management to our client, project team, and technology support groups

   e. How we intend to follow any program/corporate related standards in terms of project reporting, budgeting, time recording, human resources, hardware and software, and facilities acquisition and deployment

4. What is changing within the business over the next six to nine months in terms of

   a. New or changes to existing business policies and procedures within our scope of interest

   b. New or changes to business processes and human resources

   c. New or changes to business OLTP or any existing OLAP based systems within our scope of interest

5. What type of data warehousing architecture component(s) needs building or changing

6. What resources we have on hand to initiate the planning and analysis of the business solution and what additional resources are required to support the process

7. How we intend to measure success and plan for growth by defining our strategy for

   a. The data warehouse architecture

   b. Our approach to metadata management

   c. How we intend to develop or extend our data staging environment

   d. Our strategy for data management in terms of

      i. Centralizing or distributing the data

      ii. How we intend to deal with data replication at the mart level

      iii. Our data warehouse database software support and growth strategy (for relational, multidimensional, or both)

      iv. Our plan for archiving stale data

      v. Our backup and recovery strategy (which can be integrated or leveraged from our approach to data staging in that backup versions of data loads can be used to recover our database)

   e. Our approach to information access enabled through decision support tools

   f. Our intended strategy for platform, operating system software, and network logical and physical network design

There is a significant and broad area of issues and concerns to consider when initiating a data warehousing project effort. The key here is to focus on the essential activities and not take on more than we can reasonably manage and complete within the proposed timeframe. Some strategies for paring down and focusing the preceding topics can be found in Section Two. Other more nebulous areas we need to consider include

- Where is our sponsorship is coming from (e.g., IT, Line of Business, Corporate)?
- What is the perception of our client (tactical operational reporting or competitive assessment and analysis)?
- Where we are from a data management perspective and what has to be built (e.g., Do we have a data staging environment already in place or do we have to build one?) How wide a technology net do we have to cast to get the job done? The wider the net, the longer the project will be and the more problems and issues will arise as a result of enlarging the scope.
- Do our vendors support us or are we controlled by them? Some data warehousing projects are no win situations right from the start due to the direct (contractual) or indirect (political) control the vendor or vendor consortium has over the group or individual in control of the project budget.
- What is the knowledge level of the business in this technology? If we ask a sampling of business users what they know of and/or expect from this technology, how consistent is their answer? And how consistent is the same answer coming from the various IT support groups? Will a series of education and awareness setting presentations be required as you busy yourself getting the project infrastructure established and your sponsorship confirmed? Do we have to work a sales cycle with our management team to identify or reconfirm their commitment to the project as a necessary first step?
- Where does our project sit from an IT perspective in terms of its priority for resources and its level of support from IT managers? Do we expect to be delayed or hindered in our efforts or will we be actively supported? Is the warehouse seen as a threat to anyone's position or influence within the IT organization? From a staff perspective, is the warehouse seen as an opportunity or threat to job stability and career growth?

The most effective way to address these concerns is to establish a contract between yourself and the project champion, or sponsor, in the form of a project mandate or charter. In concert with this we need to establish a project objective for the first few months of the engagement so that the necessary infrastructure issues can be addressed. What we review is the necessary program and project management activities as well as provide insight into the analysis process for collecting enough requirements to quickly and effectively begin the design of the data warehouse project increment.

In proceeding from planning to analysis we must take into consideration the following

1. Available level of staffing and their core competency
2. What external consulting (if any) is required to complete the planning and analysis
3. The necessary program and project management methods and tools
4. The methodology and analysis tool set that will be required
5. The facilities and resources required to complete the planning and analysis process in terms of work space, telecommunications, work stations, and project support resources
6. Required planning for the selection and deployment of the necessary vendor products and services to populate the design and implementation environment
7. Establishing what is expected from the IT organization in terms of design and implementation resources support

THE PROJECT PLANNING AND ANALYSIS PROCESS

Data warehousing is an iterative process. There are, however, some activities that do not have an ending. These activities continue on an ongoing basis and are not solely dependent upon any one data warehousing project. These types of activities include

- Program office management
- Infrastructure definition and development
- Implementation and warehouse performance monitoring and evolution planning

Activities with a definitive beginning and ending incur the project planning process which deals with the work steps necessary to initiate the project, confirm scope and sponsorship, and establish the necessary infrastructure. The project initiation stage consists of the work steps, milestones, and deliverables defined here.

PROJECT PLANNING ACTIVITIES

Prerequisites

The following activities and deliverables should have been completed prior to initiating the project planning process.

Process	Deliverable(s)
1. Project core team staffing	Project start up team
2. Project control and budgeting	Project budget and management reporting
3. Project infrastructure definition	Project facility and workstation setup for the core team

PLANNING STAGE WORK STEPS, MILESTONES, AND DELIVERABLES

This process covers the necessary program and project management activities required to run and monitor the project from its inception to completion. Depending upon the size and scope of the effort undertaken, not all these activities or tasks are anticipated on any one engagement. Those activities and deliverables that are not essential to this process are indicated with an (O) behind them. Please note that if a program office has already been set up for the data warehouse environment, then all program activities can be ignored. If a data warehouse program office is not required, then all (P)-level activities indicated in the project planning process need to be completed. Milestones indicated by an (M) are review points in the project where results achieved and budget expended must be approved by the business before further activities can be initiated.

The following section describes a task list to consider in initiating a data warehouse program office and necessary project infrastructure activities.

These tasks will run over the first few months of the engagement as the project planning process is kicked off. Once established this process need only be reviewed for potential updates to already established procedures and organizational structure. This task list is listed on the attached CD and can be imported into a spreadsheet or project planning tool for your use and customization. This checklist covers required tasks for both the program office setup and project management activities. Please note that some tasks are duplicated under the initiate data warehouse project task. If a program office is not deemed to be necessary based upon the size or scope of the proposed project (e.g., a small data mart project is required that does not influence or affect any other line of business), then the duplicated project activities can be considered instead.

1. Initiate data warehouse program
  1.1. Set up data warehouse program office.
    1.1.1. Define program management environment.
      1.1.1.1. Define management and budget control structure.
      1.1.1.2. Define DW program office team reporting structure.
      1.1.1.3. Define program organization (roles and responsibilities).
      1.1.1.4. Train program office personnel.
        1.1.1.4.1. Develop/acquire core team training material.
        1.1.1.4.2. Conduct core team training.
      1.1.1.5. Publish communication and location information (O)
    1.1.2. Define DW program policies and procedures.
      1.1.2.1. Define scope, policies, goals, and objectives.
      1.1.2.2. Define change management, risks, and issue controls.
      1.1.2.3. Define DW program methodologies and tools.
      1.1.2.4. Define DW program and project work breakdown structure.
    1.1.3. Prepare and approve program mandate and approach (M).
      1.1.3.1. Assemble policies, procedures, goals.
      1.1.3.2. Assemble proposed staffing model and budget projections.
      1.1.3.3. Assemble quality, risk, and change management processes.
      1.1.3.4. Assemble methodology, tools, and reporting procedures.

1.1.3.5.   Assemble program to project work breakdown structures.

1.1.3.6.   Review, revise, and obtain approval for the proposed approach.

1.1.4.   Kick off DW program.

1.1.5.   Monitor the DW program.

1.1.5.1.   Monitor policy, procedure, and reporting compliance.

1.1.5.2.   Control quality and risk.

1.1.5.3.   Establish steering committee reporting process schedule and report progress (M).

2. Initiate data warehouse project

2.1.   Set up project

2.1.1.   Define project management environment.

2.1.1.1.   Define management and budget control structure.

2.1.1.2.   Define DW project team reporting structure.

2.1.1.3.   Define project organization (roles and responsibilities).

2.1.1.4.   Train project planning team.

2.1.1.4.1. Develop/acquire core team training material.

2.1.1.4.2. Conduct core team training.

2.1.1.5.   Publish communication and location information (O).

2.1.2.   Define DW project policies and procedures.

2.1.2.1.   Define project scope, policies, goals, and objectives.

2.1.2.2.   Define change management, risks, and issue controls (P).

2.1.2.3.   Define DW program methodologies and tools (P).

2.1.2.4.   Define project planning and analysis phase work breakdown structure.

2.1.3.   Prepare and approve project mandate and approach (M).

2.1.3.1.   Assemble policies, procedures, goals (P).

2.1.3.2.   Assemble proposed staffing model and budget projections.

2.1.3.3.   Assemble quality, risk, and change management processes (P)

2.1.3.4.   Assemble methodology, tools, and reporting procedures (P).

2.1.3.5.   Nominate project sponsors/champions and establish project steering/review committee.

2.1.3.6.   Define project sponsor/steering committee roles and responsibilities and approval process.

2.1.3.7.   Review, revise, and obtain approval for the proposed approach.

2.1.4.   Kick off DW project.

2.1.4.1.   Nominate business and technology customers.

2.1.4.2.   Identify support organization representation.

2.1.4.3.   Prepare project kickoff materials.

2.1.4.4.   Conduct kickoff session with customers and support organization.

2.1.5.   Monitor the DW project.

2.1.5.1.   Monitor policy, procedure, and reporting compliance.

2.1.5.2.   Control quality and risk.

2.1.5.3.   Establish steering committee reporting process schedule and report progress (M).

2.2.   Conduct business opportunity assessment.

2.2.1.   Identify business and technology customer interviewees.

2.2.2.   Develop business and technology assessment process.

2.2.3.   Conduct opportunity assessment.

2.2.4.   Prepare findings for review and approval (M).

2.3.   Conduct current state technology assessment.

2.3.1.   Define current state assessment process.

2.3.2.   Identify candidate systems for investigation.

2.3.3.   Conduct data quality audit of source systems.

2.3.4.   Review current and proposed IT software, server, and network architectures.

2.3.5.   Identify gaps and redundancies.

2.3.6.   Conduct IT organizational assessment.

2.3.7.   Prepare findings for review and approval (M).

2.4. Develop a business case.

2.4.1. Develop benefits value analysis process.

2.4.2. Identify financial analysis method (ROI, NPV, cost displacement).

2.4.3. Conduct benefits analysis of the proposed opportunities.

2.4.4. Conduct financial analysis of proposed investment costs in technology and resources.

2.4.5. Identify gaps and redundancies in current business organization.

2.4.6. Prepare findings for review and approval (M).

2.5. Prepare and approve project mandate and approach (M).

2.5.1. Acquire/develop or access a project repository.

2.5.2. Conduct repository support team training and/or acquire data administration support staff and facilities to provide repository management support.

2.5.3. Assemble planning phase deliverables for review and approval.

2.5.4. Revise project plan and mandate (charter) document for the analysis phase.

2.5.5. Prepare planning phase presentation materials.

2.5.6. Conduct planning phase review session.

2.5.7. Review, revise, and obtain approval for the proposed approach (M).

2.5.8. Update project repository with planning phase deliverable.

Planning Stage Deliverables

The following section describes the deliverables that are produced out of the activity list as previously described.

Work Breakdown Structure Deliverables Designations

Two types of deliverables are listed for this stage.

1. Technology dependent output containing the detail specifications for the data warehouse hardware, software, and network architecture such as code, procedures or models

2. Technology independent output (in the form of documentation), illustrated in **bold,** that includes the results of technology dependent output production for end user review

   a. **Program office communication, change management, and issue management process (O)**

   b. **Project team change management and issue management process (if not provided by the program office)**

   c. Data warehouse methodology and tools selection

   d. Project development team environment and staffing

   e. Project sponsor/steering committee

   f. **Project review and approval process through the program office or project team**

   g. **Business opportunity assessment**

   h. **Business case**

   i. **Current state business systems assessment**

   j. **Revise project plan, budget, and project mandate document or charter**

DATA WAREHOUSE ANALYSIS PROCESS

The data warehouse analysis process is iterative in nature. Its purpose is to quickly and accurately drive out essential business requirements for the decision support application as well as to define the data staging and data management (database design) approach to be adopted during design and implementation. The analysis phase can consist, therefore, of the work steps, milestones, and deliverables defined here.

ANALYSIS ACTIVITIES

Prerequisites

The following six activities and deliverables should be completed prior to initiating the analysis process.

Process	Deliverable(s)
1. Project setup	Control structure, development, environment, and staffing

Process	*Deliverable(s)*
2. Project development team training	Trained development team
3. Business and IT maturity assessment	Business and organizational study
4. Current state technology assessment	Current state assessment report
5. Business value and ROI assessment	Business case
6. Project scoping and definition	Approved initial project plan, budget projection, and project mandate or charter

ANALYSIS STAGE WORK STEPS, MILESTONES, AND DELIVERABLES

This process covers the user requirements gathering activities necessary to establish a baseline for iterative development. Depending upon the size and scope of the effort undertaken, not all these activities or tasks are required on any one engagement. Those activities and deliverables that are not essential to this process are indicated with an (O) behind them. Please note that if a program office has already been set up for the data warehouse environment, then all program activities can be ignored. If a data warehouse program office is not required then all (P)-level activities indicated in the project planning process need to be completed. Milestones, indicated by an (M), are review points in the project where results achieved and budget expended must be approved by the project sponsor before further activities can be initiated.

The following section describes a task list to consider in conducting project analysis. These tasks will run over the next two to three months of the engagement (depending upon project scope). This task list is listed on the attached CD and can be imported into a spreadsheet or project planning tool for your use and customization.

3. Analysis Stage

3.1. Define analysis phase environment.

    3.1.1. Refine management and budget control structure.

    3.1.2. Refine DW project team reporting structure.

    3.1.3. Augment the project organization (roles and responsibilities with required analysis phase staffing and support).

    3.1.4. Train project analysis team.

        3.1.4.1. Acquire additional analysis phase team members.

        3.1.4.2. Develop/acquire core team training material.

        3.1.4.3. Conduct core team training.

    3.1.5. Refine DW project policies and procedures for the analysis phase.

        3.1.5.1. Review/refine planning phase deliverables.

        3.1.5.2. Review/refine change management, risks, and issue controls (P).

        3.1.5.3. Refine DW program methodologies and tools (P).

        3.1.5.4. Refine project analysis phase work breakdown structure.

3.2. Develop business requirements.

    3.2.1. Conduct business requirements analysis.

        3.2.1.1. Schedule end user requirements gathering sessions.

        3.2.1.2. Conduct end user requirements sessions.

            3.2.1.2.1. Determine all tactical reporting requirements.

            3.2.1.2.2. Determine all strategic analysis requirements.

                3.2.1.2.2.1. Determine all dashboard or EIS based requirements.

                3.2.1.2.2.2. Determine all decision support or analytic requirements.

                3.2.1.2.2.3. Determine all data mining requirements.

                3.2.1.2.2.4. Determine all customer relationship management requirements.

                3.2.1.2.2.5. Determine all ad hoc reporting/access requirements.

3.2.1.3.   Publish and obtain feedback.

3.2.1.4.   Prepare requirements statement for sponsor/steering committee approval.

3.2.2.   Develop subject area data model (in concert with the business requirements sessions).

3.2.2.1.   Refine/establish data modeling/repository tool environment and update process.

3.2.2.2.   Populate initial subject area project model from the corporate subject area model (if one is available) (O).

3.2.2.3.   Identify/model fundamental entity types (dimensions) for analysis.

3.2.2.4.   Identify/model business requirements processes (facts or events) for analysis.

3.2.2.5.   Define all base, derived, and key based attributes.

3.2.2.6.   Document all required business rules and determine what initial summarization data will be required for fact and dimension table attribute aggregation definition during the design phase.

3.2.2.7.   Refine source system strategy.

3.2.2.7.1.   Identify systems of record from source system(s) (internal or external for data capture) and ownership; determine a strategy for missing or currently unavailable data.

3.2.2.7.2.   Determine required granularity and required currency for data loading.

3.2.2.7.3.   Develop source system change notification process.

3.2.2.8.   Establish data quality management process.

3.2.2.8.1.   Determine data quality transformation, audit, and repair process.

3.2.2.8.2.   Determine data quality thresholds (level of required accuracy) by entity and attribute).

3.2.2.8.3.   Develop data quality stewardship process and/or level or involvement of the business users in data ownership.

3.3.   Develop DW architecture.

3.3.1. Analyze and develop a strategy for the data management environment.

    3.3.1.1. Develop a strategy for capacity management and database monitoring.

    3.3.1.2. Develop a strategy for database backup and recovery.

    3.3.1.3. Develop a strategy for data archiving.

    3.3.1.4. Develop a strategy for database design, data indexing, and surrogate key management.

    3.3.1.5. Develop a strategy for aggregate navigation by users writing ad hoc requests.

    3.3.1.6. Select a server architecture approach (one, two, or three tier).

    3.3.1.7. Select a DBMS(s) compatible with the server architecture.

3.3.2. Analyze and develop a strategy for the data staging environment.

    3.3.2.1. Develop a strategy for accessing data from source systems.

    3.3.2.2. Develop a data transformation strategy.

    3.3.2.3. Develop an approach for data repair and data verification.

    3.3.2.4. Develop an approach for data replication and data distribution.

    3.3.2.5. Develop a strategy for creating derived data and data summarization.

    3.3.2.6. Develop a strategy for data loading and index re creation.

3.3.3. Analyze and develop a strategy for the information access environment.

    3.3.3.1 Develop an approach for executive dashboard and/or EIS development.

    3.3.3.2. Develop a strategy for DSS tools selection and implementation.

    3.3.3.3. Develop a strategy for supporting tactical reporting from operational data stores.

    3.3.3.4. Develop a strategy for supporting data mining and predictive modeling against relational as multidimensional databases.

        3.3.3.5. Develop a strategy for end user tool certification for writing ad hoc data requests.

        3.3.3.6. Develop a strategy for a common user interface using WEB based functionality provided over the business Intra or Internet.

        3.3.3.7. Develop a strategy for end user support (help desk) and problem escalation and resolution.

    3.3.4. Analyze and develop a strategy for the technology infrastructure environment.

        3.3.4.1. Develop a vendor management strategy.[1]

        3.3.4.2. Develop a hardware, software, and communications layer production certification strategy (O) (consult IT support for guidance and direction for the adoption of their processes).

        3.3.4.3. Develop a data staging and information access testing strategy

    3.3.5 Analyze and develop a strategy for metadata management.[2]

3.4. Prepare and approve analysis phase.

    3.4.1. Assemble analysis phase deliverables for review and approval.

    3.4.2. Revise project plan and mandate (charter) document for the analysis phase.

    3.4.3. Prepare analysis phase presentation materials.

    3.4.4. Conduct analysis phase review session.

    3.4.5. Review, revise, and obtain approval for the proposed approach (M).

    3.4.6. Update project repository with analysis phase deliverables.

---

[1] Review Chapter 11 for a detailed description of the vendor management process and deliverables.

[2] Consult Section One for a detailed description of the metadata management process and deliverables.

Analysis Stage Deliverables

The following section describes the deliverables that are produced out of the activity list as previously described.

Work Breakdown Structure Deliverables Designations

Two types of deliverables are listed for this stage.

1. Technology dependent output containing the detail specifications for the data warehouse hardware, software, and network architecture such as code, procedures, or models.
2. Technology independent output (in the form of documentation), illustrated in **bold,** that includes the results of technology dependent output production for end user review.

   a. **Project analysis team environment and staffing**

   b. **Refined project management and control processes**

   c. Refine DW development methodology and tools

   d. **Business user requirements (process model)**

   e. **Subject area data model**

   f. **Metadata management approach**

   g. **Data quality management approach**

   h. **Data management environment approach**

   i. **Data staging environment approach**

   j. **Data access environment approach**

   k. **Technology infrastructure management approach**

   l. **Revise project plan, budget, and project mandate document or charter**

CHAPTER THIRTEEN

Determining User Requirements: Techniques for Data Warehouse Requirements Analysis

INTRODUCTION TO USER REQUIREMENTS ANALYSIS

In the last chapter we reviewed the overall planning and analysis process for initiating a data warehousing project. In this chapter we drill down to the core methods and investigative techniques and questions that enable us to complete the work steps and deliverables described in Chapter 12. From an analysis perspective, the essential activities for data warehouse analysis include

1. Subject area data modeling
2. Data staging and data quality analysis
3. Information access requirements collection

SUBJECT AREA DATA MODELING

In developing our project data models for the data warehouse, we need to keep four key principles in mind.

1. Data warehouse data modeling is geared toward information analysis and retrieval and not data capture.

2. Three sets of models are required to separate and maintain our company's business rules from how they are physically implemented as governed by our data warehouse data architecture.

3. An iterative process is necessary to capture and maintain the project metadata that utilizes project case tools and program level repositories as the project proceeds from analysis into design and implementation.

4. Analysis modeling and documentation guidelines are required to allow for the reuse and management of deliverables at a cross project or program level.

1. Data warehouse data modeling is geared toward information analysis

The guiding principles behind the design of the data warehouse environment are radically different from its operational systems cousin. In the traditional world of data collection and tactical reporting, the focus is on collecting the data correctly and providing accurate reporting on today's business. From a modeling perspective, this resulted in the development of a number of information engineering based methods such as canonical synthesis and normalization. These techniques are employed using an entity relationship modeling method to capture and eliminate data anomalies, so that transaction level data could be captured and stored quickly and accurately. This whole paradigm is reversed in the data warehousing world. Our focus is not on transaction level data processing, but rather on presenting and aggregating the data to provide useful and valuable information for business decision support processing. Transaction based, row level data capture is replaced by multimillion row data updates to our warehouse. Data accuracy is ensured by our loading environment, thus eliminating the need to normalize the data in either the warehouse or the mart. Since the warehouse reflects a historical perspective to data capture, row level updates and deletes are replaced with new row inserts so that the essential history, or story, behind each business event is not lost. With such a volume of data being collected, it is essential to provide various levels of detail so that the right perspective on the information can be provided at the user level.

From a design perspective, design of the data warehouse and data mart following a denormalized process provides three benefits.

a. Easing the partitioning and replication of data from the warehouse down to the mart, eliminating an extra level of data transformation.

b. Facilitating drill through using DSS tools as the warehouse is mined for detail data or related data that are not maintained at the mart level using an integrated database schema.

c. Providing a uniformity of business metadata definition and description regarding the key business events or content (facts) and their related contextual or subject area (dimension) information. (This is an aspect often forgotten or not understood by database administrators and systems analysts.)

However, if your requirements do not reflect a time variant or historical aspect, are not corporate wide or subject oriented, do not require data integration, but rather require transaction or row level updates, then what we are modeling is not a data warehouse. In such instances what we are moving toward is an operational transaction system that can be implemented as an operational data store and/or a traditional OLTP relational database.

Many MPP level hardware vendors provide good service in the operational management space but call themselves data warehousing providers. What actually is built is terabyte level operational data store, with little ability to integrate or span data across multiple years without losing essential contextual (business rule) information. The reason is that in a normalized (transaction oriented) database design, the business rules that were implemented as foreign key links between the various tables reflect only current state business reality. If this reality changes, then the physical schema must be changed as well. Once the physical schema is changed our history is lost. This critical differentiation must be kept in mind as we design data warehouses. In a denormalized star schema representation we are seeking to put into place a time variant or business rule independent database design that can manage both the content and context behind our business information across time. The residual benefit in this approach is that it saves the DBA the significant challenge and headache of unloading a reloading up to terabytes of data every time he or she has to implement a new business rule in the warehouse.

The final aspect to this equation is the most important: the end user. By implementing a denormalized star schema approach, the data are presented in a form that is much easier for the end user to comprehend. Instead of being presented with (in some cases) what looks like a circuit diagram of tables to navigate, the end user can review a handful of base level dimensions wrapped around the fact tables. Even with aggregates and limited outrigger or normalized dimension tables for the larger dimensions such as customer, the model is much easier for the end user to comprehend and use when conducting ad hoc analysis. In addition, with the data warehouse and data marts presenting the same look and feel of the data, the end user can more seamlessly navigate across fact tables drawing in and drilling down to the most appropriate level for his or her analysis. Developing predefined routines and query reports also becomes much easier to implement and maintain.

2. Three sets of models are required to manage the data warehouse data architecture

Why three models? If we look back at our approach for data warehousing, we discussed it as consisting of a three schema architecture—conceptual, logical, and physical. This is an important differentiation to keep in mind, as it allows us to maintain our business view separately from how it was physically implemented. This approach allows us to rapidly regenerate the technology influenced (logical) and/or technology dependent (physical) level each time a major change occurs without having to re create the entire architecture. Modeling in a three schema environment requires that our repository manages three different sets of data models, each interlinked and version controlled. It also requires that the data modeling case tool be able to model in two approaches (normalized E/R) for the conceptual or business level and denormalized (or star schema) at the logical and physical level.

At the conceptual level our model consists of one or two dozen subject area data models. Each model manages the various versions of each fundamental or core data concept such as customer, location, or geographic region. What these do not model is any business event or transaction based information such as purchasing, accounting, finance, inventory control, or materials management processes. With the exception of the time dimension, the data models at this level manages the basic information concepts of the business. These models provide the data warehouse data modeler with a detailed understanding of what information can be found for a key business concept, such as a customer. Furthermore, they describe the various types or categories that exist within the subject area (e.g., a person or organization being various subtypes of a customer), and information about the attributes or properties in use at a specific point in time. With this understanding, the data warehouse data modeler can more easily and accurately denormalize all or part of this subject area model into the required dimension(s) of the data warehouse. These models also provide a starting point for OLTP normalized project data model design by specifying the fundamental and attributive entity types for the logical data model.

At the logical level, the modeling process changes to either normalized entity relationship modeling for operational data store or transaction based database design or star schema denormalized database design for data warehouse or data mart development. At this level the required business events are captured in the model that become additional fundamental and attributive/associative entity types in the OLTP design and fact tables in the star schema design.

The final level of translation is at the physical level where the logical model undergoes some denormalization in the OLTP side, reducing the third or fourth normal form logical view into second normal form to improve performance. Artificial or surrogate keys are also added at this level, incorporating the necessary level of data insularity, thereby improving access performance and indexing for the transaction systems. For the warehouse we look toward creating one or more levels of aggregation to provide drill down, surrogate keys, which offer better time variance independence for user keys and improved physical performance as well as create multiple indexes to facilitate rapid access.

The problem today is that most data modeling is done at only the physical level with the logical level being a version one view of the physical. This initial logical view is overwritten by most case tools as it prepares its language dependent DDL view for schema generation. This logical view is also overwritten by the DBA as he or she prepares it for physical implementation by adding surrogate keys and normalizing or denormalizing the data model design. In such cases this problem requires that we create a separate copy for the case tool model for modification before proceeding with the generation and tuning of the database ddl.

The conceptual view is seldom available or created and is looked upon as unnecessary overhead by DBAs and systems analysts who, due to time constraints and limited visibility, are unable to support the strategic view. Yet, it is the conceptual layer that is the most important view of all, especially when dealing with the ability of the end user to understand corporate data. Once in place, it is relatively easy to maintain the three views once a basic discipline in the form of a procedure is put into place. The benefits to IT and the business are considerable, resulting in

1. Business user understanding and access to nontechnical based information

2. More rapid OLTP and OLAP logical design due to reusability of the most difficult types of entities to model (e.g., customer, product, location)

3. Extensibility for data repair and data reengineering due to a common definition for corporate data that can be mapped to its various physical views, allowing for more rapid system of record identification

A data administration organization should be utilized to provide support for this three schema data architecture and be the go to group to obtain access to these models for data warehouse design.

3. An iterative process utilizing case tools and repositories are required to manage the project metadata

Much like the data warehouse software and hardware architecture, a metadata strategy and architecture must be determined during planning and analyzed for completeness during the analysis phase. At the data warehouse tool level, we are concerned with how the various decision support and data management tools share metadata. At the business level we are concerned how this information is managed and presented to the end user in the form of end user interfaces. Metadata is the glue that holds our data sources together, whether they be in data warehouses, operational data stores, or data marts. Therefore, as we proceed from analysis to design and implementation of our data warehouse project, it is important to ensure that the metadata concerning the various technical and business aspects of our project are kept in sync.

We must ensure that the case tool and supporting repository or work group software we select allow these metadata to be stored, shared, and updated as required. As each new development, enhancement, or maintenance project is initiated we must make sure that during the planning, analysis, design, and implementation phases metadata are collected and maintained as metadata are passed from the conceptual to the logical and physical layers. A sample metamodel for just the data layer of the metadata model is provided here to illustrate what must occur at the tool level.

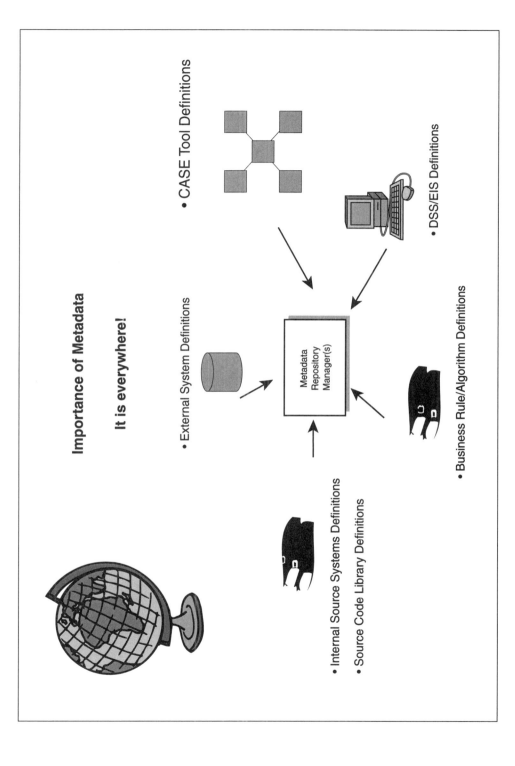

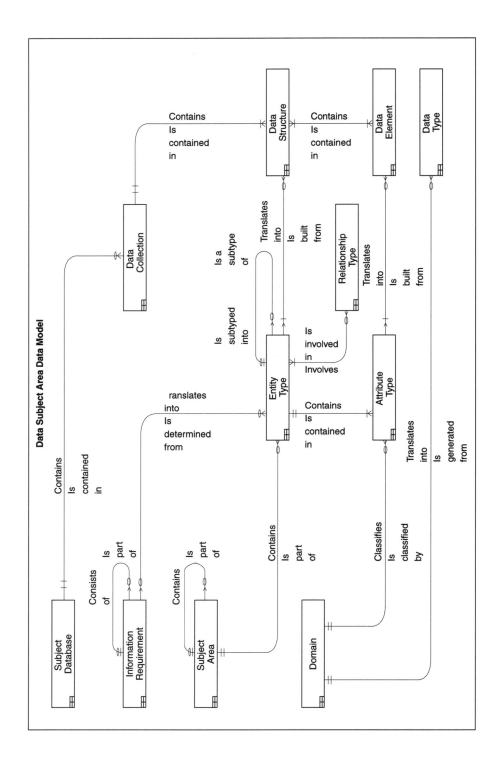

Data Subject Area Data Model

*4. Analysis modeling guidelines are required to provide deliverable
reusability and to ease documentation integration and understanding*

One of the responsibilities of the program office is to establish and provide access to various work aids such as modeling guidelines. These guidelines need to address four issues.

1. How best to use the case tool and/or repository manager in terms of
   a. Modeling conventions to be employed
   b. Data security and access to administrator or product manager level information in each product
   c. Procedures for when to pass information between the various case tool(s) and repository manager

2. Which modeling scheme or language to follow (e.g., IDEF, Martin, Chen)

3. How to migrate models from a conceptual to a logical and physical level without losing information, which includes
   a. Data quality management checkpoints and review procedures
   b. Procedures for migrating and maintaining work group or temporary (work station) versions as versus production level (shared server) models

4. What information to maintain about each model in terms of
   a. Diagrams and how they should be documented
      i. *Textual information related to how definitions should be formatted in terms of*

5. Subject area names and reference information for mapping up to the conceptual level and physical database design catalog references for mapping down to the physical level

6. Entity and relationship documentation outside the data model diagram (what definition and business rule information should be collected)

7. Version control and ownership

8. Data quality audit information in terms of level of accuracy as described in the model or level of integration possible at the corporate level

   a. Related or reference information that exists in other forms that was used to create or augment the model in terms of documents, or multimedia files

9. How new development, or test versions, of data warehouse deliverables are to be maintained separate from the production view or version for

   a. Tracking changes to models and its related information

   b. Monitoring changes to documents, presentations, plans, budgets, etc.

   c. Controlling changes to software, hardware, and network configurations as they are developed and move from test to production

DATA STAGING AND DATA QUALITY ANALYSIS

Data staging and data quality analysis for migrating data from internal and external sources to a data warehouse and or mart(s) require analysis of a number of options. As we develop our requirements for building the data staging environment, we need to consider, on a case by case basis, the nature and origin of our data sources since they can include

1. Internal nonrelational transaction systems

2. Internal PC based systems (flat files from packages and spreadsheets)

3. Internal operational data stores

4. Other data warehouses and data marts

5. External source systems where the file formats may be unstable and/or subject to change on a month by month basis

   We may also wish to utilize our data staging environment to service the OLTP environment as well as the OLAP architecture. In many environments this is not an easy task, due to the extreme differences that exist between the two environments. In the OLTP environment we may be dealing with massive and frequent record add, change, deletes, and updates requiring real time or daily processing and synchronization of data across multiple systems. In the OLAP or data warehousing environment we may require massive updates as well, depending upon the currency required in the data warehouse/data mart. Therefore, it is important to decide on the purpose of the data staging environment "hub and spoke" or dual or traditional data warehouse staging before proceeding with its design.

Other considerations in creating the requirements for our data staging environment include

- The time window available to conduct extractions, data repair and validation, transformations, and loads
- The expected reduction in processing time as new source systems, or warehouses, come online
- The time required to compare and validate the last set of load files against the current set to determine what delta changes exist for loading into the warehouse or mart
- The time required to back up the data warehouse/data mart
- The time required to create new instances of all aggregate/summary tables
- The time required to restore an old image of the data warehouse in the event of a corrupt load process that can be recovered only with a database restore
- The backup and restore capabilities of any multidimensional data mart databases.
- The time required to schedule OLTP and OLAP database updates if sharing the same data staging environment following the "hub and spoke" process

Once we decide on our data staging operational requirements, we then need to understand our source system limitations and impacts on what we have determined so far. For each type of source system we need to determine how we will access and create our load files in terms of

- The wholesale movement of data from operational DBMS and comparison against the last set of load files
- The usage of application created delta file of changes
- The alteration of application code to create a delta file
- The trapping of changes at the DBMS call level.
- The trapping of changes on a log file (reused from DBMS or separately created)

- Comparison of before and after record images from journal files
- Access to archive files for loading of history into the warehouse and the establishment of the appropriate context (dimension) information

All but the first item necessitate changes to either the source system application code or supporting DBMS or file structure. If changes are made or required to the code or DBMS, you may end up impacting either the performance or availability of these systems. Therefore, the only practical solution (in most cases) is to access the entire source systems DBMS either during off online hours or its mirror image copy to conduct the necessary extracts for comparison against the last load.

We must also consider the capabilities and capacity of the DBMS and its database server in defining our data staging requirements. We must also consider

- How much data can the DBMS realistically handle?
- How is the data stored, compressed, encoded, indexed? How are null values to be managed?
- Is locking be suppressed during the load?
- If and how will request be monitored and suppressed?
- Can the DBMS allow for parallel data loading and can this load process be customized by the DBA and tuned for optimum performance?
- How will the technical metadata be loaded into the data warehouse?

The other aspect to consider is data security and who has access to verify what goes into the warehouse and who should have access to this information. Four tips to consider in dealing with data security as part of the data loading process include

1. Deciding on a strategy for encoding highly summarized global data
2. Reducing data security constraints on load data as levels become more granular
3. Remembering that encoding load data incurs a high translation overhead
4. Layering security constraints against load data by establishing criteria such as secured to top secret (highly summarized CEO, CFO data)

Once our data access and data staging requirements are determined by selecting our approach from the options here described, we need to consider the issue of data quality. Data quality for a data warehousing involves four concepts.

1. Determining the level of field level accuracy (e.g., are null values in a field acceptable). What are the possible variations or permutations of data values of same or like data from different source systems and which value should be taken as the correct source (system of record)?

2. Determining the level of contextual accuracy (i.e., the same information coming from different sources with each using a different set of criteria, or time periods, to collect the information).

3. Determining how derived field level information and aggregate information are created.

4. Determining the data audit process and its impact on the load. For example, should only bad load records be discarded to a log file and the load proceeds. Or, should the entire load be aborted or rolled back?

INFORMATION ACCESS REQUIREMENTS COLLECTION

Six different techniques can be utilized to collect and understand client requirements for information before discussing the various presentation approaches. The most common methods employed today include

1. Individual or group interviewing
2. Brainstorming
3. Joint Application Design (JAD)
4. Prototyping
5. Data modeling
6. Process modeling

The sequence of these techniques is

1. Background materials and systems research and assessment
2. Brainstorming and/or interviewing

3. JAD, which includes data and process modeling

4. Prototyping and revision of the data and process models

As requirements are collected and understood in terms of a star schema data model and the prototype description or process model, the project then proceeds to design and implementation. The primary deliverable out of the analysis phase is the subject area data model increment or project data model. The eight procedures for building this model are

1. Select the part of the various subject areas to be built (consult the conceptual data model for a list of SAs to consult as maintained by a data architecture group).

2. Determine the required operational characteristics of each dimension and fact table to be modeled by

   a. Removing any purely operational data (user audit information)

   b. Adding an element of time to each key if not already present

   c. Creating a new (surrogate) key if required for each dimension

   d. Adding any appropriate derived data

   e. Transforming conceptual current state data relationships into data artifacts (new data items to be stored in the dimension or fact table)

   f. Accommodating the different levels of granularity by creating new tables and/or new data fields

   g. Merging fundamental and attributive entity types from logical operational data models into common structures (where keys are the same or similar)

   h. Creating required arrays for storage within the dimension or fact table

3. Integrate the data model with the existing conceptual or logical level data warehouse data model.

4. If data integration problems arise as a result of this process, determine how you will manage common keys and attributes with different corporate business rules and formats by

   a. Adding new data to existing data and/or converting old data

    b. Adding new data as of this day forward and do not convert the old data

    c. Creating a new dimension, or fact table, containing only new data as of this day forward

5. For the design and implementation phase, calculate the amount of new data to be added in terms of rows and bytes.

6. Determine if new summarizations are required to roll up the new data.

7. For data staging we must review the data at the entity and attribute level and determine any new requirements for

    a. Reviewing and/or revising conceptual or business naming conventions

    b. Determining what new derived data need to be added and documented

    c. Reviewing changes to existing key structures and date time stamps

    d. Specifying changes to any physical characteristics

    e. Specifying how data artifacts (relationships) are managed across time in the form of new fields and date time stamps.

8. For data mapping of the data staging process for each attribute modeled within each dimension and fact base level or aggregate table we must determine

    a. Establishing the system of record

    b. Defining any defaults where a key or attribute does not have a source value

    c. Creating logic for translating values from multiple sources and formatting changes

    d. Defining new or recalculations of derived values

    e. Specifying logic required to create summarizations and aggregations

    f. Determining source and target (data staging) record layouts

    g. Determining if change data capture is needed

    h. Defining how source records are identified (direct or through interfaces)

    i. Determining how data refresh for the dimension and fact tables occur (e.g., by journaling, capturing delta changes at source, creating DBMS updates)

   j. Documenting which data sources or views should not be used to create the data updates

   k. Identifying the number, size, and frequency of updates required from each internal and external source file(s).

The other major deliverable out of the analysis phase is the process model. The purpose of the process model is twofold. Its first function is to illustrate the sources and transaction types for loading the data staging environment. The second purpose is to define the end user access and data quality management process based on

1. The canned or predictable processes required to access and format data for end user consumption in terms of user views

2. The ad hoc process in accessing data at any level in the warehouse

3. The data quality audit processes in verifying data loading into the warehouse

4. The data access authorization (security) processes in governing access to the various levels of the data warehouse

5. The change and problem management processes required to support access to the data warehousing environment

These requirements, once modeled, are then used as input into the design and implementation phase for selecting, designing, and implementing software.

In the design and implementation phase (discussed in Chapter 14), the various front end user tools are evaluated and selected based upon the level of functionality required by the end user group as documented in the process and data models. Depending upon the breadth of the user community, one or more analytic tools may be required. What the analysis process should determine is the general criteria for this selection, design, and implementation process in terms of either creating the required user interfaces or customizing package OLAP software.

The seven types of analytic requirements we need to consider include

1. Tactical canned reporting

2. Tactical ad hoc analysis

3. Analytic aggregate reporting across time

4. Analytic detail reporting across time

5. Analytic drill down based on ad hoc analysis across time

6. Customer analysis through segmentation and product/service promotion and review

7. Data mining and predictive modeling

Each of these categories necessitates investigation into different tools and procedures during the design and implementation phase.

- Tactical reporting requires collecting requirements leading toward the deployment of report writer software.

- Tactical ad hoc analysis requires access to SQL (or a user friendly interface) to a query governor that determines if base, or aggregate tables, should be accessed to satisfy the query.

- Analytic aggregate reporting requires an EIS based tool that requires an Intranet, or Internet friendly user interface, to access and present the information.

- Analytic detail reporting requires either an EIS or DSS based tool with the same user interface requirements.

- Analytic drill down is an extension of the preceding and requires the DSS tool to present the data in different formats (e.g., bar charts, pie charts, graphs, spreadsheets).

- Customer segmentation and relationship analysis requires the employment of a completely different category of tools that provides customer life time value analysis capabilities. These are then connected into procedures that create and track promotions and campaigns of new or enhanced products or services.

- The most complex of all requires data mining access or drill through access of end user data requirements. This access is usually required on an ad hoc, or timed basis, from multidimensional based servers analyzing knowledge using neural net or related processing to develop predictions or responses to sensed changes in the business climate.

Access requirements determination also includes the gathering of the number and expected frequency and their sources of origin of canned and ad hoc requests for data across the data warehouse architecture. In data warehousing, this estimate can be off by many hundredfold. However, to provide input for capacity management planning, an initial estimate should be determined and adjusted through the design and implementation phase.

◆

CHAPTER FOURTEEN

Designing and Implementing the Data Warehouse

INTRODUCTION TO DATA WAREHOUSE DESIGN AND IMPLEMENTATION

In Chapter 12 we reviewed the data warehouse planning and analysis process, followed by a review of the required techniques in Chapter 13. In this chapter, we complete the process by moving our project forward through the design and implementation phase. It is during this phase of the data warehouse life cycle that the truly iterative nature of the process occurs.

The purpose of this phase is to

1. Validate the planning and analysis process and update our understanding of user requirements

2. Provide an end user system and database architecture that includes an increment of the various layers of the data warehousing architecture

3. Verify our expected return on investment by adjusting our performance measures and metrics

4. Put into place the various capacity management and support processes required for the evolution of the environment

During the design and implementation phase, we must also address the following activities:

- End user and IT operational support training

- System and database testing and production implementation
- Organizational development and redesign (for both the business user and IT community)
- Help desk and IT process support
- Information access and data quality policy and procedure processing
- System and database documentation and presentation
- Disaster recovery planning and design

Prerequisites

The following activities and deliverables from the planning and analysis stages should have been completed prior to initiating the design stage.
The following planning stage processes should have been completed.

Preplanning Stage Processes

1. Project core team staffing
2. Initial project control and budgeting
3. Initial project infrastructure definition

Planning Stage Processes

1. Define program management environment
2. Kick off DW program
3. Define project management environment
4. Prepare and approve project mandate and approach
5. Kick off DW project
6. Conduct business opportunity assessment
7. Conduct current state technology assessment
8. Develop a business case
9. Prepare and approve project mandate and approach

Planning Stage Deliverables

1. Program office communication, change management, and issue management process

2. Project team change management and issue management process (if not provided by the program office)

3. Select data warehouse methodology and tools

4. Project development team environment and staffing

5. Project sponsor/steering committee

6. Project review and approval process through the program office or project team

7. Assess business opportunity

8. Business case assessment and verification

9. Assess current state business systems

10. Revise project plan, budget, and project mandate document or charter

The following analysis stage processes and deliverables should have been completed prior to initiating the design stage.

Analysis Stage Processes

1. Define analysis phase environment

2. Develop business requirements

3. Develop DW architecture

4. Conduct source systems assessment

5. Define data management approach

6. Define metadata management approach

7. Define data staging approach

8. Define data warehouse technical support infrastructure

9. Define data access environment approach

10. Prepare and approve analysis stage

Analysis Stage Deliverables

1. Project analysis team environment and staffing

2. Refine analysis stage project management and control processes

3. Refine analysis methodology and tools

4. Determine business user requirements model (process model)

5. Subject area data model definition

6. Metadata management approach document

7. Data quality management approach document

8. Data management environment approach document

9. Data staging environment approach document

10. Data access environment approach document

11. Technology infrastructure management approach

12. Revise project plan, budget, and project mandate document or charter

DESIGN STAGE WORK STEPS, MILESTONES, AND DELIVERABLES

The project design stage deals with the required work steps to define the decision support system and supporting data warehouse database/marts. Those activities and deliverables that are not essential to this process are indicated with an (O) behind them. Milestones, indicated by an (M), are review points in the project where results achieved and budget expended must be approved by the business before further activities can be initiated.

The following section describes a task list to consider in conducting project design. These tasks will run over the next two to three months of the engagement (depending upon project scope). This task list is listed on the attached CD and can be imported into a spreadsheet or project planning tool for your use and customization.

Design Stage Activities

4. Initiate business system design stage.

    4.1. Review analysis stage results.

        4.1.1. Review analysis stage results.

        4.1.2. Review design stage scope.

    4.2. Create business system design stage systems evolution repository.

        4.2.1. Set up design stage systems evolution repository.

        4.2.2. Migrate business requirements models.

4.3. Designate design stage responsibility/control procedures.

4.4. Define data warehouse/mart database architecture.

    4.4.1. Translate the business area data model.

        4.4.1.1. Create the database design for the data warehouse/data mart, or

        4.4.1.2. Customize package data warehouse database to reflect the business requirements data model (O).

    4.4.2. Create the data staging environment.

        4.4.2.1. Install server and application software into the staging environment.

        4.4.2.2. Create data staging flat file layouts.

        4.4.2.3. Map source system records/files to data staging tables and create transformation process/code.

        4.4.2.4. Select/load source system data into the data staging environment and verify/log results.

        4.4.2.5. Map data staging tables to data warehouse/data mart tables.

        4.4.2.6. Select/load source system data and conduct data quality audits over data content, context, and currency.

        4.4.2.7. Design data recovery processes.

            4.4.2.7.1. Design data backup and recovery procedures.

            4.4.2.7.2. Design disaster recovery procedures.

        4.4.2.8. Design data access security requirements.

            4.4.2.8.1. Design user class access requirements.

            4.4.2.8.2. Design operational access requirements.

            4.4.2.8.3. Review and approve systems security recommendations.

    4.4.3. Obtain approval for data warehouse/mart database and data staging design (M).

4.5. Define business decision support system components.

    4.5.1. Define decision support application procedures.

        4.5.1.1. Define application procedure SQL code.

        4.5.1.2. Design online system component structure.

4.5.1.3. Design and validate procedural interfaces.

4.5.1.4. Refine logical database design access (user views).

4.5.2. Define data warehouse/mart testing process.

4.5.2.1. Define data staging testing and migration procedures.

4.5.2.2. Define decision support system testing and migration procedures.

4.5.3. Build prototype or refine enhance current test version.

4.5.3.1. Select client/server hardware and software platforms.

4.5.3.2. Conduct software training (O).

4.5.3.3. Define prototype.

4.5.3.4. Test and refine prototype.

4.5.3.5. Define system and database control and monitoring procedures.

4.5.3.6. Obtain approval for prototype or enhanced version (M).

4.6. Define data warehouse system dynamics and technology environment.

4.6.1. Define procedure volume.

4.6.1.1. Define data access volume (number of concurrent sessions and expected query size).

4.6.1.2. Define data staging update frequency.

4.6.2. Define systems delivery platform.

4.6.2.1. Identify a processor environment.

4.6.2.2. Identify a communications environment.

4.6.2.3. Identify a software environment.

4.6.3. Define data warehouse/mart organizational structure.

4.6.3.1. Define IT organization responsibilities.

4.6.3.1.1. Define data warehouse/mart support organization roles and responsibilities.

4.6.3.1.2. Designate staffing and conduct training.

4.6.3.2. Define business user organization roles and responsibilities.

4.6.3.2.1. Define organizational/procedural changes.

4.6.3.2.2. Define data stewardship/data quality roles, procedures, and responsibilities.

4.6.3.3.   Design training program.

     4.6.3.3.1. Design user online/manual help requirements.

     4.6.3.3.2. Develop a training strategy.

     4.6.3.3.3. Determine courseware requirements.

     4.6.3.3.4. Design operational support training procedures.

     4.6.3.3.5. Design business user decision support access training procedures.

4.6.4.   Identify an implementation approach.

     4.6.4.1.   Design an implementation plan.

     4.6.4.2.   Design the production and support environment.

     4.6.4.3.   Obtain approval for implementation (M).

     4.6.4.4.   Install prototype.

     4.6.4.5.   Activate/refine prototype and prepare for full production release.

4.7.   Review and approve stage results.

4.7.1.   Review/refine systems migration plan.

     4.7.1.1.   Review/refine migration estimates.

     4.7.1.2.   Refine the scope of design.

     4.7.1.3.   Document stage results.

     4.7.1.4.   Integrate design stage libraries.

     4.7.1.5.   Obtain approval for the design stage (M).

Design Stage Deliverables

The following deliverables are produced out of the work activities as described here.

Work Breakdown Structure Deliverables Designations

Two types of deliverables are listed for this stage.

- Technology dependent output containing the detail specifications for the data warehouse hardware, software, and network architecture such as code, procedures or models

- Technology independent output (in the form of documentation), illustrated in **bold,** which includes the results of technology dependent output production for end user review

  1. Data warehouse/mart database
  2. **Data warehouse/mart database design documentation**
  3. Data staging environment
  4. **Data staging environment documentation**
  5. Data warehouse architecture
  6. **Data warehouse architecture documentation**
  7. Prototype/refined decision support business system
  8. **Prototype/refined decision support business system documentation**
  9. **Testing process**
  10. **Training process**
  11. **Organizational design**
  12. Data backup and disaster recovery design
  13. Data security design
  14. **Data security design documentation**
  15. **Data backup and disaster recovery documentation**
  16. **Implementation stage plan and budget**

IMPLEMENTATION STAGE WORK STEPS, MILESTONES, AND DELIVERABLES

The project implementation stage deals with the work steps required to finalize the implementation and review of the decision support system and supporting data warehouse database/marts. Those activities and deliverables that are not essential to this process are indicated with an (O) behind them. Milestones indicated by an (M) are review points in the project where results achieved and budget expended must be approved by the business before further activities can be initiated.

The following section describes a task list to consider in conducting project implementation. These tasks will run over the next two to three months of the engagement (depending upon project scope). This task list is listed on the attached CD and can be imported into a spreadsheet or project planning tool for your use and customization.

Implementation Stage Activities

5. Initiate implementation and assimilation stage.
    5.1. Review design stage results.
        5.1.1. Review design stage results.
        5.1.2. Review implementation stage scope.
    5.2. Obtain access to the implementation stage environment.
        5.2.1. Obtain production library access.
        5.2.2. Obtain equipment/communications access.
        5.2.3. Review/refine end user and operations security profiles.
    5.3. Conduct end user training.
        5.3.1. Review staff training profiles.
        5.3.2. Select staff for training.
        5.3.3. Construct training environment.
        5.3.4. Conduct staff training.
        5.3.5. Update staff training profiles.
        5.3.6. Review and approve training results.
    5.4. Install business decision support system release.
        5.4.1. Migrate code to the production systems repository.
            5.4.1.1. Migrate systems evolution database products.
            5.4.1.2. Migrate systems evolution applications and manual procedure products.
            5.4.1.3. Migrate data staging environment.
        5.4.2. Conduct data conversion/migration for initial full load.
        5.4.3. Initiate operational procedures.
        5.4.4. Conduct post implementation systems products review.
    5.5. Review and approve implementation stage results.
        5.5.1. Monitor system effectiveness.
        5.5.2. Obtain authorization to conclude release.

Implementation Stage Deliverables

The following deliverables are produced out of the work activities as described here.

Work Breakdown Structure Deliverables Designations

Two types of deliverables are listed for this stage.

- Technology dependent output containing the detail specifications for the data warehouse hardware, software, and network architecture such as code, procedures, or models
- Technology independent output (in the form of documentation), illustrated in **bold,** which includes the results of technology dependent output production for end user review

1. Trained IT and business users
2. Help desk
3. **Business and IT help documentation**
4. **User training program results**
5. Production business decision support system and operational procedures
6. **Business decision support system release review**

Impacted Design Stage Work Steps

6. Design stage impacts (in **bold**).
   6.1. Review analysis stage results.
   6.2. Create business system design stage systems evolution repository.
   6.3. Designate design stage responsibility/control procedures.
   6.4. Define data warehouse/mart database architecture.
      6.4.1. **Translate the business area data model.**
         6.4.1.1. **Create the database design for the data warehouse/data mart, or**
         6.4.1.2. **Customize package data warehouse database to reflect the business requirements data model (O).**

6.4.2. Create the data staging environment.

    6.4.2.1. Install server and application software into the staging environment.

    6.4.2.2. Create data staging flat file layouts.

    6.4.2.3. Map source system records/files to data staging tables and create transformation process/code.

    6.4.2.4. Select/load source system data into the data staging environment and verify/log results.

    6.4.2.5. Map data staging tables to data warehouse/data mart tables.

    6.4.2.6. Select/load source system data and conduct data quality audits over data content, context, and currency.

    6.4.2.7. Design data recovery processes.

        6.4.2.7.1. Design data backup and recovery procedures.

        6.4.2.7.2. Design disaster recovery procedures.

    6.4.2.8. Design data access security requirements.

        6.4.2.8.1. Design user class access requirements.

        6.4.2.8.2. Design operational access requirements.

        6.4.2.8.3. Review and approve systems security recommendations.

6.4.3. Obtain approval for data warehouse/mart database and data staging design (M).

6.5. Define business decision support system components.

    6.5.1. Define decision support application procedures.

        6.5.1.1. Define application procedure SQL code.

        6.5.1.2. Design online system component structure.

        6.5.1.3. Design and validate procedural interfaces.

        6.5.1.4. Refine logical database design access (user views).

    6.5.2. Define data warehouse/mart testing process.

        6.5.2.1. Define data staging testing and migration procedures.

        6.5.2.2. Define decision support system testing and migration procedures.

6.5.3.   Build prototype or refine enhance current test version.

6.5.3.1.   Select client/server hardware and software platforms.

6.5.3.2.   Conduct software training (O).

6.5.3.3.   Define prototype.

6.5.3.4.   Test and refine prototype.

6.5.3.5.   Define system and database control and monitoring procedures.

6.5.3.6.   Obtain approval for prototype or enhanced version (M).

6.6.   Define data warehouse system dynamics and technology environment.

6.6.1.   Define procedure volume.

6.6.1.1.   Define data access volume (number of concurrent sessions and expected query size).

6.6.1.2.   Define data staging update frequency.

6.6.2.   Define systems delivery platform.

6.6.2.1.   Identify a processor environment.

6.6.2.2.   Identify a communications environment.

6.6.2.3.   Identify a software environment.

6.6.3.   Define data warehouse/mart organizational structure.

6.6.3.1.   Define IT organization responsibilities.

6.6.3.1.1. Define data warehouse/mart support organization roles and responsibilities.

6.6.3.1.2. Designate staffing and conduct training.

6.6.3.2.   Define business user organization roles and responsibilities.

6.6.3.2.1. Define organizational/procedural changes.

6.6.3.2.2. Define data stewardship/data quality roles, procedures, and responsibilities.

6.6.3.3.   Design training program.

6.6.3.3.1. Design user online/manual help requirements.

6.6.3.3.2. Develop a training strategy.

6.6.3.3.3. Determine courseware requirements.

6.6.3.3.4. Design operational support training procedures.

6.6.3.3.5. Design business user decision support access training procedures.

6.6.4.   Identify an implementation approach.

6.6.4.1.   Design an implementation plan.

6.6.4.2.   Design the production and support environment.

6.6.4.3.   Obtain approval for implementation (M).

6.6.4.4.   Install prototype.

6.6.4.5.   **Activate/refine prototype and prepare for full production release.**

6.7.   **Review and approve stage results.**

6.7.1.   **Review/refine systems migration plan.**

6.7.1.1.   **Review/refine migration estimates.**

6.7.1.2.   **Refine the scope of design.**

6.7.1.3.   **Document stage results.**

6.7.1.4.   **Integrate design stage libraries.**

6.7.1.5.   **Obtain approval for the design stage (M).**

Impacted Design Stage Deliverables

1. Data warehouse/mart database

2. Data warehouse/mart database design documentation

3. **Data staging environment**

4. **Data staging environment documentation**

5. Data warehouse architecture

6. Data warehouse architecture documentation

7. **Prototype/refined decision support business system**

8. **Prototype/refined decision support business system documentation**

9. Testing process

10. Training process

11. **Organizational design**

12. Data backup and disaster recovery design

13. **Data security design**

14. **Data security design documentation**

15. Data backup and disaster recovery documentation

16. **Implementation stage plan and budget**

Constructing the Architecture: Techniques for Data Warehouse Design and Implementation

INTRODUCTION TO CONSTRUCTING THE ARCHITECTURE

In the last chapter we reviewed the design and implementation process for constructing and implementing our data warehouse or data mart. In this chapter, we drill down to the core methods and investigative techniques and questions that enable us to complete the work steps and deliverables described in Chapter 14. From a design and implementation perspective, the essential activities for data warehouse design and implementation include

1. Database(s) selection, design, and optimization
2. Decision support technology selection, customization, and implementation
3. Data staging selection, customization, and implementation
4. Technical infrastructure selection, configuration, and implementation
5. IT and business organizational design and implementation

DATABASE(S) SELECTION, DESIGN, AND OPTIMIZATION

The selection, design, and optimization of the data management layer within our architecture is driven by 12 factors.

1. The database management system (DBMS) currently in use by your organization and the ability of the IT organization to support a change

2. The nature of the data warehousing/data mart project in that an operational data store or data warehouse is best served running relational software while data mining and predictive modeling systems often better utilize a multidimensional environment

3. Compatibility to the current or proposed server and operating system software environments in terms of performance, scalability, and parallelism

4. How the DBMS handles data partitioning and what control, if any, does a database administrator have over this process. The various types of data partitioning to consider include

   - Time (year, month, event)

   - Geography (region, market)

   - Frequency (volume and size)

   - Granularity (highly, lightly summarized or base level data)

   - Functionality (by business area such as marketing, sales, finance)

   - Customer/product based (product group, customer segment)

5. How the DBMS addresses data distribution (a core requirement for global or geographic disparate systems)

6. How does the DBMS manage indexing (does an index have to be dropped and re created each time an update is done)? Is parallel indexing available?

7. How will data compression impact performance?

8. Does the DBMS provide adequate backup, recovery, and journaling and logging capability?

9. What type of database monitoring is provided, and is it optimized for OLAP or strictly OLTP processing?

10. How does the DBMS address date time stamping and version control for identifying candidate data for scheduled archiving?

11. Is the DBMS proprietary or open, and does it follow an open systems standard?

12. Can the DBMS catalog be queried and/or accessed for technical metadata management?

When considering the primarily read only nature of this environment, ask yourself the following six questions.

1. How does the DBMS handle denormalization in terms optimizing logic in reading all the dimension tables prior to accessing the fact tables?

2. Does the DBMS include a query navigator of ad hoc query management of access to aggregate and base table? In addition, can the DBMS set query thresholds separately from the application software (to prevent the "query from hell")?

3. Does the DBMS include built in data security and data access controls for different levels of access to highly and lightly summarized data? What types of field level data security controls are available for access to granular or base level data?

4. How does the DBMS manage record locking? What level of granularity is involved in record locking, and can field and row level locking be turned off when data refreshes are scheduled?

5. Is parallel loading available, and how compatible is it to the MPP and NUMA architectures?

6. What kind of availability is required based on the nature of the DBMS? If 7 x 24 up time is required, how can the DBMS deal with the backup and data refresh process in terms of data mirroring capability? What types of storage media are supported by this DBMS?

By running each product through this list of questions, you should be able to determine what kind of DBMS will best suit your needs.

DATA WAREHOUSE DATABASE DESIGN CONSIDERATIONS

Designing a data warehouse is a process done from the fact table(s) out. The fact tables are the largest tables in terms of numbers of rows in your database, but also the thinnest in terms of numbers of columns they contain. Fact tables are called thin, tall tables as they provide information in the form of summaries, totals, and derived values to business questions. Therefore, fact tables are primarily numeric in nature. The context for these questions are framed by the related dimension tables. Dimension tables contain all the necessary contextual information. They contain a large number of wide columns containing descriptive and numeric information. Unlike the fact tables, which consist almost entirely of numbers in one form or another, the dimension tables contain structured (name, number, code) and unstructured (text, graphical, multimedia) data. Aside from the small time dimension table that contains numbers and descriptions for calendar and business event dates, the dimension tables usually contain under a million rows of data describing the products, services, and customers of your business. The related fact tables, on the other hand, could span a billion rows or more of data.

While we design the grain of our data warehouse first and then design our dimensions around it, loading the warehouse is done in reverse. To build the necessary framework to populate the fact table's concatenated key requires that we refresh the dimension tables first, prior to populating the fact tables. To provide data insularity, it is also wise to create a surrogate or artificial key for the fact table to store the data. This allows the users over time to change the value or structure of user codes and numbers (and they will do that more often than you think) without losing history or changing the context of the data. The surrogate key, therefore, not only insulates us from change but also provides a performance boost by indexing our fact table off a single, rather than a string of values.

The following checklist is designed as an extension to the work breakdown structure discussed in chapters 12 and 14. Here we describe a more detailed process for data warehouse database design.

Data Warehouse Database Design Process Checklist

1. Prepare for logical to physical database design transition.
    1.1. Review and consolidate all planning and analysis stage results that impact the design of the data warehouse database architecture.
    1.2. Establish core team for database design and data staging review.
    1.3. Establish a repository for physical DBMS design.

2. Migrate and translate the logical data model (translate entities and relationships into tables and foreign key references).
    2.1. Denormalize the conceptual model's fundamental and attribute entity types into the project database design model's dimension tables.
    2.2. Denormalize the conceptual model's associative (business event based) entities into the grain of the fact table(s).

2.3. Create fields from the conceptual model's list of attributes and apply the necessary Data Definition Language (DDL) format to each table. (Please note that one conceptual model attribute will map to multiple OLTP or OLAP based field level definitions over time, due to database language coding and level of data integration across systems.)

2.4. Create derived columns and document algorithms. Map derived columns to attributes.

2.5. Create summary tables and map to the conceptual model entity types.

3. Conduct data loading and database time variant design verification.

3.1. Create a load record format for each base and aggregate level dimension and fact table and determine a data loading strategy for each nonderived field.

3.2. Add element of time and or version control to each table.

3.3. Add a system date time stamp to each table.

3.4. Create the time dimension table and load procedure.

4. Conduct database allocation.

4.1. Determine volume and size of initial system of record load.

4.2. Determine index space volumetrics.

4.3. Determine ongoing data loading frequency and sizing.

4.4. Determine batch and/or online loading implications.

4.5. Determine number, type, location, and expected frequency of pre-defined and ad hoc requests for data from the business decision support tools.

4.6. Assess network bandwidth and review capabilities of DBMS bulk loading.

4.7. Horizontally partition tables.

4.8. Vertically partition tables.

5. Develop database access and retrieval indexing.

5.1. Design indexes for each required key and nonkey field in the dimension tables.

5.2. Design indexes (following a round robin process) for each key field combination possible or desired from the fact table(s).

6. Assemble, review, and approve data warehouse database design for implementation.

CHANGING IMPERATIVES: WHY NORMALIZATION IS NOT A GOOD THING FOR DATA WAREHOUSING

The normalization process was designed for the OLTP environment where accurate and nonredundant transaction level data capture was imperative. Nonredundancy ensured accuracy of the stored data and sped up data capture where millions of small rows needed to be updated as fast as possible. These dictam do not apply to data warehousing. Accuracy of data capture in warehousing is controlled by the data staging environment.

In the warehouse, data redundancy is a good thing since it simplifies the database design and allows for more rapid data retrieval since fewer tables are required for query processing. Data currency is also usually not as strict as in the OLTP world. The denormalization process also makes the database schema much easier for an end user to understand and navigate for ad hoc queries. Data update is also different in that millions of small transactions are replaced by a relative few containing millions of rows each. Finally, the most important consideration is time variance. Normalization focuses on developing and maintaining a DBMS structure that optimizes current state business rules. When an important business rule changes we must make a physical change to the structure of the DBMS. If we apply this principle to the data warehouse, we lose history in not being able to completely track content as well as context changes when the business changes across time.

DECISION SUPPORT TECHNOLOGY SELECTION, CUSTOMIZATION, AND IMPLEMENTATION

Selecting, customizing, and installing decision support software is the most difficult and critical part of the data warehousing process. These front end tools and the user desktop operating system are what the user sees and knows as being the data warehouse. The most elegantly designed data warehouse databases have failed because of problems, issues, and challenges at the front end. Often IT organizations become involved and "direct" the selection of the front end tools that best suit either their technology preferences and/or implementation and support concerns. In such scenarios the user needs come second. It is important for us as technology professionals to be involved in this critical process. It is *how* we become involved that must change. Our role in the selection and implementation of decision support tools must focus on two critical factors:

1. The user's view of his or her technology requirements (by user class) can pose considerable challenges. Often this can become a political issue so don't push back too hard if the technical issues are not serious inhibitors. You may also be able to wean them off a poor choice by previewing other options with them. This issue is often complicated by the fact that at the data warehouse level multiple user groups with different information needs become involved. Always remember, data warehousing is an architecture process (no one tool will ever fit or satisfy all end user needs).

2. Presentation of prescreened technology choices that we know work with our architecture. To prevent serious technology challenges it is often best to offer the user a series of choices during the design stage where various tools can be previewed based on the user profile. For example, try out two or three different report writing tools for users who require canned tactical reporting. Do not present them with DSS or EIS tools until they are ready to make the business and psychological leap to the next level.

Data Access Environment Tool Set Process Checklist

The following list can be customized for use during the analysis and design stages of the data warehousing work breakdown structures as discussed in chapters 12 and 14.

1. Collect and understand the user requirements by user class.
   1.1. Define operational analyst requirements (precanned tactical management analysis of daily, weekly, or monthly data (usually within the current fiscal year).
   1.2. Define business analyst requirements (precanned and decision support tools with different data presentation formats such as pie charts, spreadsheets, graphs, etc.) for sweeping data across multiple fiscal years.

1.3. Define executive and director level requirements (desktop dashboard [usually web based] analysis of highly summarized and broad or corporate wide data) that sweep data across multiple fiscal years and geographic locations for comparative analysis of emerging market trends and management challenges.

1.4. Define marketing and product/service analyst requirements (data mining, predictive modeling, and campaign or promotion analysis tools that preview customer behavior and buying patterns over selected new or improved products and/or services across multiple fiscal years).

2. Conduct industry surveys and prescreen two to three vendor products by class by user group.

3. Conduct cyclical tool set reviews of the screened products.

3.1. Undertake two to three iterations of tool review with the user group using predefined scripts that test the functionality and feel of the tool sets in a comparative manner.

3.2. Conduct in parallel an internal DW team review to test the features, functions, and longevity of the tools from a strictly technological perspective. Selection criteria for these tools should include

   a. Ability to support rapid application development/construction
   b. Ability to support drill down and drill up
   c. Ability to perform advanced mathematical calculations
   d. Available level of expertise or familiarity with the product
   e. Back end integration (logical and physical database level)
   f. Data and information access capabilities
   g. Debugging and testing features
   h. Front end integration capability (Three tier architecture compliance)
   i. Proposed or available server platform
   j. Query or ad hoc language support
   k. Security
   l. User interface and ease of use

3.3. Conduct a financial and market stability analysis of the preferred tool sets.

4. Develop a short list and contract the required vendors. We can then decide on the scope of our required services in terms of strictly product installation and support and/or consulting to quick start the customization process.

5. Review and approve the results of the information access buy or build selection process.

6. Initiate the customization of the installed software by user class, or in the event that no external product was selected initiate the production of the business system internally by utilizing preselected systems development software (which would have replaced step 3 if a purely internal or home grown process were preferred).

In selecting and implementing the information access environment software, four additional considerations worth noting include

1. The available or proposed network architecture
2. Integration and presentation of metadata
3. Location of the end users for performance management and product support
4. Location of the required vendor(s) for product support, maintenance, and product update presentations

DATA STAGING SELECTION, CUSTOMIZATION, AND IMPLEMENTATION

The data staging environment is an engineered environment, consisting of data servers (engineered for DBMS rather than data staging use), extraction, transformation software, and available database management system software. It does not usually consist of any direct hardware or software products (products engineered for data staging only), but rather reuses or makes use of other components of the data warehousing architecture. Some new products address this issue under the "hub and spoke" architecture process where data staging software is engineered to work as an integral part of the processor and DBMS technology. The data staging environment under this scenario will sit on top of the data warehouse or data mart sharing resources and linking in directly to the DBMS.

Much as does data warehousing, data staging can become an all encompassing process covering OLTP corporate data integration services as well as historical data update services. In developing a data staging environment, it is best to initially focus on one or the other and scale up over time to become a true data hub environment feeding both OLTP and OLAP databases. The OLTP version focuses on real time or near real time (within one business day) data synchronization of corporate data (usually customer based) across transaction systems. If we are developing an ODS (operational data store) environment, with this objective in mind then the data staging environment should not be built with the same processes we consider for the time variant, historical nature of the data warehouse. In functionally differentiating the two, the OLTP version requires

- Nontime variant data (current state data only)
- Nonsubject oriented focus
- Integrated data, but subject to constant change as source system schema changes occur
- Add, change, and delete transactions
- Small transactions with potentially high volume
- Roll up or aggregation logic requirements
- Row level record locking and rollback issues
- Normalization of staging tables to conform with the structure maintained in operational databases
- Real time or batch updates depending upon the currency requirements of the data

For data staging environments that are to feed data warehouses or data marts, the criteria for consideration include

- Integrated data
- Time variant data (need to track contextual data for business rule clarification)
- Subject oriented data and not application oriented data focus
- Remapping of source records and fields to denormalized data staging target tables as the OLTP schemas change

- Potentially large batch jobs containing millions of rows of data (batch window management issues)

- No add, change, delete transactions, simply incremental updates of the current state across the internal and external source systems

- Denormalized data staging record layouts for direct bulk loading into the warehouse

- Aggregation and summarization logic

- Data warehouse indexes to be dropped and rebuilt to speed up the load

- May require traditional DBMS journaling or logging to be turned off to speed up the load process

- Data validation prior to the load to minimize the reinstallation of a backup and roll forward if loading to a VLDB environment

DATA LOADING STRATEGY CONSIDERATIONS

How will we access the source systems to build an initial load and second deal with incremental data updates based upon a fixed schedule? A number of options exist here, including

1. Accessing relational and hierarchical journal log files for change data capture by comparing before and after record images from journal files

2. Creating an audit file for each application in the appropriate load format for the staging environment

3. Direct loading from operational systems, as this may cause performance problems at both ends; intermediate batch flat files are recommended instead

4. Trapping changes to the DBMS in a separate log file as they occur (not recommended also due to performance issues and application system change issues)

5. Bulk downloads based on date timeframes from source systems processing in background (or using data mirroring) to the staging environment for verification against the last set of load files to identify change records for loading into the warehouse (a recommended option)

When considering a data staging strategy for OLAP and/or OLTP our combinations for data movement are

- Operational to operational
- Operational to operational/decision support
- Operational to decision support
- Operational/decision support to operational/decision support
- Operational/decision support to decision support
- Decision support to decision support

Depending upon the combination chosen from the above list, consider loading only additions or changes to the data warehouse from the source systems. Deletions of stale or little used data are left for archiving/clean up processes as part of a year end activity.

Will source system archive data be required? If so, what impact (if any) will this have on the design of the data warehouse? What contextual issues must be addressed to make the archived data understandable in today's business environment? Format data staging record layouts as close as possible to the data structures defined in the data warehouse. Put a time stamp and/or consider versioning all records so that the data warehouse can be added, thereby reducing the frequency of physical schema changes (when dealing with the VLDB environment this may become less of an option other than on a quarterly or yearly basis).

Data Staging Environment Development Process Checklist

The following checklist can be used to verify your OLTP or OLAP based data staging development or enhancement process in conjunction with the work breakdown structure discussed in chapters 12 and 14.

1. Develop data staging strategy.
    1.1. Establish the data staging approach (strategy) and document (OLTP or OLAP).
    1.2. Develop an initial list of source systems for consideration as the system of record for the data warehouse or operational data store.
    1.3. Define data currency, context, and accuracy thresholds to be maintained.

1.4. Define a data audit/verification approach.

1.5. Define data cleansing/transformation guidelines and recommendations.

1.6. Define the organizational infrastructure and recommended implementation approach (for the training, development. and support of the data staging environment).

1.7. Define data staging technical infrastructure functional architecture and recommended implementation approach (hardware, software, and network).

1.8. Determine resource costs and implementation timeframes.

1.9. Develop and approve a data staging strategy mandate or charter based on the information collected here.

2. Refine a list of existing internal, external, and derived data sources

2.1. Identify all existing systems, tables, files, spreadsheets, et al., within scope.

2.2. Determine volatility and data access strategy for each source.

2.3. Identify data repair, consistency, accuracy recommendations, and collection/auditing procedures for each source.

2.4. Develop and approve a source system assessment document and set of related procedures.

3. Define data staging database.

3.1. Review/refine data warehouse or operational data store database structure.

3.2. Create compatible data staging tables and loading procedures from the data staging environment to the data warehouse.

3.3. Map source systems to data staging tables and create loading procedures from source systems to the data staging environment or create direct update procedures for OLTP data integration across source systems.

3.4. Complete all system of record analysis and identify any data integrity, security, or currency issues.

3.5. Conduct data stage testing and refine.

3.6. Develop operational procedures and training material.

3.7. Develop a data mapping deliverable.

4. Conduct a milestone review of the data staging process.
   4.1. Prepare final version of all deliverables and procedures for implementation review.
   4.2. Conduct review and refine as appropriate.
5. Conduct training and install the data staging environment and supporting operational procedures.
6. Obtain final sign off and migration of operational procedures to the data staging support organization.

TECHNICAL INFRASTRUCTURE SELECTION, CONFIGURATION, AND IMPLEMENTATION

Like the program management layer of our data warehousing architecture, the technical infrastructure layer is an ongoing project independent process. When we talk about extensibility and scalability of our *environment,* we are discussing our technical infrastructure. In developing and maintaining the various iterations of our warehousing and related operational data store environment, the following eight components require planning, analysis, design and implementation, and monitoring. These components include

1. The selection and definition of our testing, integration, production, and disaster recovery environments.
2. The definition and implementation of vendor performance management procedures.
3. The definition and implementation of a hardware upgrade, network retrofit, and software release certification process. This is a separate testing and verification process outside the testing and implementation of data warehousing system services.
4. The definition and implementation of a data warehousing testing process for data and application releases.
5. The definition and testing of a data warehousing training and help desk support environment.
6. The definition and implementation of data warehouse production operations scheduling, monitoring, and archiving.

7. The definition and implementation of data warehousing internal and external data access (local, remote, Intranet, or Internet) data security and data usage monitoring. This also includes performance threshold monitoring and capacity management and planning.

8. The definition and implementation of a data warehousing services charge back environment.

Topical items from this list are to be expanded upon in the final chapter of this section as well as discussed more fully across Section Four. Some key activities to consider in establishing this layer of the data warehouse architecture follow.

Technical Infrastructure Planning, Design, and Implementation Checklist

1. Warehouse infrastructure planning

    1.1. Establish a core team and develop a budget plan.

    1.2. Establish IT sponsorship for the process.

    1.3. Develop an initial position statement or approach for this environment for IT steering committee and/or sponsorship review.

    1.4. Define a functional framework (logical architecture model) for the components and procedures for this layer.

    1.5. Establish a list of recommended technology components and standards.

    1.6. Review and approve the proposed approach, functional architecture, and technology components and standards.

2. Warehouse infrastructure design

    2.1. Define vendor to internal IT involvement responsibility.

    2.2. Determine which components to buy versus build.

    2.3. Conduct the vendor selection and evaluation process (refer to process defined in Chapter 11: Finding, Evaluating and Contracting Vendors for details).

    2.4. Install or refine the data warehouse development environment.

    2.5. Confirm production hardware, software, and network tools and technology selection upon the conclusion of DW prototyping and/or piloting.

2.6. Determine the required supporting organizational structure and conduct development team training.

2.7. Design the testing/acceptance/production migration process and technical requirements for implementation.

2.8. Develop a product certification process for testing and the installation of new product releases within the data warehouse development environment.

2.9. Compile a proposed implementation and support plan.

2.10. Develop and obtain IT approval for a data warehouse technical infrastructure recommendation report.

3. Establish the data warehouse development/testing environment

3.1. Acquire/install and configure the development processors.

3.2. Acquire/install and configure network gateway.

3.3. Acquire/install and configure operating system and network protocol, database, and application software.

3.4. Verify client to data and application server connectivity and drivers.

3.5. Coordinate data staging, data management, and data access layer management development and testing.

3.6. Develop backup, recovery, performance monitoring and availability, chargeback, and disaster recovery environment requirements and procedures.

3.7. Develop a production environment transition plan.

3.8. Develop and obtain approval for the technical infrastructure design stage environment technical components, staffing, and procedures.

4. Establish the data warehouse technical infrastructure production environment

4.1. Confirm completeness of all design stage technical infrastructure components, processes, human resources, and facilities.

4.2. Prepare and coordinate a production implementation or rollover schedule.

4.3. Confirm client server connectivity, software functionality, and gateway requirements.

4.4. Test local and remote client access to production facilities.

4.5. Test host network connectivity and source system to server bulk file transfer capability.

4.6. Fine tune production job scheduling and monitoring procedures.

4.7. Install and verify all production technical infrastructure components and facilities.

4.8. Coordinate and monitor vendor contract compliance and production performance.

4.9. Coordinate and monitor production cutover of data warehouse database and application system components and procedures.

4.10. Review and approve the production technical infrastructure implementation.

Technical Infrastructure Environment Considerations

Implementation and start up, especially for a new or relatively immature production environment, present their own set of unique challenges and issues, including

- The stability of the selected suite of products, network, and facilities. Are you leading or bleeding edge? Did you have to conform to the constraints of the existing IT architecture due to budget constraints, and what are these implications?

- Initial versus ongoing demand for data loading and data access services.

- Actual capacity required versus initial or planned capacity and the timeframe and budget allocations for upgrade or replacement. Are they sufficient?

- A successful data warehouse implementation means large and often unpredictable growth with no fixed end point in mind. OLAP based applications have no functional end point such as transaction processing systems where the complete life cycle is known in advance.

- Planned reduction in vendor licensing costs through sharing of database instances across parallel capable server technology (MPP and NUMA).

- Migration from two to three tier and from SMP to MPP or NUMA.

- Evolution to 64 bit VLM processing.
- Access and integration to new communication standards and capabilities.
- Use up disk (relatively inexpensive) rather than memory (most expensive) in capacity management planning.

IT AND BUSINESS ORGANIZATIONAL DESIGN AND IMPLEMENTATION

The final and most important aspect to consider in our data warehousing environment process is people. As discussed in Sections One and Two, we must consider how to be successful with our technology implementation to support

- The cultural values and expectations of the business
- Business organizational (roles, responsibilities, and rewards) changes that complement rather than contradict the decision support systems features and benefits
- Complementary IT organizational change implementation, which helps our organization evolve from a reactive, paranoid, and inward looking function to an outward, responsive service organization that adapts rapidly to business and technology change

The high stakes in organizational design and implementation at the business and technology level can result in the loss of millions of dollars in accrued costs and lost benefits if not handled correctly.

From the business perspective we must appreciate and understand the business drivers so that we can suggest effective, complementary changes to their organization—changes that will not disrupt their work flow and will support the new or enhanced decision support systems. For example, if the measurement model for staff is based on old business procedures and expectations, then the new procedures for conducting knowledge centric business will be accepted and supported. At the same time, we cannot let the operational nature, mind set, and technology prejudices of our operational world dictate how business intelligence systems are designed and implemented. Old paradigms for systems development do not apply. IT must learn a new set of paradigms to support the knowledge collection and distribution of business intelligence and not simply data collection and processing.

The OLTP process is critical for ongoing business success. However, a new extension or evolution has occurred requiring the adoption and deployment of new mechanisms based on the acquisition of new skills. To be successful with organizational design and implementation for business and IT organizations we must

- Engage project sponsorship and proactive intervention and direction at the CEO, CFO, or CIO level
- Acquire the support of our human resources function and obtain access to external organizational design expertise (not a core competency of IT)
- Initiate the human resource process early (starting in earnest at the analysis stage) and not limit it to strictly training issues
- Accept feedback from the Organizational Design (OD) group in terms of cultural or rewards expectations in tuning the proposed functions, features, and properties of the proposed business decision support system(s)

The following checklist can be used in conjunction with the analysis and design stage work breakdown structures to complete this process.

IT and Business Organizational Planning, Design,
and Implementation Checklist

1. Develop an IT and business organizational framework.
   1.1. Assess current IT environment.
      1.1.1. Acquire OD core team staff and integrate within the overall project team.
      1.1.2. Analyze current IT environment, plans, and vision.
      1.1.3. Conduct a gap analysis of current versus future job functions and roles.
      1.1.4. Conduct a staff evaluation and fit analysis for new positions and determine the level of consulting expertise or contract employment that may be required over a specified timeframe.

1.2.   Assess current business culture.

    1.2.1.   Assess business environment and culture against proposed changes or enhancements to established business functions.

        1.2.1.1.   Map current roles and responsibilities.

        1.2.1.2.   Identify career development, training, and help facility requirements.

    1.2.2.   Assess current benefits and rewards against proposed changes to the business process.

        1.2.2.1.   Confirm business process requirements against proposed organizational structure and refine.

        1.2.2.2.   Assess benefits and rewards processes against the proposed organizational structure and refine.

    1.2.3.   Assess current staffing and skill level against the requirements and propose training, reallocation, replacement, or acquisition.

2.   Prepare training and human resources cost plan and roll out schedule for consideration based upon the results of the assessment.

    2.1.   Assemble assessment results and organizational implementation plans (one for each IT and the business units within scope).

    2.2.   Conduct review and approval sessions with IT and the impacted business units.

3.   Initiate the approved organizational plan in concert with the data warehouse design and implementation stages.

    3.1.   Develop proposed organizational design.

    3.2.   Develop proposed staff management schedule (education, retraining, reallocation, reassignment, or replacement).

    3.3.   Develop human resource communication, review, and feedback mechanisms.

    3.4.   Implement and monitor organizational change process in concert with the business process and technology implementation schedules.

Organizational Infrastructure Environment Considerations

The following list offers additional considerations that should be kept in mind when implementing the organizational planning framework discussed here.

- Different cultural values and business drivers across the business units within scope
- State of change or flux within the current IT organization
- Impending major business changes in terms of downsizing or rightsizing that may be due for implementation
- Impending acquisition or deployment of new business operations and their potential impact on the available staff level and core competencies
- Availability, interest, and commitment level of the parties concerned in the process
- Overall position of the business within its industry segment in terms of its ability to accept and rapidly adjust to the changing market (business track record of success dealing with change)

CHAPTER SIXTEEN

Production Performance Tuning

INTRODUCTION TO PRODUCTION PERFORMANCE TUNING

In the last chapter, we reviewed design and implementation mechanisms for constructing the data warehousing environment. Now we venture into the world of maintenance and review various considerations for maintaining our environment. Six factors come into play when dealing with ongoing data warehouse performance monitoring.

1. The data warehouse grows exponentially over time in terms of size and processing requirements.

2. Your capacity management estimates, even based on the most precise calculations, are most likely to be still too conservative, requiring you consider scaling up sooner than planned.

3. Data staging is an ongoing challenge, especially if your source systems are constantly in a state of flux due to problems and/or changes. Some may be due for replacement under an ERP initiative, causing massive changes to how data are sourced in the future.

4. Advances in technology in terms of network, hardware, and software require more rapid release changes to be applied (necessitating the establishment of a well thought out product certification process).

5. If not addressed during design and implementation, archiving of stale or little used data warehouse data eventually becomes an issue. Archiving is not a choice, but rather a fact of life, even for data warehouses.

6. Ad hoc query access grows over time and must be carefully monitored as unsophisticated users continue to run requests against base tables rather than summary or aggregate tables to produce totals. An ongoing training program for business analysts, executives, and decision support tool programmers keeps everyone informed as how best to tackle the current version of the data warehouse or mart and find the information they need.

PERFORMANCE TUNING MECHANISMS

Performance issues in data warehousing are centralized around access performance for running queries and incremental loading of snapshot changes from the source systems. Important choke points for performance tuning include how we address

- Query management
- Data loading performance
- Network management

QUERY MANAGEMENT

Some considerations for query management include

- Ensure that the bulk of your predefined and ad hoc queries access summary instead of detail data. Employ query navigators (if available) to redirect base table queries to the aggregate and summary table level.
- Monitor which tables and columns were accessed and the number of rows retrieved. Check response times for these queries and any impacts as (e.g., paging, locking). Another strategy for monitoring usage is to establish charge back algorithms and establish thresholds.
- For predefined queries, break them down into smaller queries for processing.
- Consider doing most of your resource intensive processing away from the current level of detail.
- Consider running large queries during nonpeak hours.

- Push query processing up from the client to the application server level. As part of end user workstation design, consider the employment of thin clients, forcing query processing and scheduling up to the server level.
- Data should be distributed in a hierarchical manner where the most common information has the least amount of distribution and the least common information has the highest level of distribution.
- Allow information access users to follow a hierarchical path when searching for data.
- Minimize the amount of cross network data retrieval and combination of data from different locations.

DATA LOADING PERFORMANCE

Performance impacts on data loading is affected by

- The decreasing batch window (even using data mirroring) to load data from more and more sources, coupled with increased usage of the data warehouse.
- The frequency and size of these loads.
- The changing nature of these loads as source systems change or are replaced.
- The increasing demand for more metadata regarding the data to be loaded.
- If load performance remains an issue, consider maintaining a synchronous replica of the full database to source data to the warehouse. (Remember disk is cheap.)

All these issues mean that we must plan for and monitor performance on an ongoing basis. Creating a performance management system that logs all relevant data or selecting a product that provides this functionality will arm you with a critical tool in the fight to keep on top of the growing data management challenge.

How you load data is even more important than what you load. Do not consider loading data based on real time source to target mapping. Data quality is hard to monitor with this method, and critical performance problems do occur that affect the source systems and the data warehouse. Some key techniques to consider include

1. Dropping all indexes and rebuilding them after the load completes

2. Turning off row level locking (if possible)

3. Utilizing the DBMS's bulk loading facilities (if any)

4. Turning off DBMS journaling

5. Ensuring that the data staging tables map directly to the data warehouse data mart tables

6. Doing as much calculation and preparation of derived data as possible in the data staging environment

7. Cleaning and transforming the data in the data staging environment prior to loading

8. Planning the partitioning or segmenting of the big dimensions of your warehouse, such as customer and product, by subtype, defining each to separate physical tables prior to mapping the data across the disk drives

9. Tuning the parallel loading features of your processors

10. Making available time window to resubmit corrections flagged as errors and dropped from the initial load

11. Determining and scaling up the bandwidth of your network to accommodate more traffic, for example, assuming 15 GB of change data per day at

    - 1 MB per second will take 4.1 hours to load
    - 10 MB per second will take 25 minutes to load
    - 100 MB per second will take 2.5 minutes to load

NETWORK MANAGEMENT

In developing a network strategy, consider the limitations of your current environment, as if it were not structured for the type of use you are now intending to place on it. Using mechanisms like ODBC to move small amounts of data in batch for periodic updates is one thing; moving massive amounts of data for both loading and querying on an ongoing basis requires careful planning. Your available network capacity impacts your data warehouse data management plan (data topology). High volume data access and data loading over slow pipes results in unacceptable performance. In an ideal world we define our database management layer first, before identifying the required network infrastructure. If a network infrastructure already exists, however, capacity planning must be completed before the data topology design for the data warehouse is finalized. Consider the protocols available with your extraction transformation software, database, and information access software. Are they compatible or extendable? With the closing of the gap between technologies such as Asynchronous Transfer Mode (ATM) and Fiber Distributed Data Interface (FDDI), the distinction between the two greatly decreases. This increased compatibility and integration eases the planning of parallel based architectures with respect to data distribution and access, ranging over today's parallel server architecture, local and wide area networks.

These parallel architectures are transparent to the end user. The knowledge worker accessing the DW decision support system views the virtual parallel system through his or her personal workstation not caring if the access is local or distributed. His or her main consideration is and will always remain based on performance, how much and how fast our architecture can provide the answers to a growing list of more complex and extensive business questions.

In developing a strategy for data staging and data replication consider the following:

- Use the DBMS's own data movement facilities to move data asynchronously between database systems.

- Use application program controlled asynchronous data movement when data from multiple sources are required to insert aggregate data.

- Data movement to multidimensional databases should rely on the data extract and movement facilities supplied by the multidimensional software vendor.

- Along the same lines, unstructured data movement should be managed by the products (e.g., document, multimedia) vendor.

- What role will data replication play in data warehouse database management? Data replication should be considered only when either
  - Data mirroring is required
  - Data distribution is required
  - Data movement of a subset of a data warehouse is required to update one or more dimensions of one or more marts that require this information

- Data replication should never be considered as a replacement for the data staging process by moving data directly from source systems to either an operational data store, data warehouse, and/or data mart.

CAPACITY PLANNING

Capacity planning consists of a number of key principles or objectives that include

- Translating expected service requirements into resource requirements and maintenance costs for the warehouse.
- Identifying alternative configurations to satisfy these requirements.
- Evaluating the impact of increased/new workload requirements on service levels for the information access and data staging environments.
- Developing both short and long range capacity plans for the warehouse.
- Assisting current configuration and performance tuning activities as indicated here for the data warehouse database environment and information access and data staging environments.

In capacity planning some key considerations include

- There is a direct relationship between data storage requirements and processing power. Processing in the data warehouse must be physically separate from the operational system due to the unpredictable nature of the query environment.
- Disk storage requirements is a sum of the level of detail stored, the length of time data are required to be kept, and the number of occurrences to be stored in each table.

Key benefits for implementing a capacity planning process for the data warehouse include

1. Improving decision making by providing
   - More complete forecasts over expected increases in future resource requirements
   - "What if" analysis over the potential impact of workload growth on service levels and resource requirements

- Ability to evaluate multiple resource combinations to determine the most cost effective option

2. Improving overall planning and control by providing

   - Better resource planning based on user service requirements
   - Enhanced reporting to track actual activities to plan in order to identify capacity problems so that solutions can be determined before they impact service levels

3. Improving productivity by providing

   - Selection, analysis and implementation of automated tools and standardized procedures that will allow for a reduction in the work effort required to prepare alternatives

4. Achieving stated objectives by providing

   - The ability to forecast resource requirements
   - A more reliable service by identifying the resources required to meet service levels
   - Information to justify additional resources based on service requirements

When considering the scalability of the technical infrastructure for capacity planning, consider

- How much data can the DBMS realistically handle?
- How is the data to be stored? How will it be compressed, encoded, and indexed?
- Can locking be suppressed?
- Can and how will queries be monitored and suppressed?

Processor capacity is a function of the workload passing through the environment, consisting of

- Background processing of incremental updates to the data warehouse
- Known or monitored business decision support processing based on
  - The number of times a process will run
  - The number of I/Os a process will use

- Whether the process has a peak period
- The expected end user response time based on the service level agreement
- Unknown query processing based on ad hoc queries are calculated by
  - Calculating expected response times in minutes, hours, or days
  - The total amount of expected I/O
  - Whether the system can be quiesced during the running of the request
  - Tuning the processor to provide more CPU resources during high peak utilization

Capacity Planning (Performance Management) Data Warehouse Checklist

As part of the technical infrastructure design the following checklist can be utilized to establish the measures and mechanisms for a capacity management process.

1. Conduct a capacity management (CP) assessment.
   1.1. Establish scope for the proposed effort. (Identify what resources should be studied such as processors, DASD, Network, or sites. Define what planning horizon is to be studied such as planning cycles and target dates.)
   1.2. Review available capacity management processes.
   1.3. Review source and target data warehouse/mart databases, data staging, and information access systems.
   1.4. Assess the proposed or current capacity of the data warehouse environment. (For example review performance reports and any current service levels). Summarize and document all concerns that are readily apparent. Identify quick hits in the form of any tuning or operational improvements.
   1.5. Review service quality. (Compare expected to actual service levels; determine any changes required to current capacity plans.)
2. Analyze business requirements.
   2.1. Define CP workloads. (Workloads are used to determine how changes in use of data warehouse monitoring resources will occur.)

   2.2. Define CP forecasts. (Forecast anticipated or projected growth [or decline] in volumes of occurrences of the business indicators for each workload.)

   2.3. Define service levels. (Document identifying anticipated service level requirements, costs, and workloads. These can also be determined from an existing OLTP Facilities Management Agreement if any.)

3. Develop/refine current procedures.

   3.1. Characterize workloads. (Break down workloads into criteria such as jobs, DASD and CPU usage, transaction volumes, and response times.)

   3.2. Determine performance modeling approaches. (Select methods for ongoing use such as benchmarking approaches or linear calculations.)

   3.3. Determine statistical data to be collected. (Determine what data need to be collected, and create, test, and install any tasks or systems software necessary to collect that data.)

   3.4. Identify limitations and constraints. (Determine what limitations there are for new/enhanced acquisitions. Analyze procedural changes, budgets, vendor agreements, and IT operations policies.)

   3.5. Develop capacity models. (Develop DW capacity models and validate them against actual results, applying forecast projections.)

   3.6. Develop CP support group. (Develop roles, responsibilities, and procedures for the CP group of the data warehouse team.)

   3.7. Develop selection criteria. (Create hardware and software selection criteria and features that are critical and need to be purchased to meet future demands.)

   3.8. Conduct vendor selection. (Consult the vendor selection process in Section Two for a detailed review of the required tasks and deliverables.)

   3.9. Analyze acquisition costs. (Review products and services costs and/or analyze strategies to reduce costs such as leasing, renting, or timing of large purchases, and prepare findings for review and approval.)

4. Assemble materials and obtain approval for implementation.

   4.1. Prepare findings for IT management review and approval.

   4.2. Refine and implement CP process in concert with DW implementation.

Section Four

Data Warehouse Support and Maintenance

OVERVIEW

In Section Three we reviewed the data warehouse project development life cycle and infrastructure activities. With our data warehouse increment in place, we can now address related issues that augment our production environment—establishing and maintaining ongoing communication and training, providing help support services, and managing technical infrastructure updates concerning new releases of hardware, software, and services. This section augments our discussion of these topics by providing in depth information focused on specific maintenance and support activities (which often are not addressed as part of the data warehouse project development life cycle).

This section covers the following topics by discussing a number of essential, ongoing concerns.

1. Keeping in touch with the business by conducting ongoing corporate education into the features, benefits, and current capabilities of the data warehousing environment
2. Gathering feedback and providing proactive support
3. Coordinating training for developers, support staff, and users of the data warehousing environment
4. Providing problem resolution management coordination and integration through existing, or augmented, help desk services
5. Planning for the migration of project team support to operations support
6. Establishing, maintaining, and reviewing development, test, and production environments as well as product/release certification to production

Section Four includes a number of mechanisms, in the form of deliverable templates, worksheets, and presentations, to assist you in your data warehouse support and maintenance efforts.

Additional information on impacted or related activities is also contained on the companion CD ROM. To drill into the complete library of data on this and all other sections, consult the CD or Section Five for a complete inventory of available materials.

CHAPTER SEVENTEEN

Communication and Training

INTRODUCTION

Communication and training are two interrelated activities. A communication program keeps the business user and IT community informed on the current and proposed future enhancements to the data warehousing environment. A communication process also offers a feedback loop to the data warehouse team to chart progress and proactively identify and resolve issues before they become a serious concern. The communication program can be augmented with an internal marketing activity that "shops" the features and capabilities of the data warehouse to the rest of the business as part of an ongoing activity. Training augments the communication process by maintaining a level competence in both the business and IT community as to the tools and mechanisms of the data warehouse. Both these initiatives are dealt with in more of a cursory fashion during a data warehousing project, since any one project release does not usually have the time or resources to develop an extensive program. Having implemented our data warehouse, we can now tackle these critical success factors as part of infrastructure support.

THE COMMUNICATION PROCESS

The purpose of the communication process is to improve the understanding, attitude, and commitment of the various players who are involved in the data warehousing process. Communication processes for data warehouse project and program support address the following areas:

- Corresponding with internal and external groups to the project
- Scheduling deliverable reviews and conducting meetings (e.g, status, issues)
- Providing assistance to quality assurance representatives
- Coordinating notification when project milestones are reached

The scope of your selected communication program should identify the audience to be communicated to, the key messages to relay, and the type of communication and its frequency. This is accomplished by

1. Offering a scheduled program of education and training

2. Developing and sustaining vision clarity for the data warehousing environment

3. Provide a feedback or suggestion loop in terms of an online or paper suggestion form and formal recognition and feedback process.

4. Reduce communication costs by consolidating and eliminating duplicate forms, resource requirements, and procedures.

5. Provide a place or group to contact outside the help desk to address concerns or to act as a contact point for marketing data warehousing services to new business units.

6. Invite participation from interested parties to data warehouse planning, analysis, and design sessions.

7. Host vendor forms on the features and functions of the current technology.

8. Coordinate site visits by interested IT and business users.

9. Coordinate visits to industry events and conferences on data warehousing

10. Identify and manage influential relationships among key data warehouse stakeholders.

Figure 17–1

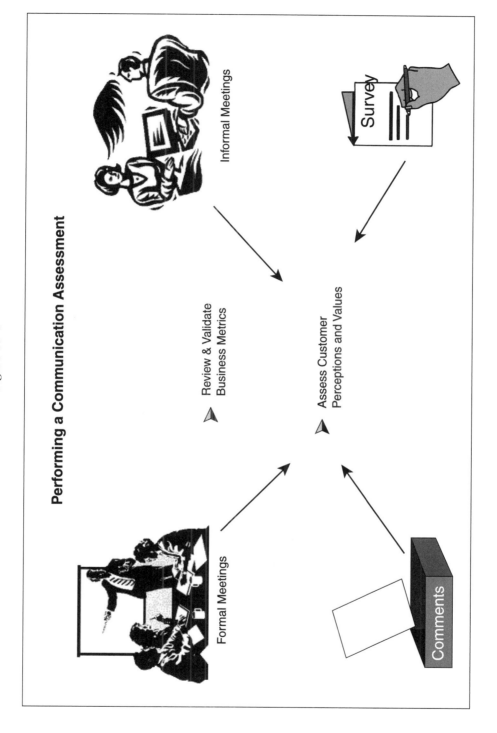

Performing a Communication Assessment

Informal Meetings

Survey

Review & Validate
Business Metrics

Assess Customer
Perceptions and Values

Formal Meetings

Comments

11. Provide project communication deliverables for review and input by business and IT participants and sponsors such as

    • Project charters or mandate documents

    • Business cases

    • Project plans and budgets

    • Current state IT and business assessments

    • Data quality reviews

    • Reviewing on line or manual help facilities and documentation

    • Testing and training processes feedback

    • Publishing a communication newsletter or brochure (on line and or paper based) promoted by a wide subscription base

    • Delivering project milestone and on request presentations to project sponsors, management, and steering committee members

The Communication Process Checklist

The following activities describe the definition and implementation of a communication program for data warehousing. A communication plan should be initiated for medium or large scale data warehousing projects discussed in Section Two. These types of projects are delivered in multiple iterations; therefore, an ongoing communication process is critical for success. Data mart projects that cross lines of business or where the focus is on corporate or executive information analysis should also consider implementing a communication program as a required infrastructure process.

1. Initiate data warehouse communication program planning.

    1.1. Establish a core team and develop a budget plan.

    1.2. Establish IT and business sponsorship for the process by conducting awareness sessions.

    1.3. Develop an initial position statement or approach for a steering committee and/or sponsorship review.

    1.4. Define a functional framework for the components and procedures to be developed.

    1.5. Establish a list of recommended technology components and standards.

  1.6. Review and approve the proposed approach, functional architecture, and technology components and standards.

2. Conduct data warehouse communication program design.

  2.1. Analyze current communication channels and mechanisms.

  2.2. Define vendor to internal IT involvement responsibility in this process.

  2.3. Determine which communication components to buy versus build.

  2.4. Conduct the vendor selection, evaluation process (refer to the process defined in Chapter 11: Finding, Evaluating, and Contracting Vendors).

  2.5. Define the timing and frequency of the proposed communication process.

  2.6. Determine the required supporting organizational structure, and conduct communication team training.

  2.7. Design and test the required organizational structure, roles and responsibilities, deliverables, and procedures of the communication program and required interfaces to the data warehouse project development life cycle, help desk function, and program office.

  2.8. Design communication and marketing procedures in conjunction with the interested business units.

  2.9. Develop components of a recognition program.

  2.10. Compile a proposed implementation and support plan.

  2.11. Develop and obtain IT approval for a data warehouse communication plan recommendation report.

3. Implement the data warehouse communication program.

  3.1. Confirm completeness of all design stage components, processes, human resources, and facilities.

  3.2. Prepare and coordinate a production implementation or rollover schedule.

  3.3. Select and train communication team members.

  3.4. Set up facilities, reporting, and feedback procedures and the supporting desktop environment.

  3.5. Install and verify all production components and facilities.

  3.6. Review and approve the data warehouse communication program implementation.

Key deliverables include

Out of this process the following documents, procedures, facilities, and systems capabilities are developed to deliver the data warehouse communication program.

1. Communication program mandate or charter containing
   - Program goals and objectives
   - Program plan and budget
   - Program organization structure and staffing approach
   - Program change management and issue resolution process
   - Program standards to be initiated
   - Program procedures to be delivered
2. Communication program facility location(s) and staffing
3. Communication program automated and manual procedures and forms to address
   - Data warehouse program office requirements
   - Data warehouse project involvement in terms of individual, team, and external feedback and review
   - Help desk interface
   - Human resources interface
   - Data warehouse program marketing

The effectiveness of your communication program will be in direct proportion to the amount of time, effort, and visibility you place on this essential infrastructure process. Good and frequent communication between development team members, users, and project managers and sponsors will assist you through the many peaks and valleys to come as you prepare to deliver and maintain your data warehouse.

THE TRAINING PROGRAM

The training program coordinates the development and delivery of the necessary education services to the data warehousing environment. A training program is geared toward providing scheduled education in support of data warehouse project increments as well as nonproject related training in the form of the general vendor tools or system training.

Figure 17-2

Training Benefits

Client Benefits

☐ Focus on Client Priorities

☐ Enhanced Client Relationships

☐ Conduct Ongoing Skills Transfer

Project Team Benefits

☐ Increased Project Satisfaction

☐ Increased Job Satisfaction

☐ Enhanced IT to Business Communication

☐ Maintained Big Picture Perspective

Training is an essential skills and confidence building exercise. People who have been adequately prepared for what is to come will perform better and more consistently than those who are cast into a new business process with little understanding of what is expected of them. Therefore, to ensure the success of our data warehouse, training should be geared toward providing

1. Training and enhancement of individual skills

2. Providing general education of the data warehouse industry

3. Defining a training curriculum in support of the data warehouse business systems, infrastructure processes, and data quality management environments

4. Developing or acquiring training software

5. Delivering or contracting the delivery of training

6. Coordinating all training plans and budgets across data warehousing initiatives

7. Coordinating with the program office and project communication teams on the training process and results achieved

8. Providing feedback on the ease of use of the technology tools and procedures to the program office and project and communication teams

9. Providing skills assessments of business and IT users of the proposed data warehousing environment

10. Providing infrastructure training to the data warehouse development and support teams on the related project management and technical infrastructure layers

The Training Process Checklist

The following activities describe the definition and implementation of a training program for data warehousing. A training plan should be initiated for medium or large data warehousing projects discussed in Section Two. These types of projects are delivered in multiple iterations; therefore an ongoing training process is critical for success in implementing and using the growing data warehousing environment. Data mart projects that cross lines of business or where the focus is on corporate or executive information should also consider implementing a training program as a required infrastructure process. The following process is developed during data warehouse planning and analysis and is rolled out during data warehouse design and implementation (if this is the first project to be delivered). Otherwise the training program can be interleaved within the data warehousing project life cycle commencing with the design stage (unless new technology or data warehousing environment processes are being rolled out for the first time).

1. Initiate data warehouse training program planning.
    1.1. Establish a core team and develop a budget plan.
    1.2. Establish IT and business sponsorship for the process by conducting awareness sessions.
    1.3. Develop an initial position statement or approach for steering committee and/or sponsorship review.
    1.4. Define a functional framework for the components and procedures to be developed.
    1.5. Establish a list of recommended technology components and standards.
    1.6. Review and approve the proposed approach, functional architecture, and technology components and standards.

2. Conduct data warehouse training program design.
    2.1. Analyze current training channels and mechanisms.
    2.2. Define vendor to internal IT involvement and responsibility in this process.
    2.3. Determine which training components to buy versus build.
    2.4. Conduct the vendor selection, evaluation process (refer to process defined in Chapter 11: Finding, Evaluating, and Contracting Vendors).
    2.5. Define the timing and frequency of the proposed training's process.
    2.6. Determine the required supporting organizational structure and conduct training developer team training.
    2.7. Design and test the required organizational structure, roles and responsibilities, deliverables, and procedures of the training program and required interfaces to the data warehouse project development life cycle, help desk function, and program office.

2.8. Design "train the trainer" procedures in conjunction with the interested business units.

2.9. Compile a proposed implementation and support plan.

2.10. Develop and obtain IT approval for a data warehouse training plan recommendation report.

3. Implement the data warehouse training program.

3.1. Confirm completeness of all designed components, processes, human resources, and facilities.

3.2. Prepare and coordinate implementation of the training program in support of data warehousing efforts.

3.3. Select and train delivery or user team members.

3.4. Set up facilities, reporting, and feedback procedures and the supporting desktop environment for the training program.

3.5. Install and verify all production components and facilities.

3.6. Review and approve the data warehouse training program implementation.

Key deliverables include

Out of this process the following documents, procedures, facilities, and systems capabilities are developed to deliver the data warehouse training program:

1. Training program mandate or charter containing
   - Program goals and objectives
   - Program plan and budget
   - Program organization structure and staffing approach
   - Program change management and issue resolution process
   - Program standards to be initiated
   - Program procedures to be delivered

2. Training program facility location(s) and staffing

3. Training program automated and manual procedures to address
   - Data warehouse program office requirements

- Data warehouse project involvement in terms of individual, team, and external feedback and review on the technology being delivered and the usefulness of the training provided
- Training program scheduling
- Training procedures for tools and data warehousing process education (e.g., education of the features and functions of a new decision support system)
- Help desk interface into training support issues
- Human resources interface for skills assessment and employee profile updating

Communication and training are two essential change management processes that enable both the technology and user communities to more rapidly accept and deploy this new business technology. By focusing on these two critical human resource development functions we have gone a long way toward assuring the success of our data warehousing initiative.

CHAPTER EIGHTEEN

Help Desk and Problem Management

INTRODUCTION

Part of the ongoing support and maintenance of a data warehouse involve how the data warehouse group, or an external IT support function manages problem resolution. A help desk acts as a coordinating body for not only collecting and logging problems with the data warehouse environment, but also determining where future requirements may lay. In some organizations, the data warehouse help service is seen as an extension to an existing OLTP help desk based program while in others a separate organization is struck to deal with the distinctive nature of this environment. Within this context, the problem management process is our vehicle for recording and resolving issues as they arise, again pointing the way toward future improvements or the need for new functionality in our warehouse. Problems can be maintenance, enhancement based, or they can point the way toward new development. The problem management process, much like the project change management process, acts as a vehicle for initiating and determining the nature of work for our maintenance, enhancement, or new development data warehousing projects (described in Section Two).

THE ROLE OF THE HELP DESK

A help desk acts as an extension to the user and as an assistant to the data warehouse support group. For the end user the help desk addresses a number of issues that include

293

1. Security and sign on (from the client network, or remote)
2. Access to detail or aggregated data stored in a warehouse, operational data store, or data mart
3. Data staging or data quality management problems
4. Ad hoc query processing
5. Predefined and scheduled reports or automated routine processing
6. System response time

For the data warehouse IT support and monitoring team, the help desk quickly points out challenges and issues revolving around

1. Installation of new functionality
2. Certification of new hardware or software
3. Facility or network capacity thresholds
4. Scheduled job performance and environment backups

The help desk, based on its authority and expertise of its staff members, resolves, redirects, or escalates a problem event that has occurred. Help desk services are provided in a number of ways including

1. By phone
2. By access to Intranet or Internet based help
3. In person
4. Through the automated help facilities available in the software or the decision support application

DEVELOPING A HELP DESK

The stages of growth for a help desk are much like that of the data warehouse. Initially, these services should be provided by the data warehouse implementation and monitoring team for a period up to three to six months, or until the new data warehouse increment is established and relatively problem free. For enhancements or maintenance efforts, this level of support can be reduced to two months and one month respectively. After establishing a help desk function as part of the role out process, responsibility for this service can be passed to IT. With the migration of this service away from the core group of expertise, training and support of help desk personnel must become part of the overall data warehouse training program. Due to the more volatile nature of this technology, support of help desk personnel is critical to their ability to provide good service. Unlike the OLTP environment, help desk personnel are faced with a large degree of the unknown, based on the ad hoc and unpredictable nature of the query environment they support. Additional challenges these staff members will face include

- Understanding the functionality of changing DSS, EIS, and modeling software
- The potential impact of rapid growth causing changes to processors, network bandwidth, and disk storage capacity
- The critical importance of error free data staging and what can happen if problems related to incremental data refresh runs are not quickly addressed

PROVIDING HELP DESK SERVICES

Help desk services are provided from a central call center, or they are distributed to the various business locations. If more hands on or personal support is required (especially during the initial months of a major data warehouse installation), this support is usually phased out of the DW group or centralized over time. Other options include "train the trainer" approach, where local representatives are given more extensive product and application based training than the average end user. Other options for providing help desk services include identifying local "power users," those more in tune with the technology or using a much broader band of the available services. These people can be tapped in a backup or support role to the help desk. To keep them interested, these talented staff can be offered "first look" and more proactive involvement in future software selections or service enhancements.

In deploying a help desk function for the first time, consider the following task list as your guide to laying out a framework for establishing this vital infrastructure service. Medium to large scale data warehousing projects (as highlighted in Section Two) should include this task list along with its associated deliverables as a critical component of their project plan.

A checklist for deploying a help desk

1. Initiate data warehouse help desk planning.
    1.1. Establish a core team and develop a budget plan.
    1.2. Establish IT and business sponsorship for the process by conducting awareness sessions.
    1.3. Develop an initial position statement or approach for steering committee and/or sponsorship review.
    1.4. Define a functional framework for the components and procedures to be developed.
    1.5. Establish a list of recommended technology components and standards.
    1.6. Review and approve the proposed approach, functional architecture, and technology components and standards.
2. Conduct data warehouse help desk design.
    2.1 Analyze current help facilities and mechanisms.
    2.2. Define IT involvement and responsibility in this process.
    2.3. Determine which help desk components to buy versus build.
    2.4. Conduct the vendor selection, evaluation process (refer to the process defined in Chapter 11: Finding, Evaluating and Contracting Vendors).
    2.5. Determine the required supporting organizational structure and conduct help desk team training.
    2.6. Design and test the required organizational structure, roles and responsibilities, deliverables, and procedures of the help desk and required interfaces to the data warehouse project implementation and monitoring team and data warehouse program office.
    2.7. Design "train the trainer" procedures in conjunction with interested business unit support team participants.
    2.8. Compile a proposed implementation and support plan.
    2.9. Develop and obtain IT approval for a data warehouse help desk service.

3. Implement the data warehouse help desk

   3.1. Confirm completeness of all designed components, processes, human resources, and facilities.

   3.2. Prepare and coordinate implementation of the help desk in support of data warehousing efforts.

   3.3. Set up facilities, reporting and feedback procedures, and the supporting desktop environment for the help desk.

   3.4. Install and verify all production components and facilities.

   3.5. Review and approve the data warehouse help desk implementation.

Key deliverables include

   Out of this process the following documents, procedures, facilities, and systems capabilities are developed to deliver the data warehouse help desk process.

1. Help desk mandate or proposal containing

   • Goals and objectives

   • Plans and budget projections for facilities, equipment, personnel, etc.

   • Organization structure and staffing approach

   • Problem management and issue resolution process

   • Standards to be initiated

   • Procedures to be delivered

2. Help desk facility location(s) and staffing

3. Help desk automated and manual procedures addressing

   • Data warehouse program office requirements

   • Data warehouse project involvement in terms of individual, team, and external feedback and review on the technology being delivered and the usefulness of the services provided

   • Help desk staff scheduling

   • Training procedures for tools and data warehousing process education (e.g., education of the features and functions of a new decision support system)

- Help desk interface into training support issues
- Human resources interface for skills assessment and employee profile updating

THE PROBLEM MANAGEMENT PROCESS

The problem management process is the glue that holds the help desk together. This process specifies how to collect, document, answer, and/or escalate calls, requests, and queries related to issues with the data warehousing environment. Problem documentation can be completed either by the help desk representative and/or in conjunction with a form completed by the end user or IT support person requesting a service or action. All inquires, no matter how trivial, should be logged, especially during the start of a new data warehouse or mart. These bits of information can form clues to taking proactive action to bigger problems before they emerge. Having a production ready data warehouse means support must be expedited in an efficient, responsive, and businesslike manner. At stake is the ability of the business to stay competitive if the business information the warehouse contains is not current, accurate, timely, and available when needed. This thought must be kept in mind by all help desk personnel as they strive to answer those nagging questions: why queries don't run the way or as fast as they expect.

DEVELOPING A PROBLEM MANAGEMENT PROCESS

The problem management process is developed entirely from scratch or it is implemented using an available IT procedure (if one exists). Problem management routines are defined using vendor services in conjunction with their data warehouse monitoring software. It is always best to refine what is available, rather than having to build a new procedure from scratch, especially if this is the first problem management process created by your business. A good problem management process, integrated within the overall functionality of the help desk, is critical for ongoing success in data warehousing. Unresponsive or inefficient procedures inevitably lead to data warehouse performance, usability, and availability issues in the near future. Major challenges faced by some early installations do not often come to the attention of management in time. Good documentation, much like responsive, timely support is critical to our success.

PROBLEM MANAGEMENT PROCESS

The following procedure highlights a problem management process. This process utilizes the problem report and follow up action/resolution forms described on the companion CD. The two primary vehicles for problem management are the problem report forms and the problem log.

PROBLEM MANAGEMENT PROCEDURE

1. When an issue or problem is identified and raised by an end user, help desk support person or IT/DW support or monitoring team member concerning the performance of the DW records the event.

2. If the problem cannot be resolved by immediate action, then an initial entry in a problem record is created. The problem is given the status of "open" and is assigned a follow on action owner. Whoever raised the problem is designated as the problem reporter.

3. As action is taken, it is documented as an entry against the problem. Every individual taking an action on a problem makes an entry in the problem log and decides who should be notified next.

4. Numerous actions may be required before a problem is resolved. Unresolved problems are escalated through the data warehouse project's escalation mechanism on a regular basis.

5. When a problem is resolved, the follow on action owner is specified as the original reporter. The original help desk reporter should be the only individual who can close a problem unless it was reassigned during problem resolution to another person.

6. When the reporter receives notification of problem resolution, he or she determines if it can be closed. If the person or group determines that the problem cannot be closed, then it is returned to the help desk for reassignment. A decision to reopen the problem is then documented as an action entry in the problem management log.

All problems, no matter how trivial, should be documented, especially if related to new development or enhancement data warehouse project. In the event that a problem remains open and requires authority beyond that of the help desk, then the problem should be escalated immediately to the data warehouse program or project leader.

Deliverables Produced Out of This Process

Out of this process the following documents, procedures, facilities, and systems capabilities are developed to deliver the data warehouse problem management process.

- Problem management log
- Problem report form
- Problem action form
- Problem resolution form

CHAPTER NINETEEN

Certifying Software and Installing Hardware Upgrades

INTRODUCTION

Updates to our data warehouse will be inevitable; so, too, will be changes to package software, hardware servers, and our supporting network infrastructure. Three strategies are available to make changes to this technical layer depending upon the scope, timeframe, and criticality of our data warehouse environment. These strategies include

1. Installing new software releases or patches, hardware components or upgrades, and network connections (logical and physical) directly in the production environment
2. Installing new software versions, hardware upgrades, and network improvements in a temporary test environment and migrate or reconnect/reconfigure to production once certification testing has concluded
3. Installing our technical infrastructure changes into a permanent test or maintenance environment and migrate/reconfigure the production environment once certification testing has concluded

Three implementation approaches exist to implement these strategies

- Peer to peer
- Master to slave
- Hybrid

The Traditional Approach (Peer to Peer)

The traditional approach has each environment act as a distinct entity. This entails a large first data warehouse iteration, to be followed by smaller migrations of critical components over time. Because we are moving between distinct environments, this approach is the most time consuming and costly to adopt as a standard practice on an ongoing basis. This approach, however, safely isolates certification testing from the production environment.

One Master Environment (Master Slave)

The master/slave approach utilizes one environment for integrating changes and upgrades (from master to slave). The benefit of this system is that new functionality and components are integrated and tested in one place as various new features and capabilities are "bolted on." Under this scenario the master releases control to the slave once certification is completed.

A Hybrid Approach

In some cases, a combination, or hybrid, approach is adopted based on the type and nature of the certification requirement. For example, a traditional approach may be adequate for migrations of software releases but not so for upgrades to the network topology.

These three aspects of software and hardware installation are further complicated by the differing requirements between software, hardware, and networking components, since the features and functions of each product should align (e.g., a DBMS with strong parallelism features should be deployed on data servers with the same properties). For implementation of new software, hardware, and network devices our considerations should include

1. For software releases, we are concerned with the potential impact of changes to code and data structures. Even a simple unload/reload can become quite time consuming, especially if we are dealing with a VLDB implementation. In such cases, the users lose access to their data for a period of time unless some type of data mirroring is employed. At this level we are concerned with managing changes to

a. Information access services consisting of

   I. *Database services containing database access requirements and synchronization/staging and replication*

   II. *Data sharing services consisting of local and remote processing*

   III. *Media management services consisting of document and folder management*

   IV. *File services*

   V. *Code table services*

   VI. *Transition services*

2. For hardware component installation or upgrades to servers or disk, there is the challenge of testing and certifying the enhanced capacity without affecting end user performance and the stability of the environment, on or after the upgrade is made. The options available largely depend upon the processor technology used since Cluster, SMP, MPP, and NUMA architectures have differing requirements for how the client and desktop technology are deployed. Here we are concerned with changes to

   a. Transaction services consisting of resource and transactions management, transaction partitioning, and TP monitor

   b. Environment services consisting of

      I. *Operating systems services containing*

   • Batch and report services for data staging containing drivers, restart/recovery, batch balancing, and reporting services

      II. *System services containing systems profiles, tasks managers, environment verification, and user and data security requirements*

      III. *Application services containing error recovery, transaction logging, common services, and external interface management*

      IV. *Client presentation services including windows operating system, desktop management, and interaction/response services that cover form filling, direct manipulation, graphics, window terminal emulation, multimedia, and report preview and printing*

3. The challenges for our network/communications environment are often even more significant, especially if our data and systems are spread across geographic regions and/or global boundaries. Enhancing the bandwidth and the ability of the network components and servers to

handle an ever increasing flow of network traffic, as well as managing the differing types of protocols, often results in significant and risky challenges if not thought out and planned for well in advance. A number of components come into play at the network level (including workflow and communication services). Components to consider for communications management include

a. For workflow services

  I. *Role management*

  II. *Route management*

  III. *Rule management*

  IV. *Queue management*

b. For communication services

  I. *Directory services*

  II. *Message management consisting of*

   • Store and forward mechanisms

   • Asynchronous data transfer

   • Synchronous data transfer

  III. *Message services that can be either function or message based*

c. File transfer services

d. Print services

e. Terminal emulation services

f. Communication system software

THE CERTIFICATION TESTING PROCESS

The following is a generic certification testing procedure for dealing with product certification issues. It describes overall management, training, procedure and script definition, and project control mechanisms that are required to provide due diligence to a testing process.

1. Initiate product certification

  1.1. Collect data warehouse environment product certification requirements.

   1.2. Review certification product(s) requested for conformance to existing or future architecture.

   1.3. Nominate core team members to the certification team based upon the scope of certification to be conducted.

   1.4. Define a certification strategy.

   1.5. Develop/enhance certification project plan and budget from the strategy.

   1.6. Identify required roles and responsibilities to implement the plan and nominate staff to each position.

   1.7. Propose certification budget and plan for approval.

2. Establish certification team environment.

   2.1. Define certification project team work location and desktop environment.

   2.2. Staff certification team.

   2.3. Obtain licensed copies of product(s) for certification.

   2.4. Develop/obtain certification procedures and test scripts.

   2.5. Train or refresh the certification team to the process.

3. Define certification test environment.

   3.1. Establish test environment for product certification.

   3.2. Obtain data warehouse release stress testing data and procedures for test verification.

   3.3. Develop/refine and install certification test procedures, script, and test data.

4. Undertake certification testing.

   4.1. Install and/or upgrade new product(s).

   4.2. Conduct certification testing of all database, decision support service, data staging, information access, and supporting network topology environment by

      4.2.1. Conducting product installation and test

      4.2.2. Testing database and application components running in that environment

    4.2.3. Conducting stress tests established from the original data warehouse release implementation

    4.2.4. Obtaining signoffs as certification testing is completed over the requested timeframe

5. Conclude certification testing and prepare for production turnover.

    5.1. Update the capacity management plan to include the new features, functionality, and capabilities of the enhanced environment.

    5.2. Schedule the upgrade to the current production data warehousing environment.

    5.3. Advise data warehouse operations support and help desk as to the timing and nature of the upgrade and potential problems and/or issues that can occur.

    5.4. Prepare or enhance existing data warehouse environment documentation.

    5.5. Update all vendor licensing/contracting agreements.

    5.6. Review and revise current service level agreements with the end users.

    5.7. Prepare and obtain documentation for end users and support groups for the new features, benefits, and/or capabilities of the new architecture.

    5.8. Update list of certified and approved products.

    5.9. Prepare certification results for review and approval.

6. Implement certified products.

    6.1. Obtain approval, confirm, and revise product implementation or activation schedule.

    6.2. Back up current production components where applicable.

    6.3. Migrate and activate new product release.

    6.4. Turn over monitoring of new product versions to the data warehouse operations support group.

    6.5. Turn over product problem management and support to the help desk.

    6.6. Close down certification cycle by

        6.6.1. Releasing the certification team to other duties

6.6.2. Closing down or returning environment components to their normal function or role (e.g., shutting down a temporary test environment)

6.6.3. Obtaining signoff for the completion of the certification process

CERTIFICATION PROGRAM DELIVERABLES

In undertaking a certification process such as this one, it is necessary to document what occurred and why and what was in or out of scope through the certification process. The generic deliverables described here discuss the types of information to be collected, which include

- Certification program
- Certification business requirements
- Certification test results

Certification Program

A certification program defines the procedures, schedules, and facilities required to conduct certification testing. It describes the technical version or view of certification testing to the information services owners of the proposed data warehouse infrastructure improvement. To undertake the technical aspect of the certification program the following information is required:

- A certification plan containing a list of steps, dates, and resources presented as a GANTT chart or spreadsheet illustrating the certification testing scope and schedule or references to where this information can be found in electronic format.

- A description of the test cycle(s) and each test cycles, test case, and the order in which they are exercised to verify the functionality of the hardware, software, or network improvement. Each test case consists of expected performance, inputs and outputs, before and after expected results, and a description of each hardware, software, or network product benchmark(s) to be met and a scoring method for testing.

- A description of the automated and manual tools and techniques, if different from the development environment, for testing tools (software and hardware support facilities), test data generation method (generators, data entry, etc.), and test bench marking approach and related techniques.
- A description of the proposed/available certification environment in terms of
  - Software, which identifies any sizing or performance requirements for certification testing if different from the development environment
  - Hardware, which describes the structure of the processor environment (application and data servers) if different from the production version
  - Communications, which identifies any wiring, cable, and networking requirements for certification testing if different from the development environment.
  - User access profiles, which identify tester user access profiles if different from the development environment. Describes the various roles and responsibilities of the certification test team if not available in the project charter.
    - Control procedures describing the validation review points for certification testing and control procedures for migration of test components to the production environment and backup and recovery process to be followed for refreshing the certification testing environment (image backups) and recovering or backing out of certification components installation in the production environment
    - Change and issue management procedures related to the initiation, testing, and conclusion of the certification process

CERTIFICATION BUSINESS REQUIREMENTS

Certification business requirements describes the scope of certification testing in nontechnical terms and any conclusions or recommendations appropriate to the generation of any future enhancements to this or similar such efforts. It is also used to convey this understanding to the business stakeholders and owners of the data warehouse. This deliverable contains the following information:

- The certification program definition explains how the certification program was developed in terms of
  - Buy or build
  - Customized from the current environment and describes the staffing model used to staff the certification program in terms of internal staff or external consulting
- A scope of testing explanation, which describes the scope in terms of duration, impact, risk, and cost of certification testing as detailed in the certification test program and includes information on
- Test schedule, which describes the test plan as a GANTT chart showing timing, testing sequence and resources, and includes
  - A plan/end user introductory seminar schedule
  - A list of facilities or contracted locations
  - Timing and availability of the certification environment
  - Allocated technology components assigned to testing (PCs, printers, etc.)
  - A list of scheduled technicians and business area end users for participation in the certification process
- Risks and issues, describing any risks associated with the certification program in terms of
  - Technical acceptance of the infrastructure improvement
  - Quality of testing or support provided describing any issues or shortcomings falling out of the generation/refinement of the certification program in terms of test coverage, timing and participation, appropriateness, and facilities access and scheduling resources
- Certification program recommendations, which identify any final productivity improvements in terms of
  - Improvement to test cases and test data or criteria
  - Improvement to the feedback mechanisms
  - Instruction support and assistance
  - Improvement to the certification plan in terms of set up, resource allocation, cost, and timeframe

CERTIFICATION TEST RESULTS

Certification test results provides an evaluation on the "state of readiness" of the data warehouse infrastructure improvement, its associated interfaces, and all data or software conversion procedures. It identifies what was tested and what was not tested, what problems or issues remain outstanding, and any procedural impacts, work arounds, or risks. Finally, it provides a recommendation whether to proceed or not proceed to implementation with the hardware, software, or network improvement. This report should contain the following information:

1. A statement of purpose explaining in a few paragraphs the purpose of certification testing and the approach used

2. Certification program results describing the success achieved and an assessment of the state of readiness of the various hardware, software, and network components

3. Support procedures test results describing the success achieved with support procedure testing as a confirmation that all expected help desk, problem logging, start up and shutdown automated, and batch and manual procedures properly support the data warehouse

4. A summary of the certification program, which details the

   • Evaluation method stating how the acceptance test program was evaluated in a few paragraphs. Methods include

     • Interviewing

     • Walk throughs

     • Kit review

     • Feedback assessment

     • Scoring results review

   • Questions used to conduct certification testing and evaluation in terms of

     • Feedback (evaluation of interviews)

     • Program validity (applicability of the certification test program to the supported decision support system and data warehouse)

The focus of these questions is to assess the validity of certification testing. Any outstanding problems or issues describing their associated impacts and any potential work arounds that were identified out of certification testing

- Any final recommendations to proceed or not proceed further in terms of
  - Possible impact on production system performance or capacity management limitations
  - Quality of upgrade based on vendor benchmark reviews and industry surveys as to the stability of the product version and/or time in the market
  - Appropriateness of product functional enhancements (complexity) in terms of ease of use and assimilation by the various classes of end users
- An appendix containing all detailed certification test program material compiled during the testing process, which contains
  - A list of score sheets containing comments from each participant or interviewee
  - Interview notes describing any general findings collected during testing
  - Industry survey results and benchmarks (i.e., TCP D)
  - Site visits, calls, or interview notes
  - Test scripts, test cases, and test scenario documentation

CERTIFICATION PROGRAM BACKGROUND INFORMATION

This section describes some essential background or reference information to keep on hand in developing and managing a certification program environment and deliverables as previously described. This information collection may also be used to measure data warehouse environmental impacts in terms of business decision support improvements and capacity management planning. To manage the data warehouse infrastructure we should maintain information on the following topics:

- Data warehouse database description
- Data warehouse management instructions
- Data warehouse support schedules
- Data warehouse technology profile
- Product evaluation test
- Vendor contact instructions
- Vendor background check
- Vendor product score

DATA WAREHOUSE DATABASE DESCRIPTION

Data warehouse database description describes supporting operational and identification criteria for both logical and physical database designs.

1.0 Data storage descriptions

   1.1 Data storage

     Specifications of libraries, files, and/or data sets where the database design is managed for

- *Development (can include a test and training subenvironment)*
- *Production (distribution environment specifications)*
- *Archive*
- *Disaster recovery (off site production copy)*

   1.2 Data standards specifications

     CASE tool, methodology, or software language standards and versions of the database design software

   1.3 Data distribution details

     Description of the data distribution environment for wide area network or remote accessing systems if appropriate

DATA WAREHOUSE MANAGEMENT INSTRUCTIONS

Data warehouse management instructions describes all instructions related to running database support routines such as backup and recovery.

1.0 Data management support and control instructions

Technical documentation that explains where to find data sets, scripts, and instructions on how to initiate the various data management processes, such as

- Backup/recovery
- Roll forward/roll back
- Unload/reload
- Journaling
- Archiving
- Disaster recovery
- Database start up and shutdown

2.0 Performance monitoring

Instructions related to predefined database performance measures in terms of checking

- The number, size, and frequency of read/writes executed by data staging transactions
- The number, size, and frequency of predefined and ad hoc queries
- Transaction time outs as a result of locked data pages or as a result of CPU paging

Data Warehouse Support Schedules

Data warehouse support schedules describes all schedules, resourcing, and vendor contact information that is required to support the production DBMS.

1.0 Data management schedule

Defines the database management schedule for the business system in terms of when

- Backups should be taken (incremental, full, and when copies should be taken for disaster recovery)
- Archiving should be done
- Timing for how and when the database is to be brought up and shut down

2.0 Data management support structure

Details the kind of support to be provided as a statement of database roles and responsibilities. Also documents any special skills required by technical support or system operators.

3.0 Vendor support

3.1 Vendor products

Specifies dataset information on vendor software as

- *Where it will be found*
- *How it will be secured*
- *How it will be updated or corrected (e.g., patched, downloaded from the Web, or how a new release or version will be installed)*

3.2 Vendor services

Specifies vendor contacts for the product/service as

- *A list of primary and alternate contact names and phone numbers*
- *Hours of availability for help desk support*

DATA WAREHOUSE TECHNOLOGY PROFILE

Data warehouse technology profile is used to convey an understanding of the information technology structure to external organizations and includes

1.0 Introduction

A brief description covering the scope and purpose of the information technology profile

2.0 Hardware environment description

A list of the major hardware components applicable to the data warehouse. This would include

- Mainframe and miniprocessors and controllers specifications
- Direct access storage devices (DASD) and tape backup facilities
- Printers (local and remote)
- Terminals and workstations

3.0 Software environment description

A list of either preferred or standard software components to be used in in house development including software development languages

- Database platforms
- GUI interface software
- Development support software (Word Processors, Spreadsheets)
- Portfolio of customized package software
- Archiving, security, and audit software
- Operating systems software (Unix, NT, VM, MVS)

4.0 Communications environment description

A list of the major communications hardware and software components.

PRODUCT EVALUATION TEST

Product evaluation test describes package performance, data capture, and user interface scoring results based on a set of specified test conditions. A test form containing package evaluation results, which includes

- Package name
- Package component identification
- Procedure to be tested
- Reviewer name
- Test date
- Test response criteria, which include
  - Procedure requirements (met/not met)
  - Degree of accessibility/ease of use
  - Response time
  - Error conditions
  - Comments

VENDOR CONTACT INSTRUCTIONS

Vendor contact instructions describe our requirements for vendor solicitation of products or services. Vendor response instructions indicate to whom and where in our organization a contractor should forward his or her response.

1.0 Corporate contact

A statement describing where the vendor response should be directed. This information includes

- Mailing address
- Contact person name
- Contact person department
- Contact person phone number/fax

2.0 Closing date

The date and time that the request will be closed.

3.0 Format instructions

A description of how the vendor is to respond to provide product update and training related information.

4.0 Statement of confidentiality

Any proprietary requirements regarding products or services that Vendors may wish to state in terms of their providing products or services before certification and roll out.

VENDOR BACKGROUND CHECK

Vendor background check describes where any additional information that was collected outside formal scoring is to be documented. A form should contain the following information:

- Results of any site visits
- Results of product demos
- Results of vendor reference checks
- Results of financial statement and accreditation checks and includes
  - Vendor name
  - Product name
  - Reviewer name
  - Comments
  - Recommendations

VENDOR PRODUCT SCORE

Vendor product score describes the weights and scores applied across package business and technology evaluation criteria. Failure to meet all mandatory requirements could result in a total score of zero. A spreadsheet containing the results of vendor scoring includes

- Vendor name
- Product name
- Reviewer name
- Review date
- Requirement description
- Requirement weighting score
- Requirement evaluation score
- Requirement total score
- Requirement weighted total score
- Section totals

CHAPTER TWENTY

The Data Warehouse Assistant

INTRODUCTION

This chapter outlines the materials on the enclosed CD ROM disk. The CD contains the electronic documents referred to throughout the text.

A README file contains the instructions for access and use of all the materials on the CD.[1] The CD contains a representative list of data warehouse product or service Vendors. With each new release of this book, more vendors will be invited to contribute material and information on themselves and the changing state of this dynamic sector of the information technology industry. The Book Material directory contains all of the author's best practice materials which cover the entire data warehousing life cycle from inception to implementation and monitoring. As in the case of the vendor list, this directory will be updated with each new release of the book with additional material supplied by the author. The author's material has been organized into folders which correspond to each Section of the book for easy access.

---

[1] Possession, use, or copying of material described in this publication beyond the single user license for the author's CD is authorized only pursuant to a valid written license from Horse & Musket Ltd. or an authorized sublicense. All trademarks and registered trademarks of products mentioned in the text are the property of their respective holders. The Vendor supplied material is for education purposes only. This material may not be copied or used in any manner other than that as specified in the book disclaimer.

REQUIRED SOFTWARE

To access the Vendor supplied material and author book material on the enclosed CD requires a PC Desktop or Laptop system with CD ROM drive. A Pentium class workstation with at least 32Mb of memory is recommended to extract and utilize some of the larger documents contained on the CD. The author and vendor material is supplied in Microsoft Office 95 format (Word, Powerpoint and Excel). In addition some PDF files have been supplied so you must have access to a copy of Adobe Acrobat (preferably version 4.0) to open some of the vendor supplied material.

CD INVENTORY

The following material is contained on the enclosed CD ROM.

- Adobe Read Me file
- *Book Material*[2]
    1. Section One The Data Warehouse Value Proposition
    2. Section Two Infrastructure Development
    3. Section Three Design, Implementation, and Assessment
    4. Section Four Data Warehouse Support & Maintenance
    5. Appendices (An electronic version of the Appendix)
- *Vendor Catalog*
    6. AVNET
    7. Business Objects
    8. Compaq
    9. LGS Group
    10. Pine Cone

---

[2] Section Five is the CD ROM and the hardcopy review of this material as contained in this chapter.

Figure 20–1

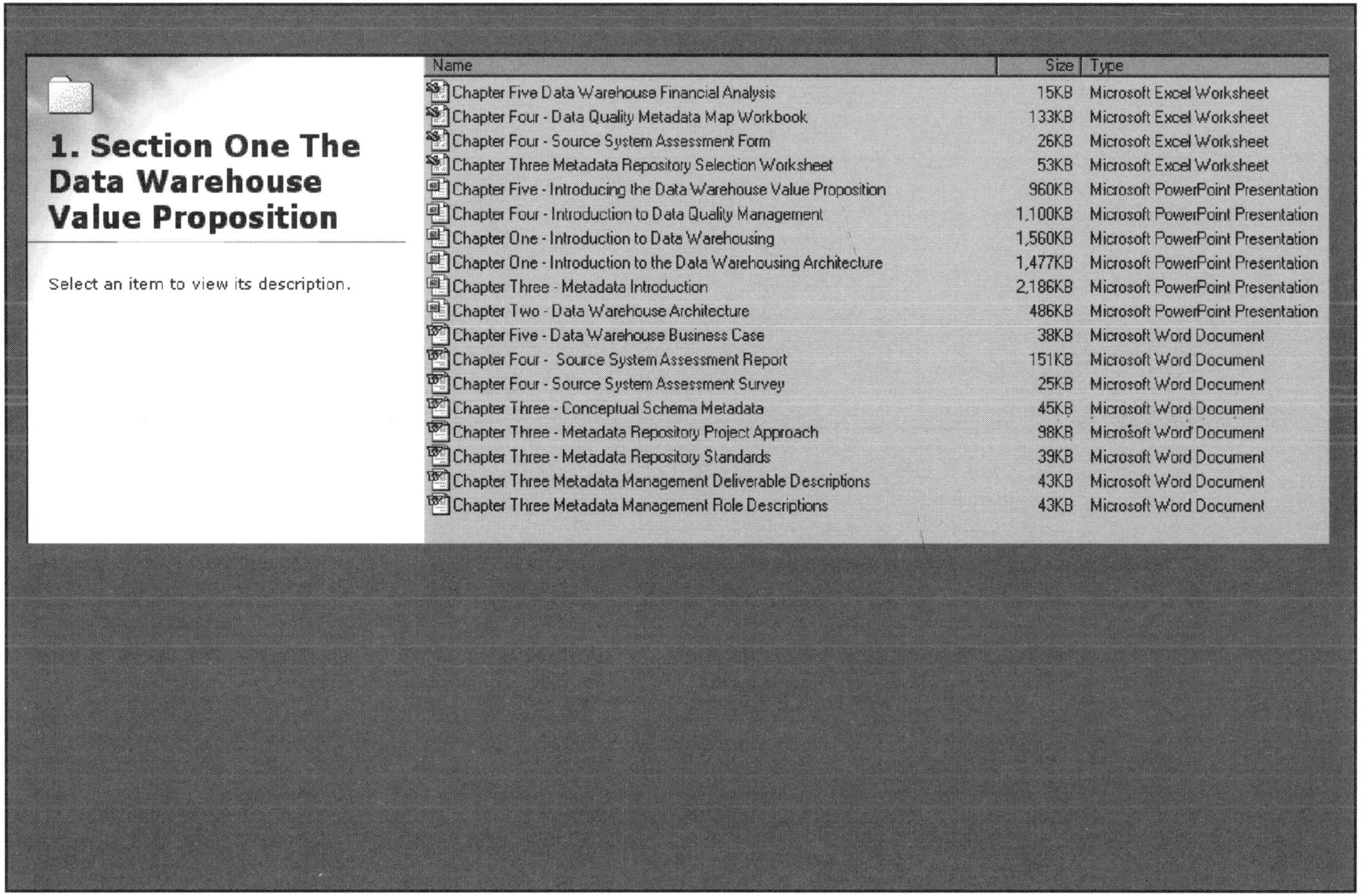

1. Section One The
Data Warehouse
Value Proposition

Select an item to view its description.

Name	Size	Type
Chapter Five Data Warehouse Financial Analysis	15KB	Microsoft Excel Worksheet
Chapter Four - Data Quality Metadata Map Workbook	133KB	Microsoft Excel Worksheet
Chapter Four - Source System Assessment Form	26KB	Microsoft Excel Worksheet
Chapter Three Metadata Repository Selection Worksheet	53KB	Microsoft Excel Worksheet
Chapter Five - Introducing the Data Warehouse Value Proposition	960KB	Microsoft PowerPoint Presentation
Chapter Four - Introduction to Data Quality Management	1,100KB	Microsoft PowerPoint Presentation
Chapter One - Introduction to Data Warehousing	1,560KB	Microsoft PowerPoint Presentation
Chapter One - Introduction to the Data Warehousing Architecture	1,477KB	Microsoft PowerPoint Presentation
Chapter Three - Metadata Introduction	2,186KB	Microsoft PowerPoint Presentation
Chapter Two - Data Warehouse Architecture	486KB	Microsoft PowerPoint Presentation
Chapter Five - Data Warehouse Business Case	38KB	Microsoft Word Document
Chapter Four - Source System Assessment Report	151KB	Microsoft Word Document
Chapter Four - Source System Assessment Survey	25KB	Microsoft Word Document
Chapter Three - Conceptual Schema Metadata	45KB	Microsoft Word Document
Chapter Three - Metadata Repository Project Approach	98KB	Microsoft Word Document
Chapter Three - Metadata Repository Standards	39KB	Microsoft Word Document
Chapter Three Metadata Management Deliverable Descriptions	43KB	Microsoft Word Document
Chapter Three Metadata Management Role Descriptions	43KB	Microsoft Word Document

Figure 20-2

Name	Size	Type
Chapter Six - Business Process Maturity Assessment	29KB	Microsoft Excel Worksheet
Chapter Eight - DW Project Planning	176KB	Microsoft Excel Worksheet
Chapter Eleven - Data Warehouse Request for Information	14KB	Microsoft Word Document
Chapter Eleven - Data Warehouse Request for Proposal	17KB	Microsoft Word Document
Chapter Eleven - Data Warehouse Vendor Selection Method	14KB	Microsoft Word Document
Chapter Eleven - Final Vendor Selection	13KB	Microsoft Word Document
Chapter Eleven - Industry Spreadsheet	20KB	Microsoft Excel Worksheet
Chapter Nine - Data Warehouse Tools Spreadsheet	41KB	Microsoft Excel Worksheet
Chapter Nine - Data Warehouse Initiation Plan	50KB	Microsoft Excel Worksheet
Chapter Seven - Data Warehouse Management Charter	87KB	Microsoft Word Document
Chapter Seven - Data Warehouse Organization Roles	63KB	Microsoft Word Document
Chapter Six - Business Process Maturity Assessment	977KB	Microsoft PowerPoint Presentation

2. Section Two Infrastructure Development

Select an item to view its description.

Figure 20–3

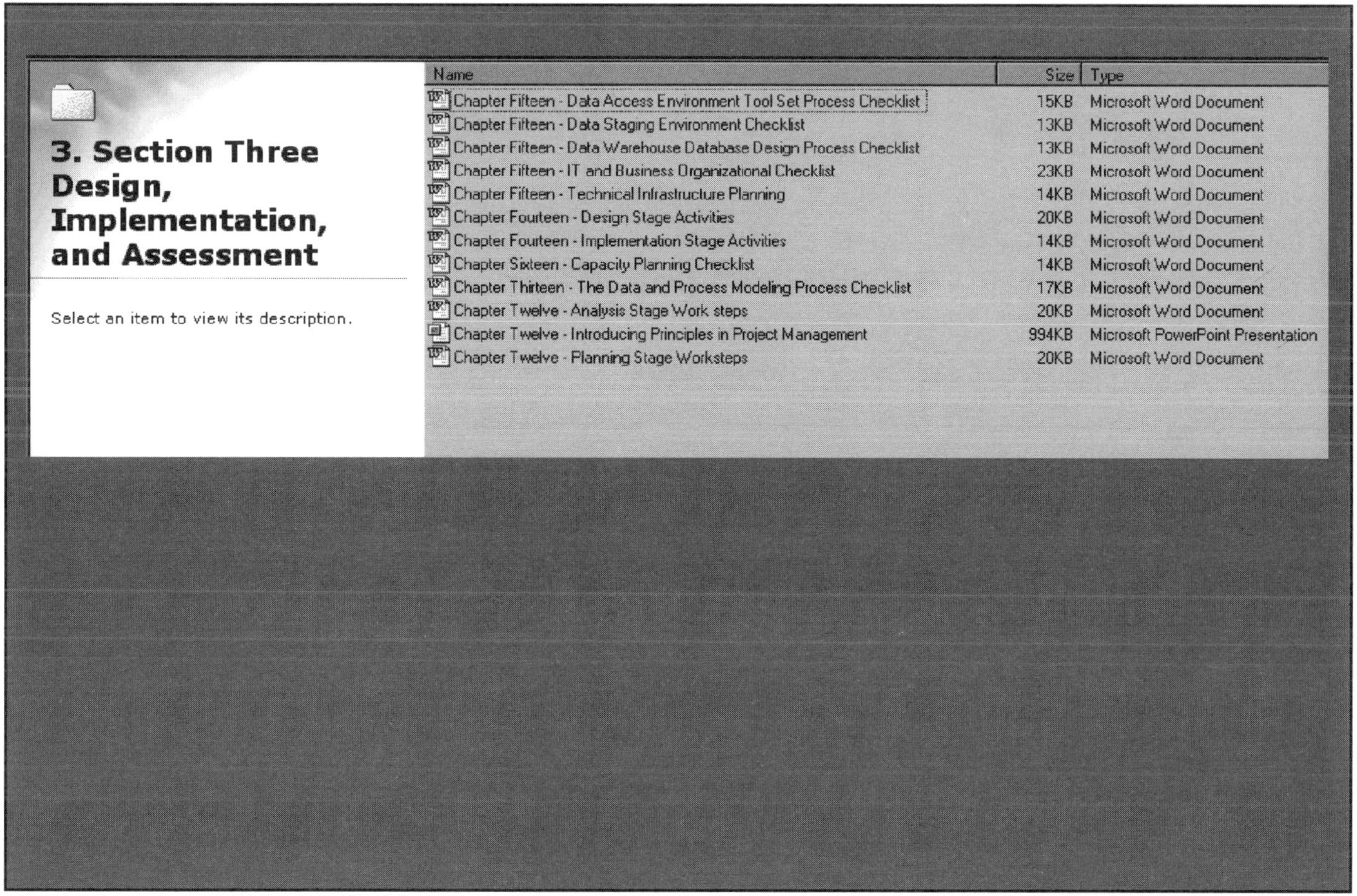

3. Section Three Design, Implementation, and Assessment

Select an item to view its description.

Name	Size	Type
Chapter Fifteen - Data Access Environment Tool Set Process Checklist	15KB	Microsoft Word Document
Chapter Fifteen - Data Staging Environment Checklist	13KB	Microsoft Word Document
Chapter Fifteen - Data Warehouse Database Design Process Checklist	13KB	Microsoft Word Document
Chapter Fifteen - IT and Business Organizational Checklist	23KB	Microsoft Word Document
Chapter Fifteen - Technical Infrastructure Planning	14KB	Microsoft Word Document
Chapter Fourteen - Design Stage Activities	20KB	Microsoft Word Document
Chapter Fourteen - Implementation Stage Activities	14KB	Microsoft Word Document
Chapter Sixteen - Capacity Planning Checklist	14KB	Microsoft Word Document
Chapter Thirteen - The Data and Process Modeling Process Checklist	17KB	Microsoft Word Document
Chapter Twelve - Analysis Stage Work steps	20KB	Microsoft Word Document
Chapter Twelve - Introducing Principles in Project Management	994KB	Microsoft PowerPoint Presentation
Chapter Twelve - Planning Stage Worksteps	20KB	Microsoft Word Document

Figure 20-4

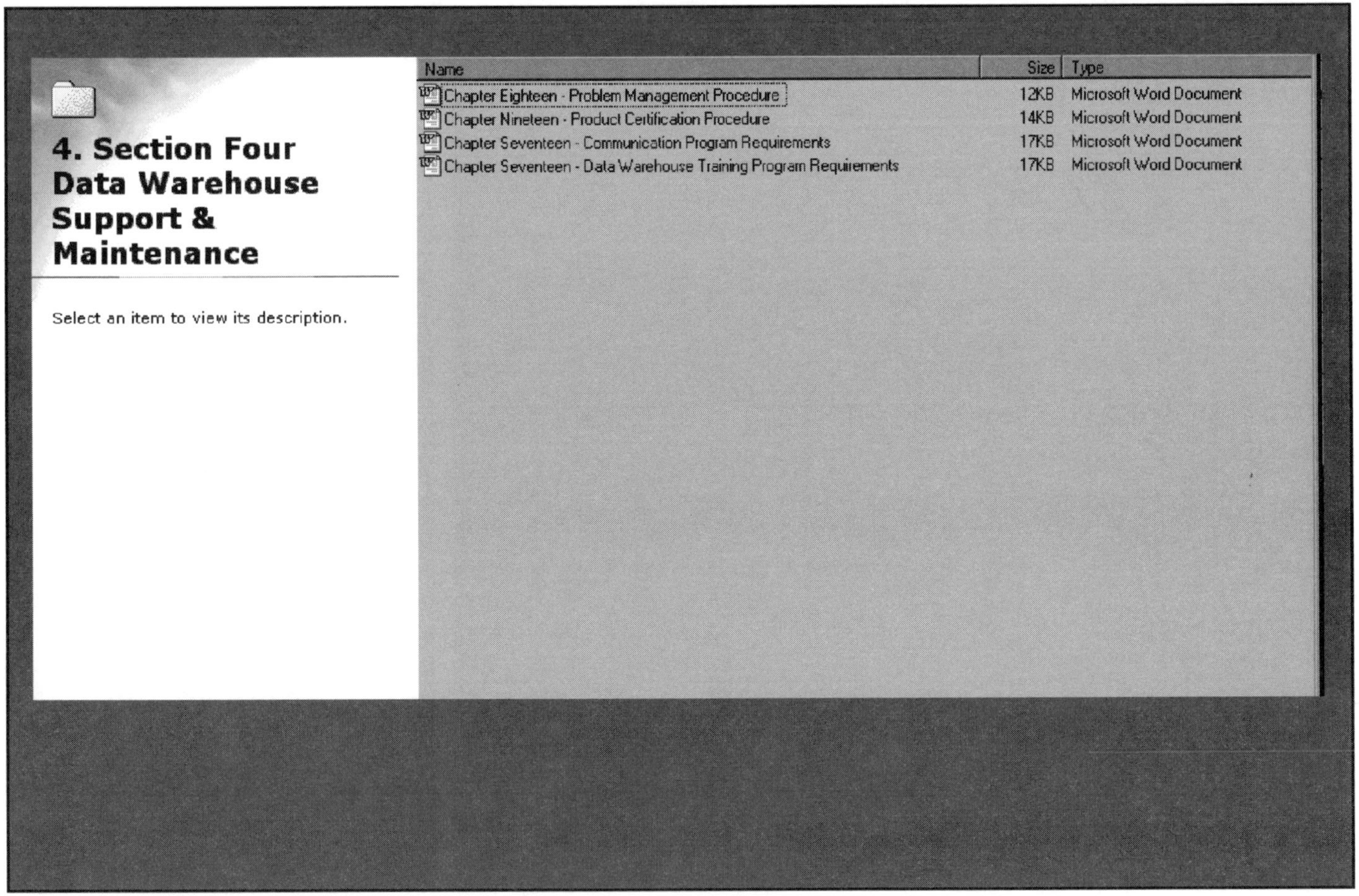

4. Section Four
Data Warehouse
Support &
Maintenance

Select an item to view its description.

Name	Size	Type
Chapter Eighteen - Problem Management Procedure	12KB	Microsoft Word Document
Chapter Nineteen - Product Certification Procedure	14KB	Microsoft Word Document
Chapter Seventeen - Communication Program Requirements	17KB	Microsoft Word Document
Chapter Seventeen - Data Warehouse Training Program Requirements	17KB	Microsoft Word Document

Figure 20-5

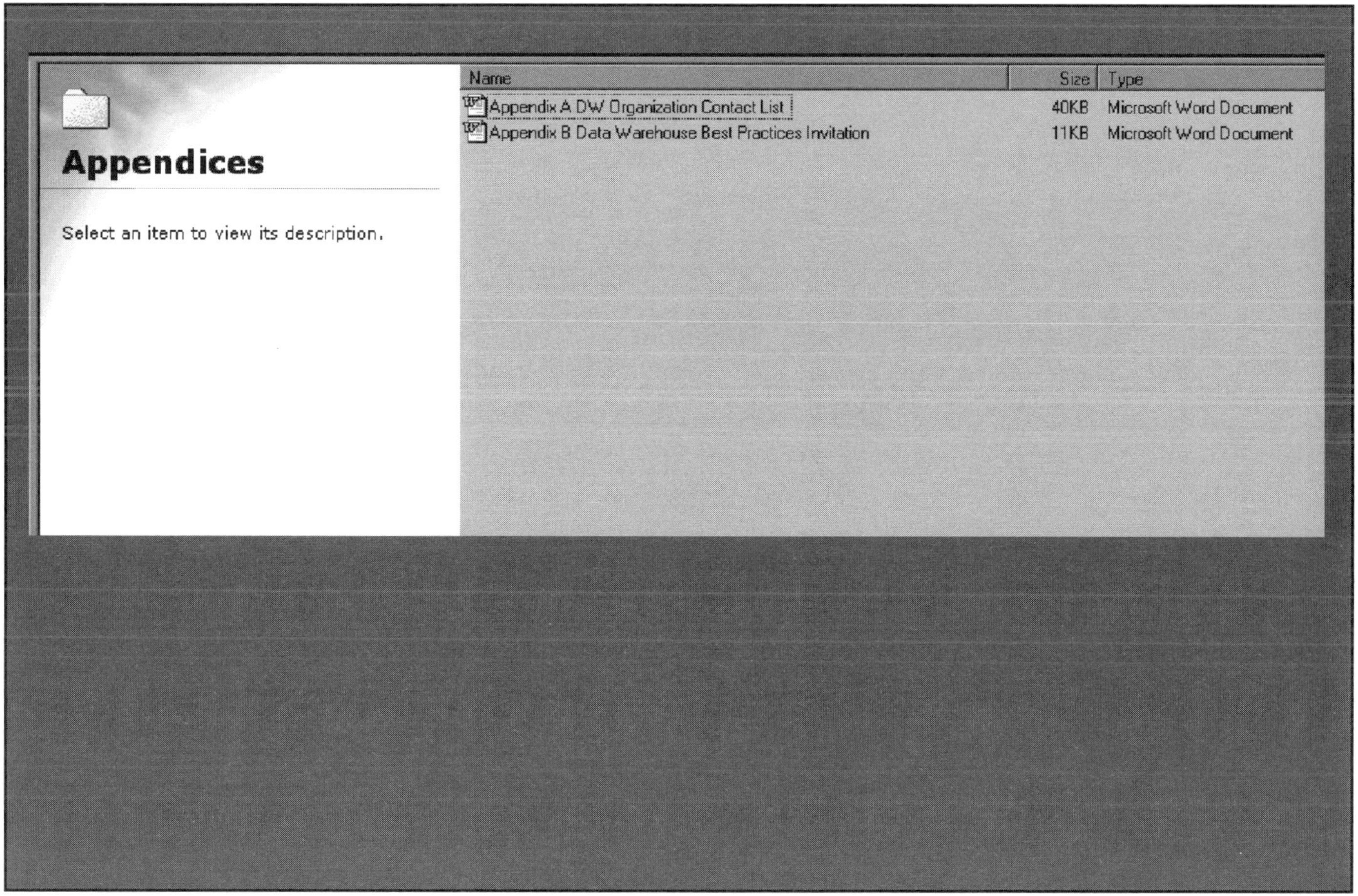

Appendices

Select an item to view its description.

Name	Size	Type
Appendix A DW Organization Contact List	40KB	Microsoft Word Document
Appendix B Data Warehouse Best Practices Invitation	11KB	Microsoft Word Document

Figure 20–6

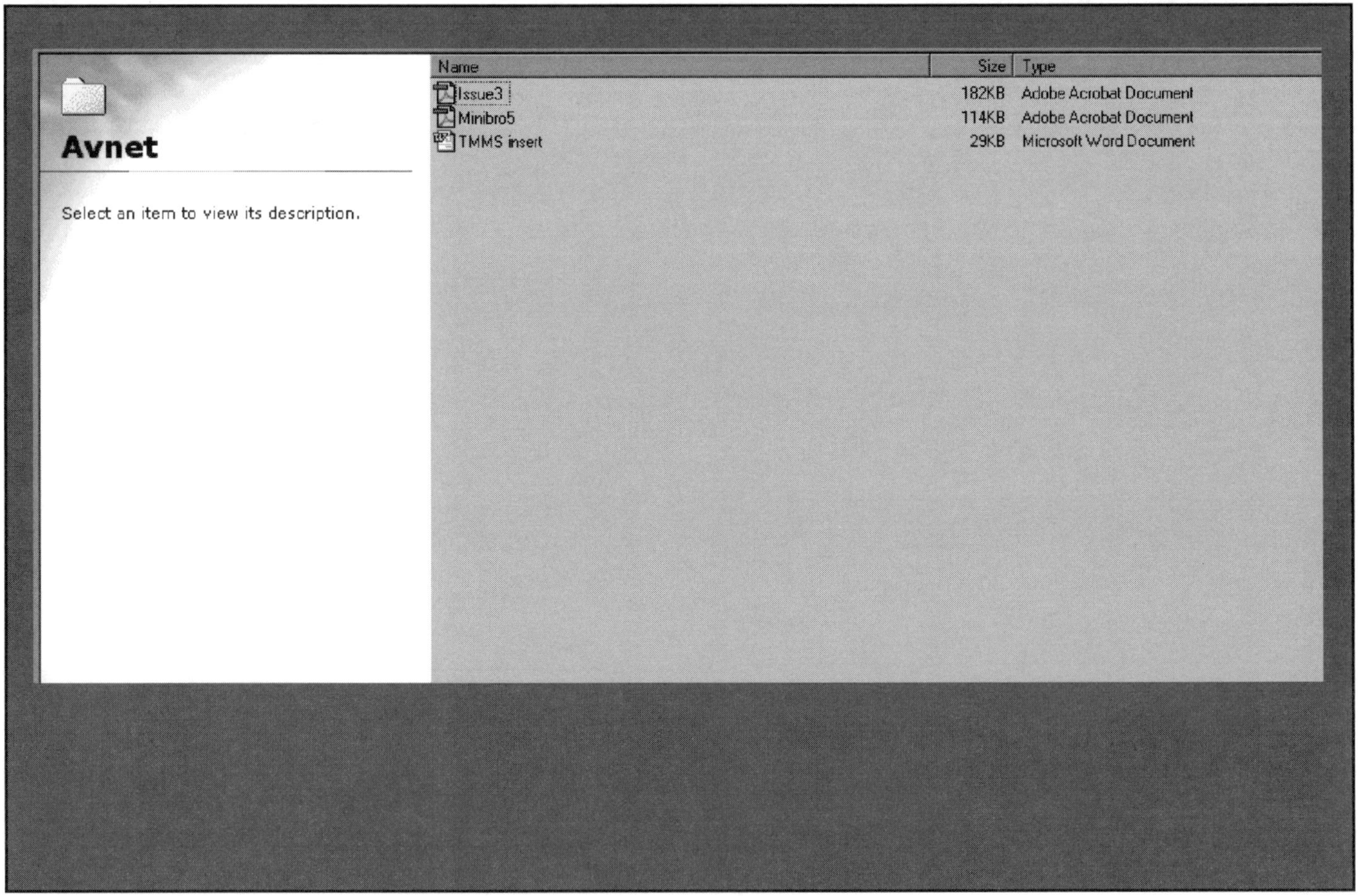

Figure 20-7

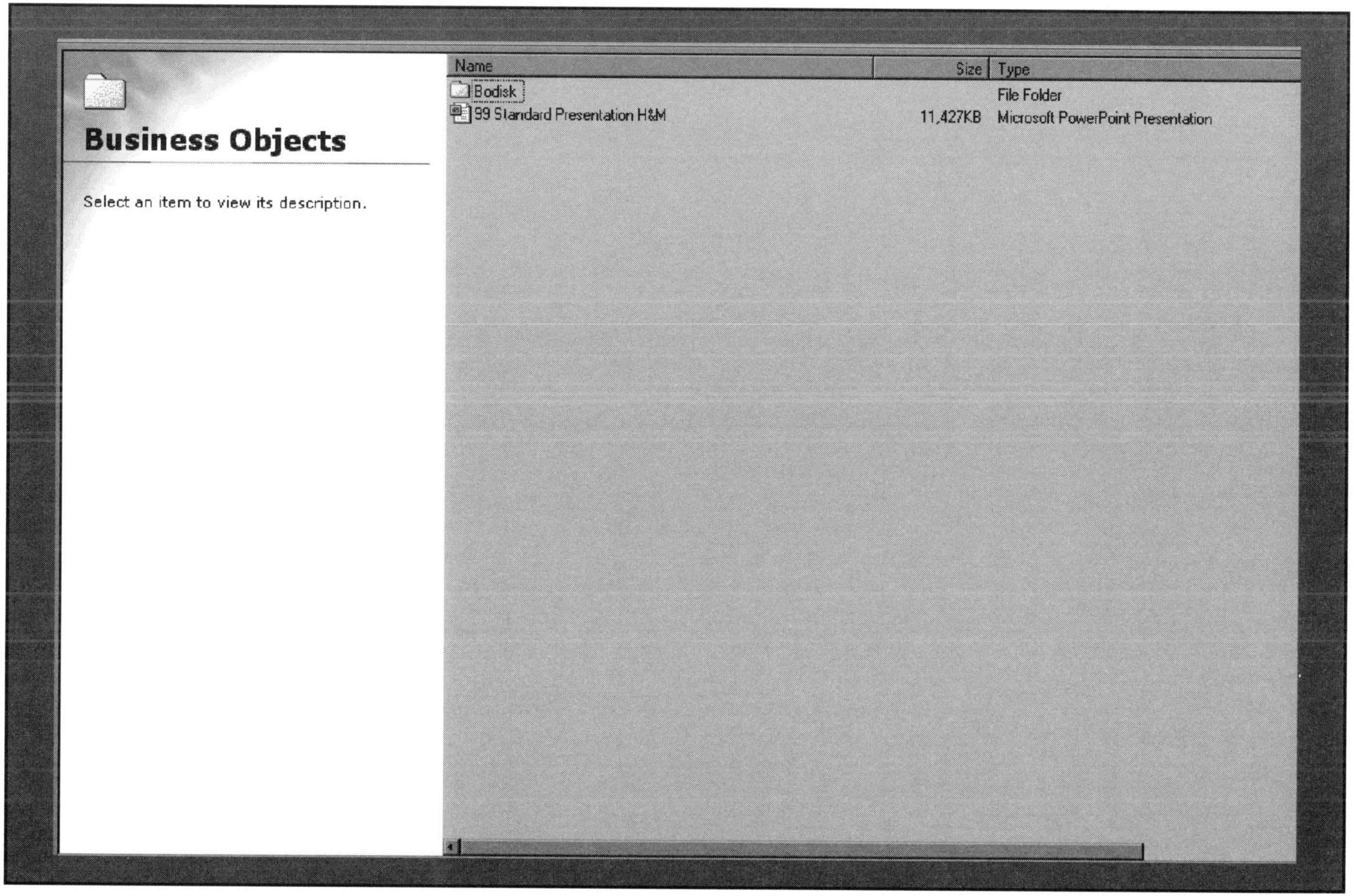

Business Objects

Select an item to view its description.

Name	Size	Type
Bodisk		File Folder
99 Standard Presentation H&M	11,427KB	Microsoft PowerPoint Presentation

Figure 20–8

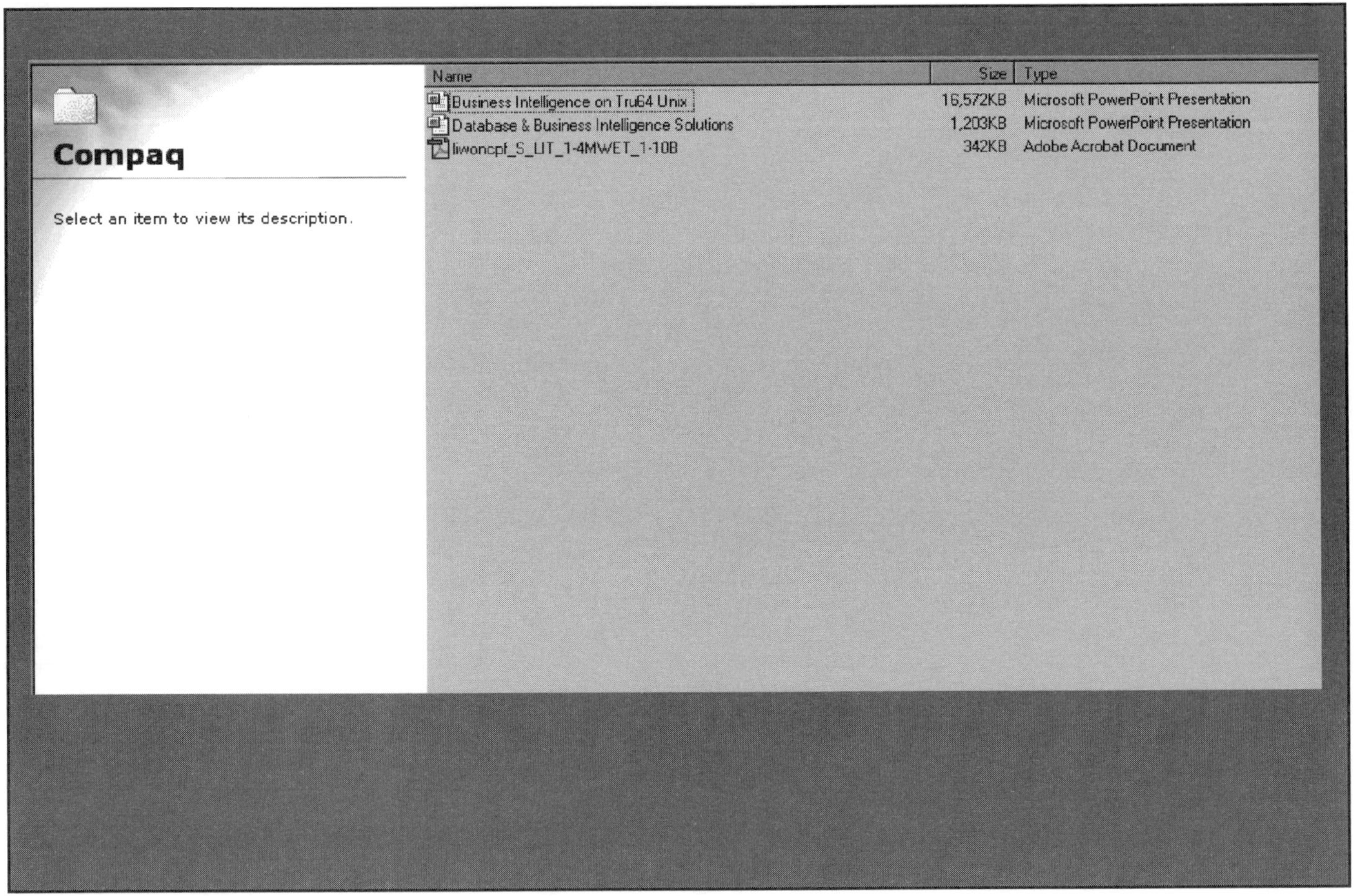

Compaq
Select an item to view its description.
Name
Size
Type
Business Intelligence on Tru64 Unix
16,572KB
Microsoft PowerPoint Presentation
Database & Business Intelligence Solutions
1,203KB
Microsoft PowerPoint Presentation
liwoncpf_S_LIT_1-4MWET_1-10B
342KB
Adobe Acrobat Document

Figure 20-9

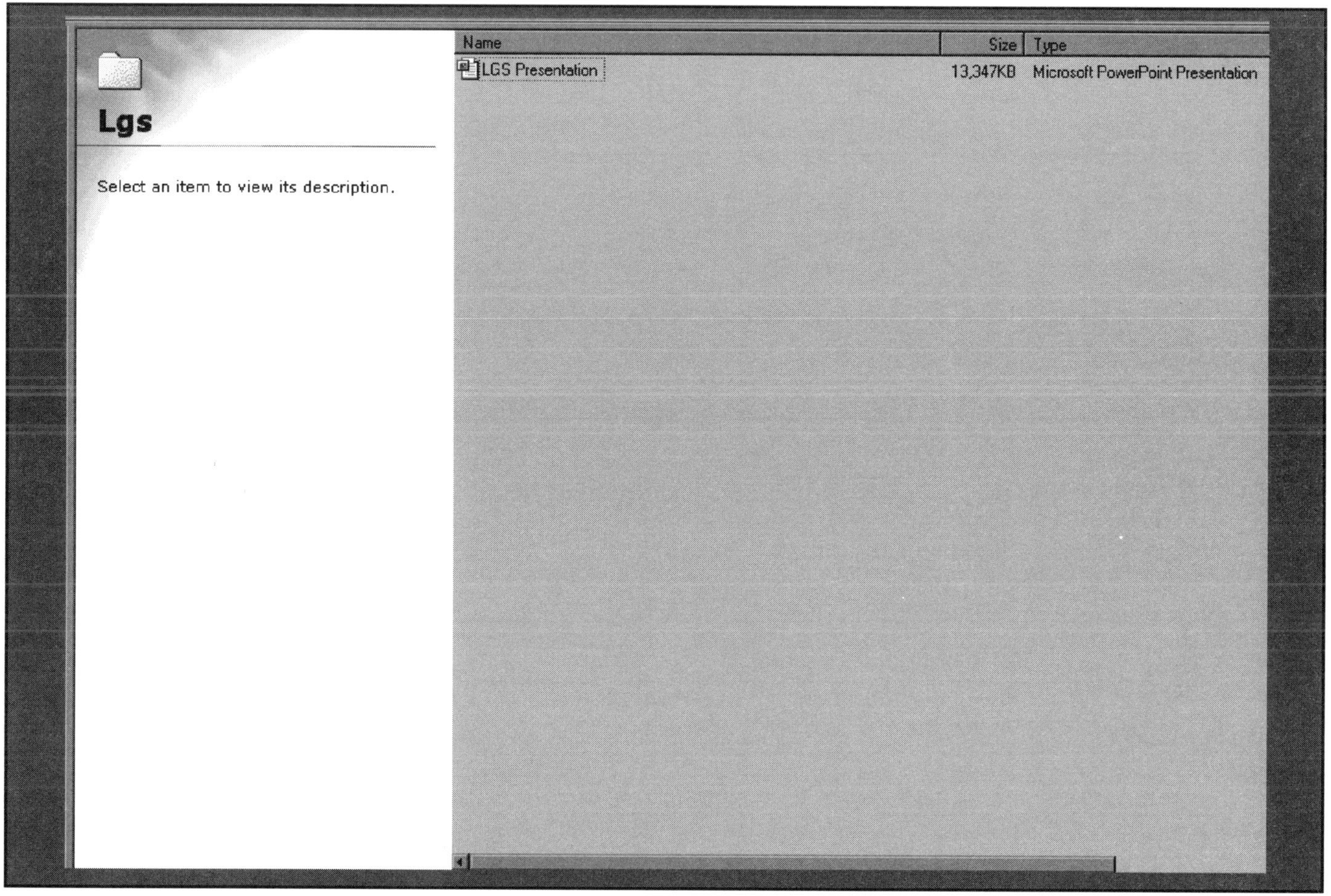

Figure 20–10

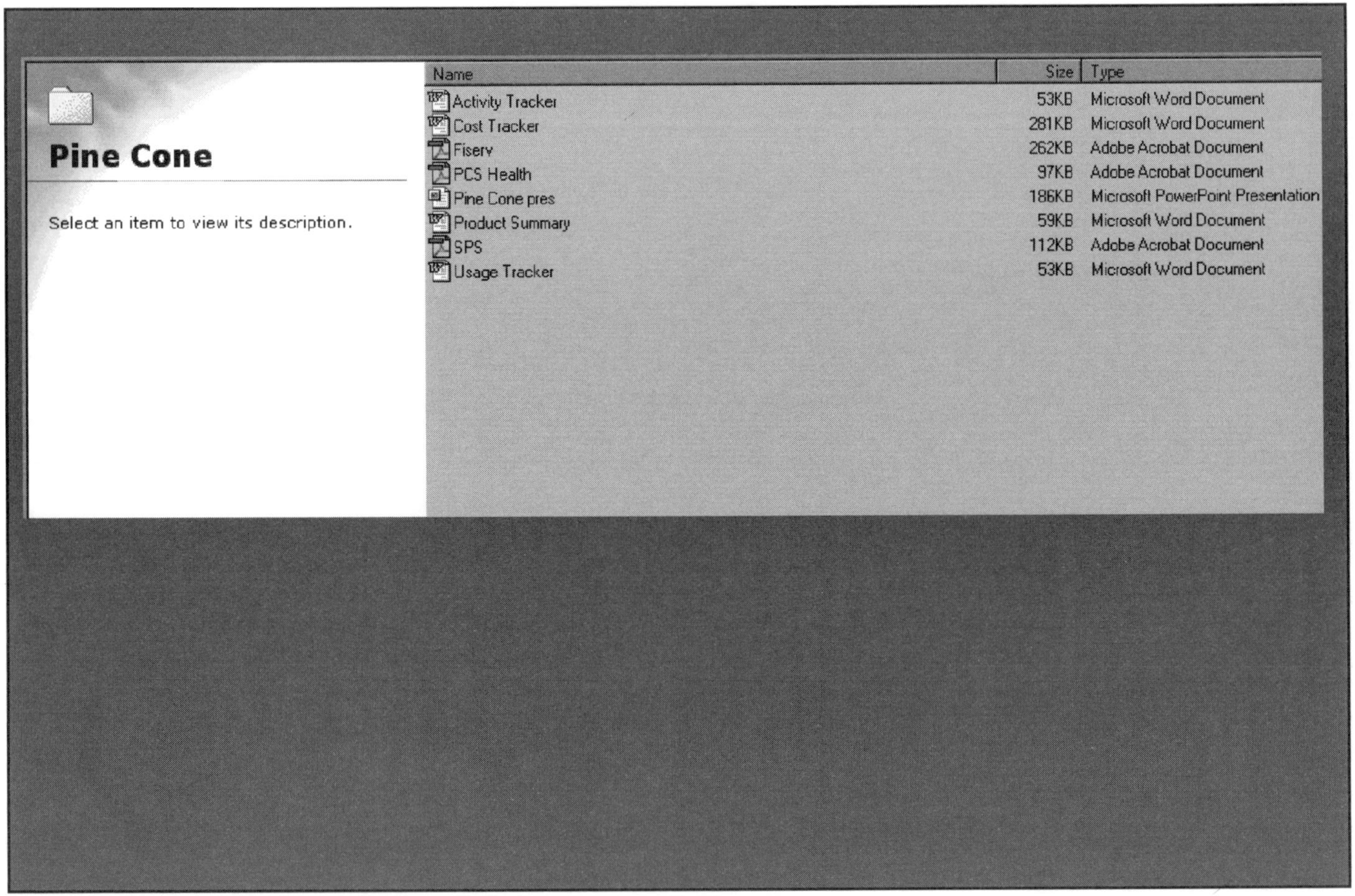

Pine Cone

Select an item to view its description.

Name	Size	Type
Activity Tracker	53KB	Microsoft Word Document
Cost Tracker	281KB	Microsoft Word Document
Fiserv	262KB	Adobe Acrobat Document
PCS Health	97KB	Adobe Acrobat Document
Pine Cone pres	186KB	Microsoft PowerPoint Presentation
Product Summary	59KB	Microsoft Word Document
SPS	112KB	Adobe Acrobat Document
Usage Tracker	53KB	Microsoft Word Document

◆

Data Warehouse Organization Contact Information List

The following list is a composite of material presented in the book an outlines the various types of data warehousing firms and how to contact them. This is *not* an exhaustive list and new entries will be added as they are identified in subsequent editions.

Vendor Name	Contact Information	Type
Dun & Bradstreet Financial Analysis	http://www.dnbcorp.com/home.cfm	Financial and Business Stability search
U.S. Financial Analysis EDGAR	http://www.sec.gov/cgi-bin/srch-edgar?	Financial and Business Stability search
U.S. Securities and Exchange Commission	http://www.sec.gov/	Financial and Business Stability search

Services & Publications

DAMA International (Data Management Association)	http://www.dama.org/damamore.htm	Data Management and Data Warehousing organizations, publications and special interest groups

Vendor Name	Contact Information	Type
Data Warehousing on the Web	http://www.datawarehousing.com	Data Management and Data Warehousing organizations, publications and special interest groups
DBMS Magazine	http://www.dbsmagazine.com	Data Management and Data Warehousing organizations, publications and special interest groups
DM Review Direct	http://www.dmreview.com/dmdirect/	Data Management and Data Warehousing organizations, publications and special interest groups
DM Review Metadata Link	http://www.data-warehouse.com/issues/_meta.htm	Data Management and Data Warehousing organizations, publications and special interest groups
Patricia Seybold Group	http://www.psgroup.com/	Data Management and Data Warehousing organizations, publications and special interest groups
The Data Warehouse Information Center	http://pwp.starnetinc.com/larryg/index.html	Data Management and Data Warehousing organizations, publications and special interest groups
The Data Warehousing Institute	http://www.dw-institute.com/comfindex.htm	Data Management and Data Warehousing organizations, publications and special interest groups

Vendor Name	Contact Information	Type
The Data Warehouse Network	http://indigo.ie/~dataware/dwnpag1.htm	Data Management and Data Warehousing organization, publications and special interest groups
The Gartner Group	http://gartner3.gartnerweb.com/public/ static/home/home.html	Data Management and Data Warehousing organizations, publications and special interest groups
The Meta Group	http://www.metagroup.com/	Data Management and Data Warehousing organizations, publications and special interest groups
Zachman Framework	http://www.ozemail.com.au/~ieinfo/zachman.htm	Data Management and Data Warehousing organizations, publications and special interest groups

Product and Services Vendors

Anubis	www.anubis.com	Constructa
Applied Data Resource Management	www.adrm.com	Applied Data Resource Environment
AppsCo	www.apsco.com	AppsMart
Avnet	www.avnetcomputer.com	DW product and services provider
Barnett Data Systems	www.barnettdata.com/htmlsems/sem02.htm	Intro to Data Warehousing: Concept to Creation
Business Objects	www.businessobjects.com	DW business intelligence, decision support systems software and services provider

Vendor Name	Contact Information	Type
CASEwise Systems	www.casewise.com	Modeler
Cayenne Software, Inc.	www.cayennesoft.com	Terrain
Compaq	www.compaq.com	DW product and services provider
Digidyne	www.digidyne.ca	DW product and services provider
Embarcadero Technologies	www.embarcadero.com	ER Studio 2.0
Enterprise Architects, Inc.	www.enterprise-architects.com/ implementationservices.htm	EAI Implementation Services
HP	http://www.hp.com/	HP Processors, Products and Services
IBM	www.ibm.com	Visual Warehouse
IBM	http://direct.boulder.ibm.com/bi/ decisionedge/index.htm	Decision Edge
Informix	www.informix.com/informix/services/ consulting/dwcons.htm	Informix Consulting: The Data Warehousing Practice
inforte corporation	www.infortecorp.com/Solutions/ KMS_DataWarehousing.as	Solutions: KMS Data Warehousing
IronBridge Software	www.ibsw.com	SQL Mill
LogicWorks (PLATINUM)	www.logicworks.com	ERWin, ModelMart, Universal Directory
LGS Group Inc.	http://www.lgs.com/Services/ Serv_Information_Warehousing.htm	Information Warehousing
Metamor Technologies, Ltd.	www.metamortech.com	MQP—Iterative Data Warehousing Methodology
Métier	www.metier.com	WareAbouts

Vendor Name	Contact Information	Type
Millennia Vision Corporation	www.mvsn.com/PracticeDW-DSS.html	Millennia Vision Corporation Data Warehousing and Decision Support Services
NCR	www3.ncr.com/data_warehouse/ services.htm	NCR's Scalable Data Warehousing— Services
Next Action Technology	www.answersets.com	AnswerSets
Oracle Corporation	www.oracle.com	Designer/2000
Oracle Corporation	www.oracle.com	Oracle Warehouse
PLATINUM technology, inc.	www.platinum.com	DB XL, Open Edition Environment
Popkin Software & Systems, Inc.	www.popkin.com/	System Architect, SA/Data Architect
Powersoft	www.powersoft.com	PowerDesigner Warehouse Architect
Prism Solutions	www.prismsolutions.com	Warehouse Executive, Iterations
PineCone	www.pine-cone.com	DW software product and services innovator. Product list includes: meta exchange, usage tracker, activator, content tracker, cost tracker and refreshment tracker
SELECT Software	www.select.st.com	SELECT SE
Relational Solutions, Inc.	www.relationalsolutions.com/Methodology.htm	Data Warehouse Methodology
SAGA Software AG	URL: 157.189.11.40/services/educ/courses/ dwi-001.htm	Data Warehouse Methodology: Implementation
SILVERRUN Technologies, Inc.	www.silverrun.co	SILVERRUN

Vendor Name	Contact Information	Type
Sybase, Inc.	www.sybase.com	PowerDesigner
Sysix	www.xsite.net/~dante/sysix/dataware/method.htm	Sysix—Data Warehouse Methodology
Tessera Enterprise Systems, Inc.	www.tesent.com	Early Harvest
Visible Systems Corporation	www.visible.com	Visible Advantage Data Warehouse Edition, Visible Analyst
Visio Corporation	www.visio.com	InfoModeler, Visio Professional, 4Keeps
Zyga Corporation	www.zyga.com	Component Engineering Methodology

---

Data Warehouse Best Practices Invitation

You are invited!

I would welcome all responses in terms of feedback, additions, queries or suggestions for extensions to the current material to be added to future editions of this book. If you wish to contribute material either as suggested input or as your own offering, I would welcome the response (with your material being presented with your name and contact information).

Vendors are also welcome to contact either myself or Prentice Hall in terms of providing information on your products or services in upcoming editions.

Please forward all queries, questions or comments to:

Richard J. Kachur
Horse & Musket Ltd.
PO Box 811 Station M
Calgary, Alberta T2P 2J6
Fax: 403-225-3356
Email: horse.musket@attcanada.net

I Look forward to receiving your input!

Index

product and service development participation guidelines, 126
project delivery team roles, 125
project management team roles, 125
supporters, 127
validators, 126
Performance management data warehouse checklist, 274–75
Performance reviews, conducting, 190
Physical multimedia architectures, 167
Planning activities, 201
Planning stage, 43
deliverables, 205–6, 232–33
processes, 232
work breakdown structure deliverables designations, 205–6
work steps/milestones, 201–6
Precanned reports, using reprot writing software, 166
Predictive modeling, 166
Preplanning stage processes, 232
Priorities, ranking, 70–71
Problem management process, 298–300
developing, 298
key deliverables, 300
procedure, 299
Process and information directory services, 33–34
Producers, 127
Production performance tuning, 267–75
mechanisms, 268–75
capacity planning, 272–75
data loading performance, 269–70
network management, 270–72
query management, 268–69
Product and service development participation guidelines, 126
Profit generation and enhancement, 73
Program management office (PMO), 15–16, 168
Program management process, 15–16
Program/project champion, 113
Program/project steering committee, 113
Project champion/sponsor, 125

Project delivery team roles, 125
Project management resource requirements, 136
Project management team roles, 125
Projects:
analysis process, 206–12
activities, 206–7
deliverables, 212
work steps/milestones, 207–11
initiating, 197–212
planning and analysis, 197–200
process, 200–207
planning stage:
activities, 201
work steps/milestones/deliverables, 201–6
Project steering committee, 125
Property description, 56
Proposed investment, defining cost/impact of, 75
Protocol compatibility, 167

Q

Quality control council, 113
Query management, 268–69
Quick strike assessment, 93–94

R

Recovery, 166
Relational based online analytical processing (ROLAP), 9, 109
Repository administrators, 46
Request for Information (RFI) process, developing, 180–83
Request for Proposal (RFP) process:
covering letter, 183–89
developing, 183
Resource costs, data warehouse development, 140
Resource requirements:
data access, 130